Brazil has developed a distinctive response to the injustices inflicted by the country's race relations regime. Despite the mixed racial background of most Brazilians, the state recognizes people's racial classification according to a simple official scheme in which those self-assigned as black, together with "brown" and "indigenous" (*preto-pardo-indigena*), can qualify for specially allocated resources, most controversially quota places at public universities. Although this quota system has been somewhat successful, many other issues that disproportionately affect the country's black population remain unresolved, and systemic policies to reduce structural inequality remain off the agenda.

In *The Prism of Race*, David Lehmann explores, theoretically and practically, issues of race, the state, social movements, and civil society and then goes beyond these themes to ask whether Brazilian politics will forever circumvent the severe problems facing the society by co-optation and tinkering with unjust structures. Lehmann disrupts the paradigm of current scholarly thought on Brazil, placing affirmative action disputes in their political and class context, bringing back the concept of state corporatism, and questioning the strength and independence of Brazilian civil society.

David Lehmann is Emeritus Reader in Social Sciences at the University of Cambridge where he directed the Centre of Latin American Studies. His publications include *Democracy and Development in Latin America* (1990), *Struggle for the Spirit* (1996), and *The Crisis of Multiculturalism in Latin America* (2016).

THE PRISM OF RACE

The Politics and Ideology of Affirmative Action in Brazil

DAVID LEHMANN

University of Michigan Press • Ann Arbor

Published in the United States of America by the
University of Michigan Press
Manufactured in the United States of America
Printed on acid-free paper
First published July 2018

A CIP catalog record for this book is available from the British Library.

Library of Congress Cataloging-in-Publication Data

Names: Lehmann, David, author.
Title: The prism of race : the politics and ideology of affirmative action in Brazil /
    David Lehmann.
Description: Ann Arbor : University of Michigan Press, [2018] | Includes bibliographical
    references and index. |
Identifiers: LCCN 2018005193 (print) | LCCN 2018020175 (ebook) | ISBN 9780472123896
    (e-book) | ISBN 9780472130849 (hardcover : alk. paper)
Subjects: LCSH: Brazil—Race relations. | Affirmative action programs—
    Brazil. | Multiculturalism—Brazil.
Classification: LCC F1463.2 (ebook) | LCC F1463.2 .L45   2018 (print) |
    DDC 305.800981—dc23
LC record available at https://lccn.loc.gov/2018005193

Cover credit: CC-BY Piniivi

For Efrat

Acknowledgments

I have been working on this subject since 2007 and on Brazil at least since I went to Brasilia as a visiting professor in 1977. During that time I have learned an enormous amount from colleagues whose precious friendships can never be sufficiently acknowledged. I am thinking of José de Souza Martins, whom I have known since 1970, Peter Fry, Monica Grin, Antonio Sergio Guimarães and Nadya Araujo Guimarães, Maria-Lúcia Pallares-Burke, Peter Burke, Myrian Sepúlveda, Marta Topel, and Patricia Birman. In Cambridge Julie Coimbra has also been part of this charmed circle and in some ways also its lynchpin.

Because so much of this research is about Brazilian academia, many of my interviewees are also colleagues, and the two relationships sometimes overlap. I have included a list of interviewees in appendix B, but here I wish to acknowledge people who have supported me in a more personal way with advice, contacts, comment, and information.

Leonardo Avritzer, Stanley Bailey, Renato Becho, Steve Berg, Leslie Bethell, Véronique Boyer, Nigel Brooke, André Cicalo, Robson Cruz, Joan Dassin, Jerry D'Avila, Andrew Francis, Peter Fry, John Gledhill, Edlaine Gomes, Renato Gomes, Ezequiel Gonzalez Ocantos, Lemuel Guerra, Monica Grin, Mariela Hita, Wendy Hunter, Amy Jaffa, Andrea Lopes da Costa, Elielma Machado, Yvonne Maggie, Veridiana Martins, Maxine Molyneux, Ruben Oliven, Guillermo O'Donnell,[†] Angela Paiva, Karla Patriota, Elisabete Pinto, Maria Alice Rezende, Luisa Schwartzman, Ed Telles, Tom Skidmore,[†] and Marcelo Torelly. Interviewees merit a separate mention and are named in appendix B.

I am extremely grateful to the British Academy, which funded my project "Multiculturalism in Latin America: A Study in the Diffusion of Ideas" (no. LRG 41979).

I am also grateful to the Rockefeller Archive Center and its very solicitous staff near Tarrytown, New York, where I was able to read and upload material from the Ford Foundation archive which is housed there.

I want to thank Francisca de la Maza and Alvaro Bello who received me in Villarrica, Chile, during my period as a Research Associate of the Catholic University's Centre for Intercultural and Indigenous Research (CIIR) in late 2016 and early 2017, enabling me to work on this manuscript.

Finally, I wish to express my appreciation to Kevin Rennells of the University of Michigan Press for his meticulous work preparing the manuscript for publication.

Parts of this book, especially the first pages of chapter 3, appeared summarized or in earlier formulations in my chapter in David Lehmann, ed., *The Crisis of Multiculturalism in Latin America* (New York: Palgrave, 2016), and in "A política do reconhecimento: teoría e prática," in Maria Gabriela Hita, ed., *Raça, racismo e genética em debates científicos e controversias sociais* (Salvador, EDUFBA 2017).

Parts have also been presented at seminars at the Brazil Institute, Kings College London, the Centro de Estudos Afro-Orientais (CEAO) of the Federal University of Bahia (UFBA), the Sociology Department at Queen's University Belfast, and at the Brazilian Studies and Latin American Studies Association meetings (BRASA and LASA) in Providence and New York in 2016.

Contents

Foreword

Antonio Sergio Guimarães

David Lehmann's book appears at a very opportune moment: it can be read in detail, providing food for careful reflection, or more quickly for those seeking a rapid overview of its subject. If I may go straight to the point, however, what struck me most forcefully in Lehmann's argument was his "structural" explanation for the adoption of race quotas in Brazil.

Seen from a traditionalist point of view, quotas present a paradox. In the early 1990s an electoral victory by Lula was nothing more than a utopian fantasy in left-wing circles, not least because it contained within itself a contradiction: not only was Lula seen to be ill-prepared for the office of president, having refused to stand for election to the Chamber of Deputies, but also the Partido dos Trabalhadores (PT) itself showed little interest in exercising power, having avoided any electoral alliances and even refusing to sign the Constitution of 1988. Likewise, even in the mid-1990s, affirmative action and multiculturalism seemed to belong to an unfamiliar international agenda, far removed from Brazilian traditions, as both social democrats and PT supporters did not fail to point out. In 1996, therefore, it was unthinkable that the country might start adopting race quotas as early as 2003.

The paradox lies precisely in the speed with which a seemingly unthinkable agenda came to be not only discussed but also implemented in a space of seven years. What can explain the capitulation of the Brazilian state to pressure from such a small group? What can explain the fact that public opinion itself moved so quickly, first taking Lula to the presidency and then accepting race quotas in the face of the almost unanimous opposition of the main news outlets and leading intellectuals?

In this book David Lehmann proposes a promising reply to the first question: the institutional structure of the Brazilian state, heir to a history of corporatism and perpetual recompositions of elite interests, and always on the lookout for ways to accommodate emerging social forces, enabled it, in his view, to come to terms with demands coming from organized sectors of popular movements and the movimento negro. What Antonio Gramsci called *trasformismo*—the absorption of representatives of the oppressed classes via the political system—is in this view an institutional arrangement peculiar to the Brazilian state that exists for the purpose of dampening conflicts and reaching accommodations between emerging social forces and more traditional sectors.

But how to explain the shift in public opinion? On this point the facts and arguments presented by Lehmann must be followed carefully, for they call for constant reflection on the part of the reader, because, although he provides all the clues, the book is open to various interpretations.

We should begin by recalling that already in the 1990s various tendencies pointed to the need to contain the growing mobilization of social forces outside the political system. We can see, first, in bills presented in the Senate and the Chamber of Deputies, that sectors of the oligarchy began to take preemptive steps toward race quotas in both higher education and the labour market. Second, a younger generation of intellectuals had already, since the 1980s, been building a new theory of Brazilian racism and the country's race relations, attacking both the "myth of racial democracy" and the "genocide of Brazil's black population." Third, after a long period of stagnation since the 1960s, the federal system of higher education was again becoming a target for the profound discontent of the middle classes, which had emerged from the rapid economic growth of the 1970s, creating broad popular support for the idea of a massive expansion of free public university education. Finally, social movements and trade unions began to produce a strong political leadership able to operate with ease in the corridors of power. Union leaders securely installed in both the public sector—mainly in education and health—and the private sector—in the metallurgical and petroleum sectors and banking—were ready to reach for the higher levels of political power.

Thus the decline in Fernando Henrique Cardoso's popularity at the end of his second period made it hard to envisage a continuation of the centre-right alliance led by the PSDB (Partido da Social Democracia Brasileira) and opened the way for a new alignment secured by the PT's victory in 2002. From then on, the accommodation of new social forces accelerated and the organized negro movements increased their access and influence. Lehmann follows the steps of a few political figures—black activists—who occupied pivotal roles in state assemblies, universities, the judiciary, and federal ministries. Quotas could now be seen as an efficient means of advancing the interests of emerging groups while protecting those of more established ones. He also makes quite a convincing sociological argument for the use of the theory of social movements as a way to understand the organization of the quotas campaign and the relative autonomy of black organizations as they gained access to state agencies.

Another point that caught my attention in this book is the role of university leaders, mainly rectors and their staffs, in the development of quota policies—a role that would be expanded in 2008 thanks to the minister of education himself. How can one understand this leadership role in the face of the substantial power of the academic and administrative trade unions? I also want to draw readers' attention to another paradox: although they almost invariably owe their election to union support, the rectors were not captured by the "class-based" and anti-quota ideology of those unions, whose focus was almost exclusively on pressing for increased government education budgets. On the contrary, perhaps seeking an independent base for their own political leadership, the rectors, and later Lula's minister of education, Fernando Haddad, were moved to open up to the demands of the black social movement so as to create a counterweight to the unions. This shift was eased, as Lehmann explains, by a discourse based on social and racial justice, which meant that the adoption of race quotas was always accompanied by, or rather stuffed into, social quotas, thus neutralizing in one fell swoop the more radical class-driven demands of the unions and the more radical race-driven demands of the social movements. As of 2008, federal ministries, the judiciary, and other state agencies had taken over the leadership of the quotas cause, and the expansion of the federal higher education system, as well as the social and racial inclusion of the "new middle class"—the beneficiaries of the PT government's income redistribution policies—found a place at the heart of the government's project.

Through this book's fluid narrative, with its firm empirical basis and solid sociological arguments, the English-language reader will be able to follow the trajectory of a social movement—namely, the quotas campaign—which reveals the mechanics of the contemporary Brazilian state and also helps us to understand the crisis unleashed by the overthrow of the PT government in 2016.

Preface

This book comes with two warnings to the reader. The first is that it is a study of a milieu of which I myself have been a member—albeit an intermittent one—for some forty years, namely, Brazilian academia. As a result I have had the good fortune to pick the brains and hear the stories of many people who would quite possibly not have responded if I had been a doctoral student at the other end of my career. This intimacy with the subject matter has also led me to write in a slightly different style than that which can be found in my work on Pentecostal churches, for example, where I am most definitely an outsider in standard ethnographic mode. The style is different both because it pays attention to the portrayal of an atmosphere and because it deals quite often with personalities, even though sometimes I hide the true identity of a source, an informant, or the holder of one or another opinion. My hope is that this makes the story more readable than it otherwise would be.

The second warning is that the book engages with some quite sensitive and controversial normative questions that have surrounded the debates about race-based quotas in the allocation of university places and public sector jobs, or affirmative actions as they are also known in Brazil. In this respect I have taken a different approach from most (though not all) writing by outsiders on race in Brazil and Spanish America, because I have listened to and considered different sides of the argument rather than declaring a partisan position at the outset. My position as an outsider has (I hope) helped me to maintain friendships even with people with whose opinions I have in the end not been able to fully agree. I am convinced that, although social scientists—local or foreign—are perfectly entitled to take openly partisan positions, to do so aggressively in their writings weakens their contribution and risks making them into mouthpieces of local political factions. The corollary is that their scholarship may be dismissed as partisan by those in the local or international arena who disagree with them. I occasionally remark in this book that scholarly activity in Brazil and other Latin American countries is excessively shaped by political-tribal loyalties. As I argued in my introduction to the recent collective work *The Crisis of Multiculturalism in Latin America* (2016), it is perverse to use the recognition of inevitable ideological bias in social science as a reason for pursuing and deepening that bias; rather it should encourage us to handle it warily. But we have to be aware that the explicit and more often implicit pressures in Latin American academic life to adopt and remain faithful to one or another ideological, political, or party loyalty can be very strong. I am no more immune to these pressures than others, but I have tried to deal as impartially as I can with the normative issues raised by the quotas debate and I hope thereby to bring about further exploration of how political philosophy—of which I am far from a seasoned practitioner—can play a role in political argument in Brazil and other countries of the region.

Nonetheless, I have in the end taken a position and I have to recognize that to spend all those years studying this subject in order then, in the end, to take a position against quotas would have been very surprising, if not perverse. In those circumstances, I would probably not have written the book at all.

London, October 2017

Acronyms

ABA: Associação Brasileira de Antropologia—Brazilian Anthropological Association.

ABI: Associação Brasileira de Imprensa—Brazilian Press Association.

ABONG: Associação Brasileira de Organizações Não-Governamentais—Brazilian Association of NGOs.

ABPN: Associação Brasileira de Pesquisadores/as Negros/as—Brazilian Black Researchers' Association.

ACMUN: Associação Cultural de Mulheres Negras—Cultural Association of Black Women.

ADPF: Argüição de Descumprimento de Preceito Fundamental—a case brought to court alleging noncompliance with a fundamental (constitutional) precept.

ANPOCS: Associação Nacional de Pós-Graduação e Pesquisa em Ciências Sociais—Brazilian National Social Science Association.

BID/IDB: Banco Interamericano de Desarrollo—Interamerican Development Bank.

BNDES: Banco Nacional de Desenvolvimento Econômico e Social—National Social and Economic Development Bank.

CCN: Conselho da Comunidade Negra—Council for the Black Community.

CEA: Centro de Estudos Afro-Asiáticos – Centre of African and Asian Studies.

CEAO: Centro de Estudos Asiáticos e Orientais—Center for Asian and Oriental Studies, UFBA.

CEAP: Centro de Articulação de Populações Marginalizadas—Center for the Mobilization of Marginalized Populations.

CEB: Comunidade Eclesial de Base—Christian Base Community.

CEBRAP: Centro Brasileiro de Análise e Planejamento—Brazilian Centre for Analysis and Planning.

CEERT: Centro de Estudos das Relações de Trabalho e Desigualdade—Centre for Labour and Inequality Studies.

CEPPIR: Coordenadoria Especial de Políticas de Promoção da Igualdade Racial—Special Coordinating Body for Racial Equality.

CHESF: Companhia Hidrelétrica do São Francisco—São Francisco Hydroelectric Corporation.

CIEC: Coordenaçao Interdisciplinar de Estudos Culturais—Interdisciplinary Cultural Studies Committee.

CNE: Conselho Nacional de Educação—National Education Council.

CNPq: Conselho Nacional de Pesquisas—National Research Council.

CONAPIR: Conferencia Nacional de Promoção da Igualdade Racial—National Conference for the Promotion of Racial Equality.

CRIOLA: an NGO devoted to women's health. This is not an acronym but a term meaning "a black woman" or maybe "a woman of dark skin."

CSO: civil society organization.

CUT: Central Unica dos Trabalhadores—National Trade Union Central—the dominant peak trade union body.

ENADE: Exame Nacional de Desempenho de Estudantes—National Student Progress Examination.

ENEM: Exame Nacional do Ensino Médio—National Secondary School Examination.

ESAF: Espaços Afirmados—Spaces of Affirmation.

FASE: Federação de Órgãos para Assistência Social e Educacional—Federation of Agencies for Social and Educational Assistance.

FGV: Fundação Getúlio Vargas—Getúlio Vargas Foundation.

FIES: Fundo de Financiamento Estudantil—Student Finance Fund.

FNB: Frente Negra Brasileira—Brazilian Black Front.

FUNAI: Fundação Nacional do Indio—National Indian Foundation—the state agency charged with protection of the indigenous population.

FUVEST: Fundação Universitária para o Vestibular—University Foundation for the Management of the Vestibular Examination (in São Paulo).

GELEDES Instituto da Mulher Negra—GELEDES Black Women's Institute.

GEMAA: Grupo de Estudos Multidisciplinar da Ação Afirmativa—Multidisciplinary Research Group on Affirmative Actions.

GPA: grade point average.

IBASE: Instituto Brasileiro de Análise Social y Económica—Brazilian Institute for Social and Economic Analysis.

IBGE: Instituto Brasileiro de Geografía e Estatística—Brazilian Geography and Statistics Institute.

IESP: Instituto de Estudos Sociais e Políticos—Institute for Social and Political Research (at UERJ).

IFCS: Instituto de Filosofia e Ciências Sociais (Institute of Philosophy and Social Sciences, Federal University of Rio de Janeiro)

IFP: International Fellowship Program.

IFPE: Instituto Federal de Pernambuco—Pernambuco Federal Education Institute.

IIDH: Instituto Interamericano de Derechos Humanos—Interamerican Instiutute of Human Rights.

ILO: International labour Organization.

IMENA: Instituto de Mulheres Negras do Amapá—Amapá Black Women's Institute.

INCLUSP: Programa de Inclusão Social na Universidade de São Paulo – USP Social Inclusion Programme.

INCRA: Instituto Nacional de Colonização e Reforma Agrária—National Agrarian Reform Institute.

INEP: Instituto Nacional de Estudos e Pesquisas Educacionais Anísio Teixeira—National Institute of Educational Research—named for Anisio Teixeira, an educator whose death during the military dictatorship has never been clarified.

IPEA: Instituto de Pesquisa Econômica Aplicada—Institute for Applied Economic Research.

ISB: Instituto Cultural Steve Biko—Steve Biko Cultural Institute.

Itamaraty: shorthand for Ministry of Foreign Affairs (named after the palace in Rio de Janeiro where the Ministry was housed until its move to Brasilia).

IUPERJ: Instituto Universitário de Pesquisas do Rio de Janeiro—University Research Institute of Rio de Janeiro.

LAESER: Laboratório de Análises Econômicas, Históricas, Sociais, e Estatística das Relações Raciais (Laboratory for Economic, Historical, Social, and Statistical Analysis of Race Relations).

LPS: Laboratório de Pesquisa Social—Social Research Laboratory.

MEC: Ministério da Educação—Ministry of Education.

MNU: Movimento Negro Unificado contra a Discriminação Racial—United Black Antiracial Discrimination Movement.

MPB: Musica Popular Brasileira—literally Brazilian Popular Music.

Term used to refer to a generation of singers and musicians who flourished in the 1960s and 1970s.

MST: Movimento dos Trabalhadores Rurais Sem Terra—Landless Workers' Movement.

NEAB: Núcleo de Estudos Afro-Brasileiros—Afro-Brazilian Studies Centre.

NGO: Nongovernmental organization.

NUER: Nucleo de Estudos Etnico-Raciais—Ethnic-Racial Research Centre.

OAB: Ordem dos Advogados do Brasil—Brazilian Bar Association.

PASUSP: Programa de Avaliação Seriada da Universidade de São Paulo—Continuous Assessment Admissions Programme of São Paulo University.

PCdoB: Partido Comunista do Brasil—Communist Party of Brazil.

PDU: Programa Diversidade na Universidade—Diversity in the University Programme.

PESB: Pesquisa Social Brasileira—Brazilian Social Survey.

PET: Programa de Educação Tutorial—Tutorial Guidance Programme (for selected students in need).

PIC: Programa Inovador de Cursos—Innovative Course Programme.

PMDB: Partido do Movimento Democrático do Brasil—Brazilian Democratic Movement Party.

PNAD: Pesquisa Nacional de Amostra Domiciliar—National Household Sample Survey.

PNAES: Plano Nacional de Assistência Estudiantil—National Plan for Student Financial Support.

PNDH: Programa Nacional de Direitos Humanos—National Human Rights Programme.

POMPA: Projeto Mentes e Portas Abertas—"Open Minds and Open Doors" Project (Steve Biko Institute).

PPCor: Programa Políticas da Cor na Educação Brasileira—Programme on Colour Policies in Brazilian Education.

ProUni: Programa Universidade para Todos—University for All Programme.

PSDB: Partido da Social Democracia Brasileira—Brazilian Social Democratic Party.

PSol: Partido Socialismo e Liberdade—Socialism and Freedom Party.

PT: Partido dos Trabalhadores—Workers' Party.

PUC: Pontifícia Universidade Católica—Pontifical Catholic University. There are several in Brazil, each of them independent.

PVC: Prevestibular Comunitario—Community-Based Prevestibular
  Course.
PVN: Prevestibular para Negros - Prevestibular Course for Black
  Students
PVNC: Prevestibular para Negros e Carentes—Prevestibular Course for
  Black and Low-Income Students.
SAT: Scholastic Aptitude Test.
SECAD: Secretaria de Educação Continuada, e Alfabetização (later
  SECADI: Secretaria de Educação Continuada, Alfabetização, Diversi-
  dade e Inclusão)—Secretariat for Continuous Education, Literacy
  Training and—later—Diversity.
SEDH: Secretaria Especial dos Direitos Humanos—Special Secretariat
  for Human Rights.
SENUN: Seminario Nacional de Universitarios Negros—National Black
  Students' Seminar.
SEPM: Secretaria Especial de Políticas para as Mulheres—Special
  Secretariat for Women.
SEPPIR: Secretaría Especial de Políticas de Promoção da Igualde
  Racial—Special Secretariat for Racial Equality Policies.
SEPROMI: Secretaria de Promoção da Igualdade—State Secretariat for
  the Promotion of Racial Equality (in Bahia).
SISU: Sistema de Seleção Unificada—Unified Selection System.
TEN: Teatro Experimental do Negro—Black Experimental Theatre.
UEMS: Universidade Estadual de Mato Grosso do Sul—State University
  of Matto Grosso do Sul,
UENF: Universidade Estadual do Norte Fluminense— State University
  of Northern Rio de Janeiro.
UEPB: Universidade Estadual da Paraiba—State University of Paraiba.
UERJ: Universidade Estadual do Rio de Janeiro—State University of
  Rio de Janeiro.
UFAl: Universidade Federal de Alagoas—Federal University of Alagoas.
UFBA: Universidade Federal da Bahia—Federal University of Bahia.
UFCG: Universidade Federal de Campina Grande—Federal University
  of Campina Grande.
UFMG: Universidade Federal de Minas Gerais—Federal University of
  Minas Gerais.
UFPE: Universidade Federal de Pernambuco—Federal University of
  Pernambuco.
UFRJ: Universidade Federal do Rio de Janeiro—Federal University of
  Rio de Janeiro.

UFRPE: Universidade Federal Rural de Pernambuco—Federal Rural University of Pernambuco.

UFSC: Universidade Federal de Santa Catarina—Federal University of Santa Catarina.

UFSCar: Universidade Federal de São Carlos—Federal University of São Carlos.

UnB: Universidade de Brasilia—University of Brasilia.

UNE: União Nacional de Estudantes—National Students' Union.

UNEB: Universidade Estadual da Bahia—State University of Bahia.

UNESP: Universidade Estadual Paulista—Paulista State University.

UNDP: United Nations Development Programme.

UNICAMP: Universidade Estadual de Campinas—State University of Campinas.

UNILAB: Universidade da Integração Internacional da Lusofonía Afro-Brasileira—University for the International Integration of the Afro-Brazilian Lusophone (Portuguese-Speaking) World.

UNIP: Universidade Paulista—Paulista University.

UNIRIO: Universidade Federal do Estado do Rio de Janeiro—Federal University of the State of Rio de Janeiro, (not to be confused with the UFRJ or with UERJ).

USP: Universidade de São Paulo—University of São Paulo.

THE PRISM OF RACE

ONE

Introduction

This book can be read in three ways: as a history of the campaign to introduce affirmative action in the form of quotas for black students in Brazil's public universities; as an engaged survey of the arguments for and against the principle of race-based quotas; and as an argument about social movements, civil society, and the state in Brazil and by extension in Latin America. These three themes are not always brought together in writings on the subject, and so different readers will have different interests and will follow the sections relevant to those interests. The themes are intertwined throughout the text because I want to convey a multilayered set of narratives and debates. The campaign was conducted by a fairly small group of people who appear throughout these pages in different settings so that their network can come to life in all its density. The arguments are presented in part as just arguments but also in the context of the inescapable personal and institutional relationships of those who propound them. The theory of social movements is included because it should enable the reader to see how this "prism of race" casts light on some deeply rooted features of Brazilian and Latin American society and political culture that must be taken into account by outsiders if they are to avoid remaining forever mere beginners in their understanding of the region.

Over some fifteen years during the presidencies of Fernando Henrique Cardoso (1995–2003), widely known as Fernando Henrique or FHC, and Luiz Inácio Lula da Silva, universally known as Lula (2003–11), Brazil was the stage for a campaign that may go down as a turning point in the country's race relations. It started with a demand that public universities which cater to but a fraction of the country's youth and an even smaller proportion of its black youth should set up programmes to improve substantially the number and proportion of those young blacks among their students. The subsequent evolution was wide ranging in its practical effects and the endpoint was momentous in terms of constitutional principle: first there was a gradual unfolding across the country's universities of mechanisms to expand the black student population; and then, in 2012, the Supreme Court unanimously confirmed the constitutional acceptability of the core of those mechanisms by sanctioning the recognition of a person's colour classification for the purpose of official allocation of resources such as university places, scholarships, and employment in public service.

This unanimous decision overturned objections to such recognition, grounded in a century of everyday practice and explicit and implicit legal doctrine, and opened the way for Congress and the government to follow in its wake. In this way "affirmative actions" (always in the plural in Brazil, as will later be explained) and quotas (or "reserved places") became a standard feature of bureaucratic and educational life, operating in the allocation of government employment as well as in the universities, and by 2016 the changing colour of the undergraduate student population in prestigious institutions was widely remarked upon.

Behind this lay a fairly small network of intellectuals and NGOs, known collectively as the *movimento negro*,[1] who worked their way through university lecture halls and meeting rooms and the corridors of the federal bureaucracy to gather support for their cause. Their campaign was not a mass movement, though it did involve occasional mobilizations on university campuses and one major national demonstration in Brasilia; on the other hand it did fit some deeply rooted corporatist characteristics of the Brazilian state that had served to handle emerging social forces in earlier periods.

The polemical aspect of the affirmative actions and the classificatory regime they inevitably implied manifested itself in rifts among academics who ranged themselves in opposed camps, conducted occasionally bad-tempered debates, and wrote frequently in the op-ed pages of the leading newspapers of São Paulo and Rio de Janeiro. This was more than point-scoring. When it comes to this subject, everyone, whatever their skin colour, and whether they say it or not, knows that they are personally implicated. The debates about racial inequality were being conducted in institutions where there were few black students and

---

1. Throughout the book the word "*negro*" is used in its Portuguese pronunciation—to rhyme with "hedgerow."

barely a handful of black professors. So, although in debates no one ever mentioned the colour of another's skin—at least not if that person belonged or seemed to belong to a different colour group—the vehemence of expression betrayed an underlying tension. This emotional charge should not, however, distract from the very important issues about the place of identity politics and reparatory justice in the frame of social justice, and about the ways to pursue racial justice in a society shaped by centuries of race mixture.

This subject has attracted so many research projects and articles that the task of summarizing and reviewing them all would be a research project in itself. Thanks to the abundance of data published by the official statistical agency, the Brazilian Geography and Statistics Institute (IBGE), and the Ministry of Education (MEC) through its research and data collection arm, the National Institute of Educational Research (INEP); by the government's own economics think tank, the Institute for Applied Economic Research (IPEA); by universities themselves; and by independent surveys, studies have been pouring out in Brazilian and international (especially US-based) publications with quantitative analyses of various aspects of the affirmative action programmes. To evaluate them all and compare their results consistently would require deep familiarity with those very complex sources and many days and weeks spent inspecting the multiple corresponding databases, making for yet another project. I do refer in detail to some of these studies, but I am aware that my observations suffer from technical limitations. There are many excellent qualitative studies as well, and, although to generalize from them is risky, the speed of change and the scale of a phenomenon covering so many institutions, plus the hazards of interpretation of quantitative data on race in circumstances in which the mere assignation of an individual is a matter of dispute, make qualitative observation absolutely essential. There have already been attempts to evaluate outcomes of affirmative actions, but they are still only preliminary exercises in the face of a vast project of social engineering that acts like a prism opening the way to insights into many aspects of Brazilian society. It is in that respect, by going beyond the initial and important question of the viability and efficacy of affirmative action in the education sphere, that this book hopes to open up new perspectives—taking a broad analytic approach of the kind that so far has been taken only by Tianna Paschel in English (2016). The story must also be held up as a multifaceted mirror to the country's race relations regime, to its political and academic cultures, to its heritage of corporatism, and to the ways in which its intellectuals write and talk about social justice and identity politics. It requires an understanding of the evolution of Brazil's higher education and the division between its public and private sectors, its hierarchy of prestige, and its headlong expansion since the 1990s. The theme of corporatism opens the way to an understanding of how political pressure works through the bureaucracy and how nongovernmental actors can, quite legally and properly, penetrate the state's resource allocation and rights-creation processes. Since these pressures go under the name of a movement, the question arises of what can count as a social movement in the contemporary Brazilian context and how we are to characterize the nexus with the international NGO system, which has become a standard feature of social movements in the entire Latin American region.

The theme of inequality itself also needs to be seen in a wide perspective, preventing us from taking ethnic divisions and identities for granted: we have to set them beside the class dimensions of inequality and ask who, to use William Julius Wilson's consecrated term (1987), are the truly disadvantaged, who are the authentically needy, and who can be called the truly deserving—if such words as "truly" and "authentically" are acceptable at all and if those questions can usefully be answered. Certainly we cannot proceed as if the ethnic dividing lines were self-evident and unambiguous: to do so would fly in the face of a mountain of literature on ethnicity from Barth to Brubaker (Barth 1969; Brubaker 2002, 2015, 2016; Brubaker and Cooper 2000). Following on inequality, the theme of social justice, then, opens the way to a reminder that these are complex philosophical questions to which answers cannot be taken readymade from the cut and thrust of polemical disputes, especially in the context of the emotive arena of race—and this same emotional temptation calls for moderation in the use of language, for it is not the task of the social scientist to pass judgment, or to attach pejorative or demeaning labels to individuals. We are not judges, and we are not detectives; we are not equipped to assign unconscious personal motives. Nonetheless, when our own profession is the object of analysis, it must be recognized that academics have interests and biographies and participate in generational, professional, and political networks, wherefore at least an attempt must be made to look at ourselves and our institutions with as dispassionate an eye as can be managed.

The affirmative action disputes were not a storm in a teacup, but they did not go on forever: in the end they faded, the enmities they had fueled simmered down, and the political class legislated for a compromise. In the view of some, by mixing racial and socioeconomic criteria in the allocation of quota places the politicians had betrayed the black cause. Not long after, Brazil sank into a disastrous period of political deadlock, spectacular corruption trials, murky political manoeuvres, and economic stagnation, in the midst of which a coalition of opponents and erstwhile allies cobbled together, who knows by what means and with what resources, a coalition that successfully impeached a hapless president on what were clearly spurious grounds, as was readily admitted by the very promoters of the impeachment. The law obliging federal universities to implement affirmative action remained, though universities entered a period of budgetary uncertainty and, in the case of the State University of Rio de Janeiro, near closure.

Like numerous studies of comparative race relations, I hold Brazil up to the mirror of its "eternal Other," the United States, and do so in terms of the concepts of affirmative action applied in the two countries. The United States is not the only other country to have adopted such policies: India has perhaps the longest track record since the principle, known as "reservation" or "reserved seats," was enshrined in the country's 1949 Constitution, and political mobilization by the most varied groups, especially lower castes and "untouchables," in the most varied contexts, remains a recurrent theme in the country's politics (Jaffrelot 2010). Malaysia has imposed a wide-ranging policy to displace ethnic Chinese from commanding positions in business and to reduce their proportion in education and public service since 1971, and South Africa has opened up quotas in universities and elsewhere on a massive scale to Africans. These and other examples suffice to show that an extensive comparative coverage would raise all sorts of new issues in sociological analysis and political theory, so my comparison of Brazil with the United States remains very much a preliminary exercise.

The comparative approach means in turn setting the debates against some ideas about social justice in contemporary political theory, above all those of John Rawls. Rawls does not deal directly with the politics of identity, but philosophers such as Anthony Appiah (2005), Amartya Sen (2009), Seyla Benhabib (2002), and Charles Taylor (1992), offer a full-scale treatment of the tension between the politics of identity and the politics of social justice, and I have included elements of those discussions as they are relevant to the present subject, because it helps to understand the assumptions about rights and entitlements that lay behind the polemics. I do not however pretend even remotely to offer a full treatment of that very distinguished literature.

The applicability of concepts of race developed in Europe and the

United States to other parts of the world has long been subject to doubt, in conjunction with calls to think about those regions as no more or less exceptional than any others. This thinking is evident in the work of authors as disparate as Jack Goody in his impassioned *The Theft of History* (2006) and Tianna Paschel, who in the course of her account of black movements in Brazil and Colombia questions "two latent assumptions: that theories of race in the United States can be extended to the rest of the world; and that the US civil rights and Black Power movements should be the benchmarks from which we define and evaluate Black struggle everywhere" (2016: 229). It is now time to go further and question the global applicability of terms like social movements and civil society in their social democratic and liberal definition and in the sense in which they are used by Anglo-Saxon and European social science (as in Touraine 1985; McAdam, et al. 1996; Tilly 1998). I do not by any means deny the applicability or relevance of a social democratic or liberal ethos to societies or cultures outside the North Atlantic generally or to Brazil in particular, but I do start from the view that as observers we are all too ready to project our values onto the social movements that attract our sympathy in distant places, or conversely sometimes to draw our values from an admiring acceptance of the virtue of those movements. The traditions mentioned also do not speak of the state in their interpretations and definitions of social movements, whereas in Latin America the state is an indispensable partner—as Touraine has said in his writings on the region (1988). I am therefore concerned to emphasize certain overlooked features of social movements and civil society, and the final chapter explores what these terms really mean in the Brazilian context and by extension in the context of Latin America.

If these are the analytical and sometimes polemical points of the following chapters, my purpose is also to tell a story, to convey the atmosphere in which Brazilian debates and struggles over race have taken place in recent decades, and to bring some of the leading players to life. Therefore, after an exposition of the term corporatism and its importance in understanding our subject, this chapter and the next one will track the history of affirmative action and actions mostly in the field in which they have been most controversially and prominently applied, namely, higher education. It will introduce the important subject of private for-profit education, operated by firms that have profited handsomely from government affirmative action programmes without ever arousing the same heated controversy as was the case with their application in the public sector. The following three chapters will dissect the arguments, the issues, and the interests involved and will place the story in the context of Brazil's political culture, of certain concepts of social justice, of a comparison with affirmative action in the United States, and of the theory and concept of social movements. The last chapter will then form a complement to the account of corporatism in this opening chapter by confronting the applicability of concepts of social movements and civil society in Brazil.

I am aware that at some points the reader may find the detailed information tedious or hard to interpret, and for this I apologize. However, I have chosen to describe arguments in detail because this is a subject in which ready-made or stylized facts are deployed too often too casually, and it is part of my task to explain the basis of those arguments. Quite often these are statistical claims, whose credibility depends on circumstances, definitions, and the nature and quality of sources. This applies with greatest force when it comes to racial classification, and chapter 3 has an extensive discussion of this question. Given the pervasiveness of race classification throughout the text, it is not feasible to stop and discuss terminology each time classification arises, so I have tried to write with caution. Another example is that of student numbers: sources do not always distinguish between full-time and part-time students for example, and this may well distort estimates of student numbers in private universities in particular. But doubts also arise in relation to their numbers in certain courses in public universities where in effect students are working part time or even full time and attending classes scheduled in the evenings. Indeed the whole area of educational statistics, of which the Brazilian MEC produces vast amounts, is a specialty in itself requiring intimate knowledge of criteria, methods, and definitions that I do not possess. I also use various sample surveys, but again I have pointed out their procedures and sometimes differences between their findings in order to avoid seizing on one or another result that happens to be convenient for my views. These words of caution also extend to qualitative work, including my own, because the sensitivity of the subject matter has to be recognized and moralistic language avoided. It is all too easy to lapse into judgments about the racist character of individuals, texts, or an entire society: in Brazil, for example, the "myth of racial democracy" is routinely dismissed as a malign fiction paraded as a cover for racist ideas and prejudice. In effect this is to attribute evil intentions to vast numbers of people, to Gilberto Freyre who coined the phrase, and to governments that for a time promoted it as a banner for Brazil on the world stage. Yet whatever the effects or implications of the idea (it hardly merits the word "doctrine"), it is incumbent on us to ask whether Freyre really held the views attributed to him or whether others supposedly inspired by them were truly bent on perpetuating racial discrimination, rather than simply consciously or unconsciously blind to it. In another example, one might attribute a degree of tone-deafness or subconscious resistance to those who prefer to ignore the anger underlying the claims and rhetoric of the movimento negro and its supporters, or who treat the issue of affirmative action in purely technical terms: are they not (subconsciously perhaps) changing the subject by raising the alternative of investing in primary schooling for example? Even then it would be wrong to use terms like "racist" to describe those people or those views, for there is no reason to believe that they are speaking in bad faith or that they intend to perpetuate discrimination, and it is not the place of a social scientist to engage in such labeling.

Three Longer-Term Implications

Although as its title implies, my research on the politics of affirmative action has led me to reflect on the nature of the Brazilian state and the country's social movements, as well as on some difficult questions of how to approach the study of race and how to write about the subject, it is also of course my purpose to contribute to the understanding of the country's race relations. In this, as in the themes of why the Congress passed its 2012 quotas law and why the quotas campaign focused so much on prestige universities, and in my interpretation of the instability of racial self-assignment, I advance interpretations which themselves require further study. Each of these three interpretations can be thought of as counterintuitive (though that depends on your intuitions): I advance the hypothesis that Congress passed the quotas law because its members saw in it a way, and an inexpensive way, to prevent Brazil from sliding toward confrontational and embittered race conflicts. They probably also thought of it as a relatively minor affair just as they probably did not regard race relations as an issue of supreme political importance, but at least, perhaps because affirmative actions do not attract budgetary allocations,[2] they kept it out of their interminable trading of political favours. In response to the question why the campaign focused so much on prestige universities (unlike in Chile where student mobilization tar-

---

2. There is a federal scheme for student hardship grants or financial support (PNAES: Plano Nacional de Assistência Estudiantil—National Plan for Student Financial Support) but they are not allocated on a race basis.

geted the entire higher education system), I advance the hypothesis that this is because the main concern of the movimento negro was access to the elite: of course they were concerned to promote racial equality in general and probably also universal social justice, but if the priorities had been elsewhere they would not have followed a strategy concentrated on the institutions which are the unavoidable and indispensable channel to elite professions. And on the difficult subject of self-assignment of racial classification, I advance the possibility that substantial numbers of people who might otherwise or previously not have thought of themselves for one moment as *negro* or *moreno* (brown) began during this period to think of themselves as such: instead of attributing their disappointments to bad luck or laziness at school, they began to attribute them to discrimination and so also thought of themselves if not as victims, perhaps at least as potential beneficiaries of official affirmative action. In a climate where the movimento negro was calling on people, sometimes in quite forceful moralistic language, to *asumir*, to face up to their black (not brown) heritage and identity, it is not surprising that the appeal of black self-assignment has broadened.

Once again, to verify such a claim of cause-and-effect would require another research project, although there is some evidence to support it in research by Luisa Schwartzman (2009b). But its long-term implications, allied to a trend toward *preto* and *pardo* identification among younger people not from the poorest income strata, which has been registered in successive censuses, along with growing *negro* identification in surveys, could be very significant indeed, and this is where we reach the most counterintuitive hypothesis—which is one about the future of Brazilian race relations. According to this theory, negros and morenos will become racially integrated as a result not of a campaign advocating racial integration but rather of one that emphasizes their difference. Black activists and sympathizers have for long been claiming that blacks, or blacks and browns taken together, are half the Brazilian population, much to the annoyance of those who either dispute the binary racial model on which such claims are based, or find this division of the nation into racial groups inherently distasteful, uncomfortable, or maybe just embarrassing. But the country is changing, because the politics of race has changed thanks to affirmative actions, the unstoppable demographics of intermarriage, and the expansion of the middle class—or at least of the lower middle class. Once recognized as constituting the majority or near-majority, negros and morenos, or just negros for those favouring a binary formula, will begin to embody Brazilian national identity and their presence in the middle class and, gradually, the upper middle class, will be normalized. Inequalities will have to then be recognized as deriving mainly from injustices in the distribution of resources, notably education and social capital. Quotas will become anomalous and possibly unsustainable because far too many people will qualify for them according to the system established in 2012—under which quota places are allocated, *inter alia*, according to the proportion of pretos and pardos in each state.

If this panorama develops then the campaign for even mildly dark-skinned people to "come out" as black, whose purpose was to accentuate contradictions and provoke confrontation, will have contributed to a kind of racial integration, while the fears of the campaign's opponents who conjured up nightmare scenarios of Brazil as a country divided racially because of these campaigns will also have been proved wrong. In this case new research is not called for: just patience to wait and see.

Corporatism

There is a classic, if now somewhat dated, interpretation of the state in Brazil, as well as in other Latin American countries, according to which the country has been ruled since colonial times by an unchanging bureaucratic apparatus staffed by a self-perpetuating elite. Thus Raimundo Faoro in the conclusion of his classic treatise on the Brazilian state, *Os Donos do Poder* ("The Power Holders"), originally published in 1957:

> The caste of bureaucrats based on the system of politically managed patrimonial capitalism, acquired for itself an aristocratic content, as a *noblesse de robe* [whose rank was attached to a judicial function] and also of title. The rise of liberal and democratic ideologies neither broke nor diluted, nor dismantled the political patronage which they exercised over the nation, and which remained impervious to majority rule. (Faoro 1975: vol. 2, 747–48)

Faoro continues in quite ornate language to deplore the endless chameleon-like changes in the outward appearance of the elite while the mass of the people oscillate between contentious outbreaks and acceptance of largesse as if from a "benevolent prince dispensing justice and protection" (748)—the prince being not so much the elite in the sense of a class of persons as a bureaucracy in the sense of an institution that rules forever and devours all that it surveys, at once parasitic and predatory, perpetuating itself through the centuries at the expense of a population of slaves and subjects.

In 1974, Philippe Schmitter, inspired by his research on Brazil but operating in a synchronic comparative framework, coined a now standard definition of corporatism as

> a system of interest representation in which the constituent units are organized into a limited number of singular, compulsory, non-competitive, hierarchically ordered and functionally differentiated categories, recognized or licensed (if not created) by the state and granted a deliberate representational monopoly within their respective categories in exchange for observing certain controls on their selection of leaders and articulation of demands and supports. (1974: 93–94)

So both emphasize the hierarchical and co-optative character of the state, but Schmitter, writing of the Brazilian state as reshaped by Getulio Vargas, is more aware of its role in managing or dampening the clash of social forces that arose in the twentieth century process of industrialization, and therefore points to representation as a counterpart to hierarchy. Similarly, Guillermo O'Donnell (thinking primarily, but not exclusively, of Argentina) used the expression "estado bifronte," which I translate as the "Janus-faced state" (1977) and Alfred Stepan spoke of "inclusionary" and "exclusionary" corporatism (Stepan 1978). The author who has devoted most energy to the question of corporatism in Latin America is Howard Wiarda, for whom almost any interaction between private interests and the state qualifies both as corporatist and as illiberal and usually undemocratic (1981: 10). Although he offers an exhaustive guide to these interactions, the approach is too narrowly focused on institutions and their formal characteristics. In the context of identity politics the only political scientist who has applied the concept is Sarah Chartock, whose 2013 article, based mainly on the case of Ecuador, provides a catalogue of "ethnodevelopment as a subtype of corporatism," including "the state structuring, subsidizing, and partial control of indigenous sector representation in ways that both keep with the old corporatist models and partially diverge from them" (2013: 69, 70). This is quite similar to my analysis, although the elements of (quite personalist) state control are much more pronounced in Ecuador than in Brazil, reflecting the regime of Rafael Correa.

Corporatism combines clientelistic and institutional features, evidenced notably in consultative and parastatal bodies where leaders of interest groups such as trade unions and employers' organizations can take part in decision-making and the allocation and even control of state resources, although in the case of trade unions on condition of a degree of subservience to the state, however radical their rhetoric (Erickson 1977; Mericle 1977). Although the state bias is in favor of business interests, as in O'Donnell's model, substantial resources are ceded to trade unions for the purpose of providing services to their members—sometimes facilitating the entrenchment and perpetuation of leading figures.

Corporatism can therefore be described as an ensemble of habits and structures of controlled inclusion by the state of social actors and constituencies through the incorporation of their leaders in decision-making and the provision of resources specific to their interests. Corporatism creates monopolies of political representation, and also monopolies in labor markets and the allocation of state resources, for example, regulating access to professions or ensuring that designated industry associations are represented in decision-making of direct interest to them—as amply illustrated by Brazil's National Education Council (CNE), on which the private sector of education is represented as of right (of which more in chapter 2). In its heyday of state-orchestrated development through import substitution, corporatism also institutionalized the representation of sectoral industry interest groups—cotton producers, sugar producers, textile producers and so on—in government policy and resource allocation, especially in protectionist import restrictions and foreign exchange allocation. The opportunities for favoritism and corruption are unfortunately evident. On the workers' side, in Brazil the political power of union leaders, enshrined in laws imposed by Getulio Vargas as part of the corporatist system, was cut down during the military dictatorship, but other aspects of corporatism were maintained, and after the passage of the 1988 Constitution Maria Herminia Tavares de Almeida, the leading authority on the subject, wrote frequently of "hybrid corporatism": despite initial liberal clamour for a complete disconnection from the state in early days of the "New Republic," supported at the time by the former union leader Lula, the attractions of the automatic and compulsory deduction of union dues from wage packets (the "imposto syndical" or union tax), before they are passed to the government and then redistributed among unions, and also of the principle of single representation per workplace, were too great for the "burocracia sindical" (Tavares de Almeida 1996; Power and Doctor 2004). Under the new

Constitution union freedoms were consolidated and elected union leaders ceased to be subject to government approval and during Lula's government the position of the trade union "peak" organization CUT was consolidated in law (D'Araujo: 73). But the position of unions was weakened in 2017 when, post-impeachment and much to the satisfaction of private sector interests, new legislation put an end, in principle, to the union tax, rendering them subject to the agreement of individual employees. As of late 2017 the principle still awaited implementation via an administrative decree ("portaria") regulating its application and it was possible that this would be held up for some time by union pressure and the Ministry of Labour's bureaucracy.

Corporatism was never hegemonic in twentieth-century Brazil or elsewhere in Latin America: even in its heyday, during the period of protectionist industrialization from about 1930 to 1982 there was also unregulated trade union activity and the economy remained capitalist, so rather than using the term to refer to the state as a whole, it should be used to describe an enduring feature of the state whose prominence was greatest during a certain period, and that coexists with both the state's repressive periods and intermittent repressive reflexes and with its more democratic periods, as well as with the many liberal and individualist features of contemporary citizenship.

Whatever the institutional changes that have occurred over the long and short runs, it is important to understand that corporatism is embedded in a perennial culture of patrimonialism. By this is meant not a specific set of arrangements, as Weber outlined (Pereira 2016), but rather a widespread assumption that holders of public office enjoy almost total security of tenure and also that holders of established positions are entitled to many perquisites, notably guaranteed pensions equal to their salaries and (for the military in particular) special medical facilities. Corporatism since 1989 has been expressed in the distribution of jobs to key actors, in the opening up of policy formulation to the participation of leading interest groups, the allocation of some largesse, and the occasional establishment of relatively small new agencies. The scale is limited, but the Janus-faced character continues: if the Cardoso government was said to be partial to big business through privatization and deregulation, the more interventionist PT governments have been notoriously indulgent toward big business through the state's enormous National Social and Economic Development Bank (BNDES) and its heavily subsidized loans, notably to the construction industry, and through tariff protection for the car industry during the post-2008 downturn to avoid increased unemployment (which eventually came, but later and harder, in 2014).[3]

The pattern of inclusion by absorption of the movimento negro within the federal state machine started during the Cardoso government as black individuals were appointed to niches within the Ministry of Justice and worked to promote the cause in diverse ways. Under Cardoso, racial equality was the responsibility of the Ministry of Justice, and the Special Secretariat for Racial Equality Policies (SEPPIR) as a separate special secretariat was only established by Lula. SEPPIR itself can be described as a corporatist initiative because it was staffed by people recruited from the movimento negro, but like the quota places themselves—whose cost is born by the universities out of their budgets—it is also low cost and not like the long-standing class corporatist bodies, which have their origins in the 1930s.

Within in the Brazilian state SEPPIR was a minnow. I was told that it "coordinated" projects to the value of R$2 billion in 2008 (c. US$120 million at the time), but they were funded from elsewhere; its own budget, according to Tianna Paschel, was a paltry US$9 million in 2015 (2016: 175), although that sounds like an underestimate for a professional staff of eighty. Originally established as a secretariat attached to the presidency with the rank, but not the resources, of a ministry, it has been downgraded in successive reshuffles to a department in the Ministry of Justice, first by Dilma Roussef and then by Temer, although it retains its name and its staff.[4] It should also be noted that, apart from the federal government, all states of the union and some municipalities now have an institution similar to SEPPIR, although their influence and resources vary; Paschel writes that they number "some 600" (177). Another corporatist initiative is the Universidade para Todos (University for All) programme—a scholarship scheme whereby private universities offer free or half-price places on a competitive basis to black and low-income students. There have been hundreds of thousands of beneficiaries, but the universities themselves benefit as much as the students since these places have been made available as "payment in lieu" of a very large amount of overdue taxes. This accounting device can be thought of as a corporatist

---

3. The BNDES became known as "bolsa empresario" in a play on "bolsa familia."

4. Not without reason had I been told by Giovanni Harvey, the senior official at SEPPIR, as early as 2008, that these secretariats "only last as long as a president unless the successor decides to maintain them."

policy because it recognizes the universities as both partners in and beneficiaries of the state's higher education policy—a relationship to which we shall return.

From the point of view of social movements, especially those representing relatively recent political constituencies like the Afro-descendant population, the opportunities offered by the enduring, albeit reduced, corporatist state are very important. Rather than building a mass base by mobilizing a vast potential following, leaders build a strategic base through the opening up of opportunities for advancement to make their voices heard and enable their followers and constituencies to gain access to state resources and entitlements. It is a piecemeal business: Paschel writes of an "ethnoracial state apparatus" (2016: 154), but although black organizations can find interlocutors and employment in many instances in the sprawling Brazilian state, they have not been included in the state apparatus on an institutional basis, in contrast to the classic corporatism under which unions were included in welfare arrangements, consultative procedures, and the system of industrial tribunals. The price for unions under the old regime, before the 1988 Constitution, was that the Ministry of Labour could intervene in their affairs under certain circumstances and could even dislodge leaders on grounds of a lack of "idoneidade ideológica" (ideological suitability). This cannot happen with the black movement (so long as political institutions remain untouched): instead, through their party connections and affinity networks, leaders and activists are given employment individually in state and federal agencies such as SEPPIR and IPEA (the government's economic think tank) and their state-level equivalents, and the numerous pressure groups, study groups, think tanks, and NGOs that make up the black movement are included in policy discussions. In SEPPIR, for example, I interviewed someone who had previously worked as an adviser to a federal deputy piloting the quotas law through Congress; someone else who was responsible for *quilombolas* (rural black communities connected to a history of fugitive slave settlements), having previously worked with them as the "coordenador"—that is, head—of an organization called "União de Negros pela Igualdade" (Union of Blacks for Equality); and a third person who had run an NGO in Rio supporting black businesses. It is an informal pattern of inclusion whereby like-minded people recruit each other into the bureaucracy, well expressed in terms like "absorption" and "state-civil society interpenetration" used by Paschel. But she also notes the weakness of the institutions established by the federal government:

not only does SEPPIR have a paltry budget, but it may also have had limited leverage even before it was "demoted": NGOs and professional associations that campaign on issues such as health, including the health of the black population (cf. Criola), also function very well independent of the state—to such an extent that in the case of AIDS policy state bureaucrats have sought them out for advice and support in persuading weak or unwilling local and state governments to implement national policies or simply spend federally allocated funds (Weyland 1995; Rich 2013). A top SEPPIR official also told Paschel that it has little power and is largely ignored by leading black-movement-linked NGOs whose reputation is strong enough to do without it (Paschel 2016: 181). Nevertheless SEPPIR came into its own as a political "articulator," facilitating political events such as marches and congresses. Since the demise of the PT government it has doubtless lost some of its leverage and may also have changed its purpose: SEPPIR was due to organize the National Conference for the Promotion of Racial Equality (CONAPIR) in December 2017, but this was postponed to the second half of 2018 (see SEPPIR announcement 21 June 2017).

Even so the penetration was still quite limited. One might, for example, have imagined that once the quotas law was passed the government and the black movement would try to oversee its implementation, but in 2013 I visited the MEC in Brasilia and found that there was no person or unit responsible for monitoring application of the quotas law. This was a matter for the universities themselves, since admissions were their autonomous prerogative. True, the government had made resources available for "permanência" grants to support students from low-income families, and this can be seen as a complement to the quotas. But those in charge of overseeing higher education were lawyers, not educationalists let alone black activists, whose job was to ensure or give advice on formal compliance rather than substantive policy goals. A year after the law was passed, the committee established by presidential decree to monitor progress in its application, which included representatives from the MEC, SEPPIR, FUNAI (the National Indian Foundation, charged with protection of the indigenous population), and civil society bodies, had not yet been constituted. A similar lack of follow-up can be seen in the wake of passage of the law requiring schools to teach African history— totemically the first law passed after Lula took power in 2004: I heard repeatedly that teachers were not trained to teach the subject or that suitable textbooks were not reaching the schools. There was no "package" linking resources to affirmative action—something very familiar in the UK academic world where conditionality and monitoring accompany every penny of resources provided to higher education institutions. Eventually, in 2015, perhaps thanks to the ephemeral tenure at the ministry of the philosophy professor Renato Janine Ribeiro, a meeting of the committee, which had been formally created by a decree in late August 2013, did take place. Apart from the federal ministries, it was attended by members of the National Students' Union (UNE), the Brazilian Black Researchers' Association (ABPN), and various organizations representing the black population, but the accompanying announcement by the ministry did not contain anything of substance.[5]

These administrative details show that the quotas law is not so much a government policy as a facilitating instrument for universities but also that the passage of members of the movimento negro through the corridors of power was ephemeral and they did not seek to perpetuate their influence through a sustained policy or if they tried they did not succeed. Rather, once the law was passed and after the restructuring of the units within the MEC that had promoted quotas—the Secretariat for Continuous Education, Literacy Training, and Diversity (SECAD) and its funding from the Interamerican Development Bank—they returned to their activism within the academic sphere.

I chose the word corporatism so as to emphasize, first, that these are ancient practices deeply rooted in the political culture and the country's political institutions and, second, that the sense of frustration over the movement's absorption by the state, expressed, for example, by Paschel, is a response to this structural feature so that a further deepening of measures to support black citizenship or empowerment is unlikely once the movement has found its interlocutors, once some of its leaders have found public sector employment, and once measures like quotas have been installed. When Paschel writes of the "absorption of activists into the state" and "the restriction and unmaking of black rights" (2016: 223), even while also recognizing that reforms have come from the top

---

5. Portaria 804—a ministerial decree—of 28 August 2013, had created this portentously named but purely deliberative "Comissão Consultiva da Sociedade Civil sobre a Política de Reserva de Vagas nas Instituições Federais de Educação Superior" to "contribute to debate" on the implementation of the quotas law passed twelve months earlier. For the text of the decree, see http://www.lex.com.br/legis_24790022_PORTARIA_N_804_DE_28_DE_AGOSTO_DE_2013.aspx. See also the 27 July 2015 statement by the MEC at http://portal.mec.gov.br/ultimas-noticias/222–537011943/21498-reserva-de-vagas-promove-a-inclusao-no-ensino-superior

and cannot be attributed significantly to "massive social movements" (222), she is reflecting again the double-edged or Janus-faced character of corporatism—"el estado bifronte" to recall O'Donnell's phrase (1977). I return to these themes in chapter 5.

It is widely assumed that the corporatist state relies on relations of personal trust and allegiance that are taken to be a core feature of Brazilian culture, embodied in the classic question asked of a person who infringes on the unspoken rules of respect: "Você sabe com quem está falando?" ("Do you realize who you are speaking to?"). It is contrasted sometimes with the Anglo-Saxon question "Who do you think you are?," addressed to people who take unfair advantage (da Matta 1991), or the reputedly typical Argentinian question "Y a mí qué me importa?" ("What the hell do I care?") (O'Donnell 1984). The phrase is a highly simplified description of the way in which social hierarchy has for generations been held together in Brazil—though less today than in earlier times. The same ambivalent "respect" also holds together the corporatist institutions and niches in the state and even filters down into the functioning of student quotas. The proliferation of affirmative actions in the allocation of resources within institutions creates ever more micro-opportunities for the exercise of this kind of personal power—and of the discretion that comes with the inherent fuzziness of the system of racial self-assignment: like generations of students before them they chase one grant or subsidy after another, now with the added chance to emphasize their status as blacks or low income earners; they attach themselves to professors who take a personal interest in them as members of a disadvantaged population and can help them out with research apprenticeships or internships (bolsas de iniciação científica). Such strategies are not unknown in academia worldwide: professors promote the cause of former pupils or people associated with their own network, specialization, outlook, or ideological standpoint. In Brazil, where cohorts and classes are very large in undergraduate courses, they are probably essential if a student wants to stand out from the crowd, and so the new generation of black and low-income students are initiated not only into the life and procedures of research but also into the "relational society" of which Roberto da Matta and Guillermo O'Donnell speak, and into which a doctoral student in anthropology in Rio de Janeiro has recently provided a lively insight (Pereira 2017).[6]

---

6. For more detail on Pereira's story see the section Affirmative action schemes and outcomes in chapter 3.

Anti-Discrimination Laws and Precursors
of the Movimento Negro

Although racial inequality only became an acutely controversial matter of political dispute, as distinct from academic debate, when it began to be formulated in terms of allocation of resources by the state, Brazil had long before then had constitutional and legislative provisions outlawing acts of racial discrimination. The first Republican Constitution of 1891, coming in the wake of the final abolition of slavery three years earlier, stated that there would be "no privileges or distinctions based on birth, sex, race, profession . . . wealth, social class, religious belief or political ideas" and the 1946 Constitution stated that the propagation of racial or class prejudices would not be "tolerated". But the first specific legislation, going beyond the declaration of principles, was the Afonso Arinos Law of 1951, which outlawed and punished those who would discriminate against a person "on grounds of racial or colour prejudice" in public venues such as restaurants and schools or in employment. The law prescribed corresponding punishments, including imprisonment, fines, and, in the case of public servants, dismissal. Its effect has been the subject of debate: according to Andrews, as of about 1990, there had been only one conviction under the law and even in that case the punishment was a mere token (1991), while Ivair dos Santos quotes rumors that in 1978 it was used by the police in Salvador to actually prevent a nationwide black movement meeting from taking place, on the grounds that a black movement also encouraged racism (2006: 44). A report in the magazine *Carta Capital* in November 2012 recalled an incident at the São Paulo Athletics Club in the 1970s in which a black man was not allowed into a carnival ball: he told the doorman that this might incur a sanction under the Afonso Arinos Law to which the reply was "Do you really think they would close this club on account of someone like you?"[7] However, Dávila's recent archival research unearthed twenty-three cases alleging discrimination between 1951 and 1988, although few were successful because of the language of the law, which either prescribed excessively spe-

---

7. *Carta Capital*, 27 November 2012, http://www.cartacapital.com.br/sociedade/o-fim-do-clube-de-regatas-tiete. A similar incident at the Clube de Regatas Tiete—an elite rowing club in São Paulo—in the 1970s led to the founding of the pioneer Movimento Negro Unificado contra a Discriminação Racial (Black Antiracial Discrimination Movement—MNU). Ironically, by 2012, because of the debts of the Clube de Regatas, its premises had been confiscated by the city and handed over to the Faculdade Zumbi dos Palmares, a nongovernmental higher education institution aimed at black students, which we shall have occasion to discuss later.

cific settings or allowed judges to make very narrow interpretations. More important, however, is his statement that the number of criminal complaints filed "is too large to count," which indicates that the law had a wider moral impact at least on the climate of opinion than others have claimed (Dávila 2016: 174).

The military government that seized power in 1964 decreed further constitutional measures (known as institutional acts), including a provision banning wage differences based on colour, but it also of course contained numerous provisions that severely restricted political and civil rights and thus the capacity to protest against discrimination. Its National Security Law of 1969 stated that incitement to racial hatred or discrimination was a crime punishable by imprisonment, but this could be used to punish protests against racism as much as racism itself, as in the incident quoted above, and leading black intellectuals who identified with antiracist causes, such as Alberto Guerreiro Ramos and Abdias do Nascimento, neither of whom was remotely a Communist, were forced into exile. Curiously, in the early years of the military regime, just as it was entering its most repressive phase in late 1968, a proposal to oblige enterprises to employ a certain proportion of blacks, had briefly been floated (Guimarães 2015: 7–9) by the minister of labour and discussed in public. In his account of the episode, Guimarães shows that, although there were many indications of recognition of the existence of racial prejudice among public intellectuals and journalists, there was strong resistance to admitting the existence of a structural pattern of discrimination in the society and there was also resistance to the prospect of blacks organizing themselves, as was occurring in the United States. As ever, the Brazilian intelligentsia could not quite decide whether the United States was a spectre, a rival, or an example to follow.

After the end of military rule the Constituent Assembly (in fact the Congress sitting as a Constituent Assembly) drew up the 1988 Constitution, which gave much closer attention to universal human rights, and also to indigenous rights, and defined a crime of racism in general (not just acts of discrimination or the propagation of intolerance). In 1989 the Congress passed the "Lei CAO" (Law number 7.716/1989, named for Carlos Alberto Oliveira, the deputy who introduced it), which translated this principle into law as a "crime inafiançável e imprescriptível," meaning that those accused cannot be bailed and there is no statute of limitations. But the punishment contemplated by this law is so harsh that at least at first the police (once again) rarely applied it: according to Antonio Sergio Guimarães it was only applied in 58 out of the 275 cases of complaints made to the police in the four-year period 1993–97, the remainder having been dealt with under nonracial provisions such as "insulting behaviour" (Guimarães 1998: 66–68).

In the mid-1990s, after one or two high-profile cases in which individuals from prominent black families entering chic apartment blocks were denied access to the "social elevator"—as distinct from the "service elevator" (Fry 1995)—states and municipalities passed laws against the denial of access on grounds of sex, colour, profession, or noncontagious disease. Thus the municipality of São Paulo, like many others, passed a law in 1996 that obliged apartment blocks to post notices to this effect, and these are now a standard feature of entrance lobbies in many cities.

But these laws did not deal with racial exclusion as a pattern, as a structural feature of society. In the words of Renato Emerson dos Santos, a prominent black movement figure, professor at the State University of Rio de Janeiro (UERJ), and in 2014 president of the Brazilian Geography Association, they did not deal with the effects of racist behavior. Also the few black voices in the public sphere were only gradually changing their tune. According to Guimarães (2003:2), these voices were principally those of cultural figures associated with theatre and film, had focused on the inadequacies of black education and organization, and adopted cultural and even psychoanalytical approaches as in the Black Experimental Theater (Teatro Experimental do Negro—TEN), founded in 1944 and led by Abdias do Nascimento, who was elected to the 1945 Constituent Assembly.

The TEN had been preceded by the Brazilian Black Front (Frente Negra Brasileira—FNB), which lasted from 1931 until, despite its stance as an organization principally concerned with educational advancement, it was shut down by Vargas in 1939. It had at one stage, had six thousand card-holding members in São Paulo and two thousand in Santos, ran newspapers and a school in São Paulo, and had branches in Campinas, Salvador, and elsewhere (Larkin Nascimento 2007: 129; Alberto 2011: 130–50). But the FNB did not leave an enduring mark, and some later movements or writers may be embarrassed by its leaders' enthusiastic espousal of nationalist quasi-fascist ideas. In 1946 and 1953 there were, respectively, a National Convention and a National Congress of Black People (Convenção Nacional do Negro and Primer Congresso Nacional do Negro): the first insisted on economic opportunities for blacks; and the second, in which Nascimento had a prominent role, focused more on cultural recognition and condemned vehemently racial "messianism" or exclusivist organizations on the part of any racial group (Guimarães

2015). The TEN itself was far more than a theatre company: rebuffed by the intellectual elite—as in the "polite" rejection of a request for support from Mario de Andrade, the leading modernist writer—it ran a newspaper that offered space to all political parties and carried its contestation of the racial exclusion suffered by blacks into the spheres of art, beauty contests, religion, and, of course, education (Larkin Nascimento 2007: 167, 176–80). The TEN, like the FNB, operated without state support; organized two national congresses on the race issue in 1945 and 1950, apparently separately from the congresses mentioned above; and published ten issues of the journal *Quilombo*. It fell victim to the repression of the military regime, which clearly saw it as much more than the "culturalist" or "elitist" operation described a little harshly by some commentators (Hanchard 1994: 99–141).[8] But in the end some might say that the FNB and the TEN were false starts, as Antonio Sergio Guimarães remarks in his review of Paulina Alberto's *Terms of Inclusion* (Guimarães 2012). Their independence vis-à-vis the state is striking compared to that of the movimento negro decades later, but the latter has been much more successful. In his exile, perhaps under the influence of black movements in the United States, Abdias came to adopt a harsher vision of the fate of Brazil's black population. In speeches and lectures in the United States and Africa he described mass European immigration in post-abolition Brazil as a strategy to perpetuate the subordination of the former slave population by importing white workers to compete with them. He also emphasized the cultural dimension of racial exclusion: for him religious syncretism was "the more all less violent imposition or superimposition of white western cultural norms and values" and compared the valorization of Afro-Brazilian heritage as no better than "ethnocide . . . immobilising and fossilizing the vital dynamic elements of African culture . . . as simple folklore" (do Nascimento 1989: 59, 61).

For a long time those who thought and spoke about these matters referred to "preconceito"—prejudice—as an individual pattern of behaviour. During the military dictatorship, especially after the mid-1970s, what came to be known as civil society (NGOs, middle-class feminist

---

8. Another theatre-based source of consciousness-raising was the artistically more radical Theatre of the Oppressed, which was led by Augusto Boal and inspired by liberation theology and the educator Paulo Freire but not focused specifically on racial oppression. It was referred to in a 2008 interview with me by the famous black actor Zeze da Motta (then secretary for human rights of the state of Rio de Janeiro) as one of several sources of her own awakening. Boal was also forced into exile during the dictatorship and gained international recognition for his venture.

movements, self-managed development projects, and Christian Base Communities [CEBs]) had a growing impact, but the themes of racial prejudice, discrimination, and exclusion were absent (Lehmann 1990; Assies 1993, 1999; Doimo 1995). With the democratic transition and its accompanying campaigns there was a growing advocacy of measures that would counter a pattern of exclusion rather than sanctioning only individual behaviour, as evidenced by the founding of the MNU in 1978 (of which more later). Guimarães points out that this was contemporaneous with the emergence of a black middle class, but it was a middle class hobbled by tacit racial exclusion especially in the upper reaches of society, and the poor quality of the state education on which its members relied for their advancement. This enduring cross-fertilization of the themes of education and race surely contributed to the protagonism of "young people who defined themselves as black and took up the role of standard-bearers for the poor, black and mestizo masses" (Guimarães 2003: 252). The story of how this demand arose from the young people themselves, which has yet to be told, is the counterpart of the academic-bureaucratic politics charted in this text. The emphasis on education is striking: if we compare it to the situation in the United States, we can see that, although many American voices are raised to denounce the disproportionate numbers of blacks, especially young blacks, among victims of police violence and violence in general, in Brazilian cities such civil rights protests have gained far less traction in the political system than the campaign to open up more space for young blacks in higher education especially, even though this is but one dimension of racial disadvantage.[9] Abundant evidence of the disadvantages suffered by blacks in dealings and confrontations with the police was already available in the 1990s: it showed they were disproportionately represented among those killed by the police, they were shockingly over-represented in the prison population, were less likely to have a private lawyer and more likely to be convicted when sent for trial (Fry 1999) and this pattern persists (Waiselfisz 2012; French 2014).

The question remains as to why the idea of quotas for university places in particular as a means of reducing racial exclusion took root so quickly and so deeply. My interviews did not deal with this question directly: in the prevailing climate of opinion, which I did not question, the

---

9. The Forum Brasileiro de Segurança Pública, in its *Anuário* (Annual Report) for 2014, states as a headline figure that 11,197 people were killed by police in the four-year period 2009–13. This is the same number as those killed by police in the United States in the period 1983–2012.

priority of university access in the promotion of racial equality was taken for granted as a matter of common sense. But in retrospect, and in the light of our knowledge of some of the darker aspects of Brazil, my answers to this question remain hypothetical. To be sure they have to do with the place of the public universities as necessary staging posts on the path into the professions and the country's upper strata, but a university degree hardly offers a guarantee of access to the elite, especially for graduates in less competitive subjects such as the humanities and social sciences. The answer would have to look on what might be called the "supply side," that is, where the activists are who have the desire and the time to promote the cause. They are not in the industrial trade unions, and they are not among the peasantry—rather they seem to be located in institutions of higher education, as members of the teaching staff as well as students. Potential activists are also present to some extent in urban cultural movements and NGOs led by popular intellectuals, such as "Afro-Reggae" and the "Observatório das Favelas" in Rio de Janeiro.[10] But they are few compared to the university faculty members and researchers who play a dominant role in campaigns for black access to higher education, and the provenance or current employment of campaigners does not provide a fully satisfactory answer to the question "Why the universities?" It is also important to couch the answer in terms of the sensitive role of higher education in Brazilian society, where all sorts of groups lay claim to setting the agenda of prestige universities: among established elites, as always, they are taken for granted as channels for the cultural reproduction of their way of life and the skills needed to sustain it. But other groups also lay claim: prominent professors and student organizations see universities as agents of social change, even fundamental change; and professional corporations (e.g., medicine and the law) rely on them to manage the standards required for admission to their professions. The op-ed pages of leading newspapers are daily populated with opinion pieces by academics. This is a subject awaiting analytical treatment in Latin America as a whole, as well as Brazil, for while it is not difficult to observe the political role of student movements and the role of the academic professoriate in forming opinions, it is too easy to take for granted the sensitivity of universities as institutions without asking why this should be so. For the moment, I merely wish to highlight the question.

In the transition period, state institutions were not entirely inactive, but what they did was limited. In the early 1980s, when direct popular

---

10. See the Observatório das Favelas' website, http://www.observatoriodefavelas.org.br

election of state governors (not yet the president) was restored, the governor of São Paulo, Franco Montoro, agreed to establish a Conselho da Comunidade Negra (Council for the Black Community) (Santos 2006).[11] Several features of this institution presaged the future of state initiatives in support of the black population, namely, a mix of bureaucracy and militancy, of formal administrative and informal political arrangements and commitments, and reliance therefore on the unpaid activism of committed black intellectuals and trade unionists. (Later on trade unionists were notable by their absence from the movimento negro.) The movimento negro seems to shy away from forming a visible presence in Congress—a caucus, or *bancada* such as evangelical politicians and other interest groups have created. Mala Htun mentions an Afrodescendant caucus which began to meet regularly in the national legislature and in 2001; she claims that there was a "first-ever meeting of black federal and state legislators" in Salvador, and she refers to the creation by the PSDB and the PMDB of "black" or "Afro" wings, such as "Tucanafro"[12] and "PMDB Afro," but these initiatives have left no traces at all (Htun 2016: 124). There seems to be a tacit preference for working in the corridors of power—best described as an inclination rather than a conscious strategic choice. The discomfort that would arise among members of the political class, who are less visibly white than the socioeconomic elite, if invited to join a "black caucus," is so evident that it is hardly surprising that potential advocates have held back; the insistent calls on students to "asumir"—to take responsibility for their black skin or black inheritance, and adopt blackness as an identity—have been rare among members of Congress, with the exception of Senator Paulo Paim who sponsored the Estatuto de Ingualdade Racial for years before it was adopted in 2012.

Both the black organizations that pressed for its creation and took part in its work and the São Paulo Conselho itself focused entirely on discrimination against individuals—notably in public administration, employment, and relations with the police. Ivair dos Santos's account (2006) describes eloquently the difficulties the Conselho experienced, despite its status as an official advisory body to the governor, in finding premises, in obtaining a telephone line, and in small but irksome things

---

11. The full title was Conselho de Participação e Desenvolvimento da Comunidade Negra, but it was known by the abbreviated version. This body was mentioned as a precursor by at least three of my interviewees, all of whom were actively engaged in campaigns for black inclusion or equality.

12. PSDB politicians are known as "tucanos" as in the toucan bird which is its emblem.

that constantly reminded its leaders of their status and colour.[13] (The parallel Council for Women's Rights did not, according to Ivair dos Santos, suffer similar slights.) There was no mention of preferential treatment or affirmative action—rather, the dominant theme was equal treatment. On the subject of education the pressure was to remove from school history books stereotypical or patronizing allusions to the black population—something that people in the FNB had already complained about in the 1930s. In 2002, pressure of a slightly different kind, more driven by identity politics, succeeded in obtaining the federal law incorporating African history into the main school curriculum.

Multiplication of NGOs in the 1990s

The period of the dictatorship after the extremes of repression abated around 1977, and the prolonged transition that ended it, saw NGOs flourishing in a range of race-related spheres, such as legal support in discrimination cases, mobilization for indigenous rights, labor law, health, and education. Organized expressions of black interests and identity began to change. One important aspect of this take-off was the prominence of women leaders like Sueli Carneiro and women-led NGOs like the Geledès-Instituto da Mulher Negra (Black Women's Institute) in São Paulo and Criola in Rio,[14] which gained a voice in the public square denouncing the pervasive presence of discrimination against blacks and black women in particular, and also denouncing the oppressive treatment of women by black men, while undertaking projects to improve their position and defend their rights (see also Paschel 2016: 59). Thus Geledès, founded and still led by Sueli Carneiro, which has flourished as a consultancy, training organization, pressure group, and consciousness-raising platform, created a campaign, SOS Racismo (after its French

13. I had the opportunity to interview Ivair dos Santos in Brasilia in 2008, when he was working both at the university and as a consultant to SEPPIR. His insights into the quotas campaign were invaluable—see chapter 5.

14. This is a list of black women's organizations from many states who signed a joint declaration in advance of the 2001 United Nations (UN) Durban World Conference against Racism, Racial Discrimination, Xenophobia and Related Intolerance (of which more later): Nzinga—Coletivo de Mulheres Negras, Minas Gerais; Maria Mulher—Organização de Mulheres Negras, Rio Grande do Sul; Ialodê—Centro de Referência da Mulher Negra, Bahia; Grupo de Mulheres Negras Malunga, Goias; IMENA—Instituto de Mulheres Negras do Amapá; Fala Preta! Organização de Mulheres Negras, São Paulo; Centro de Estudos e Defesa do Negro do Pará; AMMA—Psique e Negritude, São Paulo; CRIOLA, Rio de Janeiro; El, Rio de Janeiro; Casa da Mulher Catarina, Santa Catarina; ACMUN—Associação Cultural de Mulheres Negras, Rio Grance do Sul; Geledés—Instituto da Mulher Negra, São Paulo.

homonym SOS Racisme), to bring cases of discrimination to court, and it runs training courses in the private and public sectors to help black women get jobs and encourage companies to adopt affirmative action policies.[15] The Centro de Articulação de Populações Marginalizadas (Center for the Mobilization of Marginalized Populations—CEAP), led by Ivanir dos Santos, which started out as an operation in support of street children in Rio, spawned several independent offshoots in the city, such as Criola, and others specializing in the support of black entrepreneurs (the Instituto Palmares de Direitos Humano—Palmares Institute of Human Rights), of favelas (the Central Unica das Favelas), and of popular black-identifying culture (like Afro-Reggae). Ivanir himself was undersecretary for human rights while the mercurial evangelical Anthony Garotinho was governor (1999–2002), working under Abdias do Nascimento as the Secretary. Nowadays CEAP takes the lead in public demonstrations in defense of religious tolerance, protesting against the hostility of evangelicals toward Afro-Brazilian possession cults, and Criola joins cultural and identity-based issues with social issues, specializing in health and environmental themes, working with young people in the dance halls and "bailes funk" (funk gigs) in Rio to develop their political awareness or social conscience. These examples show black themes branching out from culture into the practicalities of black advancement and living standards, as well as antidiscrimination and broader social issues like health, so to speak colouring those causes. In the 1980s in Salvador da Bahia, the Steve Biko Institute was founded on the basis of black consciousness and black educational advancement specifically to help young blacks pass entrance competitions to study in prestige universities, and this example was followed in the early 1990s by the Franciscan friar and campaigner for "his" "povo negro" (black people), Frei David (Frei David Raimundo dos Santos, universally known as "Frei Daví"), pioneer of community-based preparatory courses for the university entrance examination (the Vestibular, hence their name, Prevestibulares Comunitarios or PVCs). We shall return to these experiences in greater detail. One can look at the pattern in two ways: from one point of view one can see a strategy of emphasizing black distinctiveness, as, for example, in

15. An article in the *Folha de São Paulo* published many years later reported that several leading firms, including the bank Bradesco, Google, and Microsoft, were joining with the black-oriented Faculdade Zumbi dos Palmares (see below, p. 185) to create a scheme encouraging black university graduates to improve their preparation for public and private sector employment. "Ação de empresas mira estudante negro," *Folha de São Paulo*, 6 November 2016.

the prominence given to sickle-cell disease which disproportionately affects people of African descent,[16] but one can also see how these NGOs seek to draw attention to the disproportionate effect of widespread social problems on the black population. For example, some campaigns summon up black identity or cultural practices (like funk and hip-hop) that are associated in the popular imaginary with the black population, as bearers or vehicles for struggles to overcome social problems, even though leaders or spokespeople do not intend to either identify those problems principally with the black population or to attach the label "black" to those practices as if it exhausted their projection or appeal. Thus, what from one point of view may seem separatist, from another appears inclusionary, and the politics of identity become intertwined with broader claims for inclusion and opportunity. We shall have occasion to discuss the two-sided potential of calls, notably from intellectuals, for individuals to "asumir"—to recognize themselves as black: again, while some might see these calls can as "separatist" or confrontational, others might see them as inclusionary, especially since they are a call for people assumed to count themselves as "mestiço," of "mixed race," or just brown-skinned to join the trend toward black identification.

The inflection of the politics of blackness and race that took place in the ten years between the transition to civilian rule and the emergence of the quotas movement is captured in a short article published by the anthropologist Yvonne Maggie (1994) about the commemoration of the centenary of the abolition of slavery in 1988. Based on a detailed catalogue of 1,702 events, of which 218 were closely observed, she documented the overwhelming predominance of cultural themes and the celebration of black culture in the form of ritual, religion, and music. The analysis showed the marginalization of dissident and dissonant voices that were drawing attention to continuing social exclusion and to the "farce" of an abolition that had scarcely opened the way to freedom. A mock poster advertising the sale of slaves put out as a stunt in extremely poor taste by employees of the Rio Stock Exchange passed without comment. (Fifteen years later it would surely have provoked an outcry and brought opprobrium on its creators.) The celebrations were marked predominantly by an emphasis on *negro* culture as a heritage of all Brazil, and the social exclusion represented in the use of the word *preto* (denoting the deepest black skin colour) was played down.

---

16. The approved formula of the US National Institutes of Health is that sickle cell anemia is "more common in people of African, African-American, or Mediterranean heritage." http://ghr.nlm.nih.gov/handbook/inheritance/ethnicgroup

The inconvenient facts of racial exclusion were largely passed over in silence: it would be several years before the denunciation of black victimhood gained a prominent place in public discourse and when that time came it brought realignments and sometimes painful personal rifts. While Maggie's position in the 1994 article was a clear if implicit plea for greater attention to be paid to the socioeconomic exclusion of blacks, ten years later she and Peter Fry—both professors at the Federal University of Rio de Janeiro (UFRJ) who had published pioneering research on the terminology of race—would be pilloried for their opposition to officially sanctioned racial classifications and reserved places or quotas for black students, while many whose writings she had invoked in support of her position at that time later stood on the other side of the divide (Maggie 2013).

Despite the proliferation of NGOs emphasizing the racial dimension of exclusion in the sphere of health, of schooling, and especially of violence, it was the campaigns for black causes in public universities that eventually brought institutional responses. The advocates started to find a place in the federal government during the Cardoso administration, which began in 1994, and gained further space beginning in 2002 under Lula, and meanwhile the themes of black activism expanded: the issue of human rights in the strict sense of antidiscrimination and the punishment of racist behavior was still there, but the colouring of major social issues was under way: education, health, and social mobility were now seen in terms not just of universal citizenship but also of black collective rights.

First Official Governmental Steps toward Affirmative Actions

Some of the people who had worked with or in the São Paulo Conselho later followed Montoro's ally Cardoso to Brasilia when he became president, notably Helio Santos, who presided over the Grupo de Trabalho Interministerial para a Valorização da População Negra (Interministerial Working Group for the "Valorization" of the Black Population), which was inaugurated on the day on which Brasilia experienced its biggest—and perhaps only—national mass demonstration in favor of the black cause: the "Marcha Zumbi dos Palmares Contra o Racismo, pela Cidadania e a Vida."[17] This was also the three-hundredth anniversary of the ex-

---

17. "The Zumbi dos Palmares March against Racism, for Citizenship and Life." Even if the upper estimate of thirty thousand participants is correct, the number is small when the size of the constituency is taken into account, as well as the number and diversity of spon-

ecution of folk hero Zumbi dos Palmares, who had held sway over an archipelago of territories in the northeast, including runaway slave communities, in the late seventeenth century (Reis 1995–96): twenty thousand demonstrators (thirty thousand according to some estimates) took part, and Cardoso received the leaders in the Presidential Palace. The word "valorização" in the name of the working group means something between recognition by others and recognition of one's own worth by oneself. This perhaps intentional ambiguity may indeed have been the reason for the adoption of that word, and it may also have reflected the ambiguities of Cardoso's own positions on these issues, as well as resistance within his party, the PSDB (Paschel 2016: 122), for while he repeatedly recognized the existence of racial prejudice in Brazil, he never laid down a clear set of policies in response, acting more like a moderator in a debate than a leader.

Cardoso was almost alone in his administration in talking about Brazil's race problem, and he did so frequently. His other "point man" on the subject was Paulo Sergio Pinheiro, whom he named head of the newly created Special Secretariat for Human Rights even though he was known as a supporter of the PT. A fellow professor at the University of São Paulo (USP) who later became the UN's Human Rights Special Rapporteur in some of the world's most gruesome crisis areas (Burma and Burundi, for example, and more recently as chairman of the Independent International Commission of Inquiry on Syria), Pinheiro said to me that Cardoso took all decisions on race issues with little consultation, if only because "if he had consulted his ministers nothing would have happened." How decisive Cardoso was may be a matter of debate but, as we shall see in the case of his Minister of Education, Paulo Renato de Souza, the resistance was palpable.

This inclination to remain above the fray is again reflected in Cardoso's remarks at the opening ceremony of an international seminar on affirmative action, which took place, unusually, in the Presidential Palace,[18] in which he invited policymakers and others to "be creative" and turn Brazil's "ambiguity and non-Cartesian characteristics," which "so often act as obstacles" in other respects, to advantage (Cardoso

---

soring organizations, including trade unions, women's organizations, and the association of lay collaborators in the social and mobilizing work of the Catholic Church (Paschel 2016: 264).

18. The seminar was organized on 2 July 1996 by the Secretariat for Citizenship Rights of the Ministry of Justice.

1997).[19] Nonetheless, Cardoso's words in the same speech have been frequently quoted and did mark a historic moment.

> We in Brazil live in a society characterized by discrimination and prejudice [in which] discrimination seems to be an established form of behaviour, constantly repeated and reproduced. It is no good taking refuge in the hypocritical attitude that this is not the way we are. No, our way is utterly wrong, because we see discriminatory behaviour and unacceptable prejudice repeated over and over again. This has to be unmasked and seriously challenged, not just in words but also through mechanisms and processes designed to achieve a transformation, a more democratic relationship between races, social groups, and social classes. (14–16)[20]

Later, in 2000, shortly before leaving office, he welcomed the Brazilian position paper for the UN World Conference against Racism, Racial Discrimination, Xenophobia, and Related Intolerance, known as the Durban Conference, and stated his support for affirmative action in general, but he still remained aloof from controversy, referring to racial quotas as a "more complicated question" (*Folha de São Paulo*, 23 August 2001, quoted in Machado 2004: 80).

In presenting the Interministerial Working Group's first report in 1996, its president, Hélio Santos, had seemed to offer a strong defense of affirmative action but not the sort one might have expected: he was not proposing any sort of preferential access for blacks to any institution or employment (i.e., quotas). Rather, he said, he had abandoned the ethnic "discourse" and was proposing an "eminently economic and operational argument" that the country could not develop harmoniously without investing in its Afro-Brazilian population (Sardenberg and Santos 1997). He may also have been deferring to Cardoso's balancing act, expressed in many different formulae, between recognizing the reality of racial discrimination and the universality

---

19. "Temos de ter criatividade . . . ver de que maneira a nossa ambigüedade, estas caracteristicas não-Cartesianas do Brasil—que dificultam tanto em tantos aspectos—tambem podem ajudar em outros aspectos."

20. "Nós, no Brasil, de fato convivemos com a discriminação e convivemos com o preconceito [. . .], a discriminação parece se consolidar como alguma coisa que se repete, que se reproduz. Não se pode esmorecer na hipocrisia e dizer que o nosso jeito não é esse. Não, o nosso jeito está errado mesmo, há uma repetição de discriminações e há a inaceitabilidade do preconceito. Isso tem de ser desmascarado, tem de ser, realmente, contra-atacado, não só verbalmente, como também em termos de mecanismos e processos que possam levar a uma transformação, no sentido de uma relação mais democrática, entre as raças, entre os grupos sociais e entre as classes."

of citizenship, as well as the value of diversity.[21] In fact we may detect the slightly contrived mutual admiration between the two as prefigured in Cardoso's earlier comments, at the installation of the Working Group, calling for an "affirmative position and not a negation of differences and of discrimination . . . in a perspective, as Professor Hélio says, of citizenship and democracy."[22] Yvonne Maggie has also noted Cardoso's apparent avoidance of taking strong positions, as well as his description of Brazil as a nation at once "multi-étnica e multicultural e mestiça"—something she regarded as a contradiction in terms. For Maggie *mestiçagem* blurs the boundaries that multiculturalism hardens, while if multiethnic refers to differences in skin colour it is misleading (Maggie 2005).

The report of the Interministerial Working Group is hard to find, but the shift toward collective entitlements and restorative justice made its definitive appearance in official documents shortly afterward with the publication of the first National Human Rights Programme (PNDH) of 1996. This was drafted by Paulo Sergio Pinheiro and developed in the wake of the World Human Rights Conference held in Vienna in 1993, at which the Brazilian delegation was led by Ambassador Gilberto Saboia— who later also led the delegation to the Durban Conference in 2001.[23] It turned out to be a very long document, containing 228 policy proposals, of which 21 were devoted to the black population, 14 to the indigenous population, and 6 to disability. Its proposals included the requirement that questions about individuals' colour must appear in "all and any information systems on the population and publicly available data banks"; the adoption by the government's statistical agency, the IBGE, of a single

---

21. For example, "When I speak of the negro, I am talking of the Brazilian, the Brazilian citizen. . . . We are not here speaking of a movement or a part of the whole: rather it is a part that forms the whole . . . a whole that today in particular is multiple, contains a great variety of racial and cultural components. And we have to develop civilized forms of coexistence that recognize and understand that Brazil has been able—or will be able—to produce a positive outcome of its diversity." Speech delivered at the Presidential Palace at the launch of the Interministerial Working Group, 27 February 1996.

22. "This really is a threat to contemporary civilization. I want to emphasize here that we are opposed to the return of this type of irrational appeal. We value the existence of many races in our population, each with its own characteristics and able to develop a shared way of life without trying to build privileges on the basis of difference. This is very important." These quotes are from a very useful paper by Andrea Lopes da Costa Vieira delivered at the ANPOCS annual meeting in October 2006 and published on the Internet: "Ações afirmativas: Construção, implementação e institucionalização: Uma análise das propostas de ação Afirmativa nos Programas Nacionais de Direitos Humanos (1996/2002)," http://www.anpocs.org/portal/index.php?option=comdocman&task=docview&gid=3422 &Itemid=232

23. Tianna Paschel provides more useful details in her highly informative account of the lead-up to Durban (2016: 123–32).

category of "negro" to replace, in its censuses and surveys, the more chromatic *pardos* and *pretos* (a highly controversial proposal as we shall see); and the implementation of "affirmative actions" in access to university and training courses.[24] Although there was no mechanism with which to compel government departments to follow these proposals, so that the IBGE has continued to use the "preto-pardo-branco" classification, this and other documents enshrined ideas, terminology, and concepts that fed into the everyday jargon of policy debate and into the preparation of Brazil's Durban position paper. It was clearly heavily influenced by the activist intellectuals of the movimento negro: but for Yvonne Maggie, by taking a position in favor of positive discrimination, the programme was breaking with the "a-racial'" and antiracist tradition in Brazilian legislation and government policy (Maggie 2013).[25]

Publication of the second PNDH in 2002 coincided with the last year of Cardoso's second period. It contained five hundred recommendations, of which twenty-nine were of specific interest to the black population. It included a new theme—the *quilombos*—and also a new usage, the term "afrodescendente," which had not appeared in the first programme. The inclusion of the quilombos reflected a growing campaign among anthropologists on behalf of rural communities.[26] When it was included in the Constitution of 1988 the word was assumed to refer to communities tracing their origins to groups of escaped slaves, but the activism among anthropologists and intellectuals and the difficulty of applying the definition in a bureaucratically consistent way led to a widening of its meaning to refer to almost any rural community able to demonstrate a shared or common ancestry. This was to lay the basis for a separate field of reparation for historic injustices in the form of official recognition of communities and claims for land restitution, to which we shall return in chapter 5 (Boyer 2014, 2016).

---

24. "Preto" could be described as a slightly archaic word meaning black, or even "very black." Like "pardo" it has survived in official documentation even while it has given way to "negro" in daily speech, especially among campaigners and the more politicized. The complete document can be found at the USP's Virtual Human Rights Library (Biblioteca Virtual de Direitos Humanos).

25. By "a-racial" she means the absence of race as a criterion of social differentiation in "radically neutral" legislation on racial matters. (Maggie 2013: 18, n. 20).

26. The word has a complicated origin, according to João Reis, in borrowings among Angolan languages where he says it first described groups at once uprooted and invading and then was adopted to refer to initiates' societies; from there, somehow, it reached the territory of Palmares, site of the legendary Zumbi's de facto autonomous territory, where the connotation of uprootedness caught on. Thereafter it became a word for communities of fugitive slaves (Reis 1995–96: 16). In some Spanish-speaking countries quilombo means "chaos" and in others "a brothel."

The third National Human Rights Program was published much later, in 2010, with twenty-five directives and eighty-two strategic objectives; this one was much longer than its predecessors, but by now the focus of public debate—and sharp controversy—on human rights had shifted to the question of truth and memory of the violations committed under the dictatorship,[27] and other issues, while race had become a vast subject of its own with its own institutions. The growing autonomy of racial equality, beyond antidiscrimination, as a subject of policy in its own right was confirmed soon after Lula took office when, in January 2003, he upgraded three bodies to "special secretariats," whose heads had the status, but not the resources, of ministers, attached to the presidency: one for human rights in general, one for women, and SEPPIR for racial equality.[28]

To Durban: The State Commits to Race-Based Quotas

Once the policy debates had shifted from antidiscrimination to collective entitlements the dominant issue became that of quotas, known in India as reserved seats and in the United States as positive discrimination. The question this raises, which is hard to answer in any but very general terms, is why the concentration on quotas in general and specifically on quotas for university admissions as the top priority in reducing racial exclusion? The answer implies counterfactuals that should at least be listed so that the quotas obsession can be put into an ideological context: other widely recognized themes that might have dominated in the context of racial exclusion received less attention and were not the subject of concrete proposals, such as the question of why black Brazilians are so overwhelmingly the majority in prisons or (the obverse of the same question) why they seem so shockingly overrepresented among victims of police brutality and killing (Sansone 2002)? Affirmative action programmes could have been adopted within the state apparatus, in the

---

27. The military successfully pressured Lula to withdraw the document and revise it to protect their interests with respect to violations committed under the dictatorship. But Dilma Roussef did set up the wide-ranging Truth Commissions at national and state levels, and their hearings have been at times moving and shocking.

28. The full titles, apart from SEPPIR, are Secretaria Especial dos Direitos Humanos (SEDH) and Secretaria Especial de Políticas para as Mulheres (SEPM). These secretariats are attached directly to the presidency and, as mentioned before, do not have the resources that a ministry has to undertake policy initiatives. In other words they are responsible for promoting policies in other ministries. They could be described as campaigning organizations embedded within the state, with a "horizontal" brief to spread their messages across ministries.

medical and teaching professions, or to help in the advancement of black staff in their careers, not just in their initial appointments. In education, proposals could have been developed to help young blacks stay in secondary school so as to complete their studies (and thus improve the results they need to enter higher education institutions) or to fund preschool education for the children of black mothers (like Head Start programmes elsewhere). In fact the *prevestibular* courses to help young blacks and people from low-income families prepare for university entrance examinations did receive support of this kind, and they were encouraged and sometimes funded as experimental exercises by the MEC's Innovative Courses Programme (Programas Inovadoras de Cursos—PIC). But the vast majority of what Renato Emerson dos Santos (in an interview) and Antonio Sergio Guimarães estimated as eight hundred such courses (Guimarães 2003: 259), were local cooperative initiatives with no consistent format or evaluation or government support (for example, Frei David's EDUCAFRO in Rio, and then São Paulo, and the Steve Biko Institute in Bahia of which more in chapter 5).

During Cardoso's second term, two ministries adopted affirmative action of slightly different sorts. In 2001 the Ministry of Agriculture announced various measures that were concerned with correcting biases in assistance to farmers and tackling rural poverty, rather than recruitment of staff to the ministry, and were focused on gender as much as race, but little is known of any results.[29]

The scholarship programme announced in 2002 by the Ministry of Foreign Affairs (Itamaraty) was more strictly in keeping with the term affirmative action, as it is understood in English, since it did not set aside quotas but was designed to improve the preparation of black candidates who were likely to have had a less-privileged education than the average successful applicant. In 2008 I interviewed a diplomat who had been centrally involved in the preparation of the Durban Conference and who, somewhat to my surprise, declared himself to be one of the fifteen black members of the Diplomatic Service at that time—a number he said was small but larger than the five who had been counted in 2005. By 2013 the Itamaraty Affirmative Action Programme was awarding ten-month scholarships of a value equivalent to a postgraduate studentship to selected black applicants. These would enable them to follow one of the courses offered by for-profit private institutions established by former ambassadors

29. These were Portaría numbers 025, 033, and 222 of 2001 and Decree 3,991 of October 2001 of the Ministry of Agriculture.

to prepare students for the Itamaraty entrance exam.[30] It is also possible for candidates to apply for a second or even third year to continue their preparatory studies. Thus a total of 526 scholarships had been awarded to 319 individuals, implying that most of them made a follow-up application and had two years of study in which to prepare. Award holders have a much higher success rate in the entrance exam than do applicants as a whole: although 18 successful affirmative action candidates out of 269 from 2002 to 2011 sounds small (6.7 percent), it is far higher than the minuscule overall success rate of 1.6 percent. This may well be simply because the affirmative action award holders themselves have been through a competitive process unlike the open exam, to which anyone can present themselves—and thousands do. In 2011 the ministry modified the programme and instituted a formal quota reserving 10 percent of places in the first round of the entrance exam for black candidates. This foreshadows the much more radical law (no. 12.990/2014) passed in 2014 reserving for blacks 20 percent of places put up for competitive examination (*concurso*) in the entire federal government, including enterprises wholly and partly owned by the state (such as Petrobras), for a ten-year period.[31]

The other major contribution to the evolution of affirmative action during Cardoso's period was the preparation for Durban itself.[32] The emphasis is very much on preparation because of the unusual participatory approach adopted by the government in the drafting of its position paper for the conference. Every country had to present a position, but Brazil's country paper was prepared by a committee half of whose members were from NGOs. Paulo Sergio Pinheiro spoke to me of his "emotion" at a reception for the delegation at which whites were a tiny minority. He said the Brazilian delegation had 275 members of whom only 3, including Saboia and Pinheiro himself, were neither black nor indigenous; other sources speak of 67 representatives and "150–200 *negro* movement actors" (Bailey 2008: 584).[33] These latter were not necessarily

---

30. The business of offering courses to prepare students for entrance examinations to the public service agencies and the professions is a vast industry in Brazil involving the publication of detailed study guides (*apostilas*) as well as classroom-based and online courses. Large bookshops devote significant amounts of shelf space to the study guides. For the Itamaraty programme's website, see http://www.institutoriobranco.mre.gov.br/ptbr/programadeacaoafirmativa.xml

31. It must be remembered that succeeding in a *concurso* will qualify a person for a position, but it does not ensure that a post will actually be available for that person to fill. In the austere fiscal circumstances post-2014 this will be particularly relevant.

32. It will be recalled that international coverage of the conference was dominated by the Israel-Palestine conflict.

33. Bailey is quoting the unpublished masters' thesis of Michelle Perla (2004). Paschel gives more details (2016).

official delegates but rather participants in the parallel NGO meeting, and some of them later appeared in government positions, like the person who under Lula became head of the newly created quilombo section of the National Agrarian Reform Institute (INCRA), Givania Silva. The document had six sections on indigenous peoples, gypsies (*ciganos*), migrants, homosexuals, disability, and the black community. In this last, out of the twenty-three recommendations six concerned land tenure problems and entitlements of quilombos and rural black populations; several other recommendations were of a general kind calling on the government to properly fulfill its commitments under the Constitution and international agreements against racism and intolerance. The last and shortest recommendation called for "quotas or other affirmative measures that increase the access of blacks to public universities." Since this report was not a policy document, let alone a document allocating resources, it would be wrong to draw any conclusion from it about the priorities of either the government at the time or the members of the delegation itself.[34] Nevertheless we can note, first, the prominence of the quilombos, which prefigures our remarks in chapter 5 on the success of the promoters of their cause in getting their demands met in Congress and the executive, and, second, the importance of the preparations for the Durban Conference in the collective memory of the movimento negro, as I could confirm in numerous interviews.

The lead-up to a conference on the scale of the Durban meeting provides a fruitful opportunity for the production of ideas and proposals, for lobbying governments, and for international networking and fundraising, and the relatively new and previously little-noticed Afrodescendant or black movements throughout Latin America seized the chance. Conferences of this kind, with their more or less open-ended agendas—unlike some whose purpose is to reach enforceable international agreements or treaties—consist of an official meeting and an accompanying, often quite rowdy, NGO meeting, which attracts more delegates and sometimes even more media coverage than the official one. Other examples include the 1995 World Conference on Women in Beijing and the Rio Conferences on Environment and Development in 1992 and 2012. In advance of the Durban meeting a preconference regional Latin American meeting was planned to take place in Brasilia in October 2000, but President Cardoso asked his friend Ricardo Lagos, president of Chile, to host it instead—and it took place at the UN's office building

---

34.]The report can be found on the independent human rights website: http://www.dhnet.org.br/direitos/sos/discrim/relatorio.htm

in Santiago.[35] Shortly afterward, at a preconference (global) meeting in Geneva in February 2001, five Brazilian NGO representatives produced a manifesto in Portuguese, English, Spanish, and French protesting the Brazilian government's decision to cancel its plans to host the Latin American preparatory conference in Brasilia.

An eyewitness account by the Chilean anthropologist José Bengoa, presented at a seminar in Cambridge in September 2005, described how at a certain point in the Santiago meeting all the representatives of black and Afro-descendant movements throughout Central and South America stood up in different parts of the hall and made the point very effectively that they felt left out and were now making their presence felt. The message was that their concerns about discrimination were overshadowed by the prominence of indigenous issues and the cultural emphasis of their framing, and that the hour of black and Afro-descendant awareness, with greater emphasis on socioeconomic inequality and, for example, discrimination in labor markets, had arrived.[36] For the black and Afro-descendant movements in Latin America this was a moment equivalent to what 1992 had been for indigenous movements, and it presaged a wave of interest in them among international development institutions.[37]

Meanwhile, back on the home front, state-level meetings took place in Belem, Bahia, and São Paulo in advance of a national preparatory meeting for the Durban event in Rio where thirteen organizations drew up a manifesto on behalf of black women at a three-day meeting in Sep-

35. Cardoso may have been concerned about the risks of controversies and demonstrations following the disastrous police action in April of that year surrounding the ceremony marking five hundred years since the Portuguese arrival. When I raised the question of the change of venue with him, however, he had no recollection of such an issue. See also Paschel's interview with the then minister of justice on this (2016: 126).

36. The Afro-descendant groups seem to have come together under an "Alianza estratégica Afro-Latinoamericana y Caribeña" at a meeting organized by the Interamerican Institute of Human Rights on 30 September 2000. The information is posted on the IIDH Instituto Interamericano de Derechos Humanos (IIDH) website, http://www.iidh.ed.cr/comunidades/diversidades/docs/div_docpublicaciones/racismo_esp/anexos.pdf. The meeting was funded, at least in part, by the Ford Foundation under Grant no. 1015-1181 (see a letter to the head of the IIDH dated 10 August 2001 held in the Ford Foundation archive at the Rockefeller Archive Center near Tarrytown, New York). Paschel again provides further details (2016).

37. For example, a Washington network on the subject was organized out of the Interamerican Dialogue think tank at the initiative of the late political scientist Donna Lee van Cott: the Inter-institutional Consultation on Afro–Latin Americans was launched in 2002, involving the World Bank, the Interamerican Development Bank, and other institutions based there.

tember 2000. The Ford Foundation funded an office in Brasilia named Escritorio Zumbi dos Palmares, led by a person closely associated with Ivanir dos Santos, to coordinate NGO contributions to the country's Durban position paper.[38] The preparatory committee also dispatched people around the country to conduct meetings publicizing the forthcoming conference and the issues, addressed by prominent advocates of affirmative action. Among these were Moisés Santana, then of the Federal University of Alagoas (UFAL); Jocelio Teles dos Santos of the Federal University of Bahia (UFBA); Wilson Mattos of the State University of Bahia (UNEB); Jose Jorge de Carvalho, the prime mover of the pioneering student quotas policy at the University of Brasilia (UnB); and Ivair dos Santos, Professor of Contemporary African Thought at UnB, whom we have encountered as one of the enthusiasts who started out in the São Paulo Conselho and then followed Cardoso to Brasilia (not to be confused with Ivanir dos Santos). The culminating event in Rio in July 2001 was chaired by one of Brazil's most prominent black politicians, Benedita da Silva, a member of the PT and therefore of the opposition to Cardoso's government, vice-governor of Rio state, and a former senator—though not, as it happens, a leading campaigner on race issues, even though she was supportive. The meeting, entitled National Conference against Racism and Intolerance (the first of the CONAPIR series), was attended by seventeen thousand people and finalized the country's document to be taken to Durban, the National Plan to Combat Racism and Intolerance. So the whole exercise was energized by people who were not under the government's control and were in disagreement with the minister of education and many in Cardoso's own party.

Conclusion: The Protagonism and Inclusion of the Movimento Negro

This chapter has told of the first steps in bringing the idea of quotas— also known in Brazil as affirmative actions, in the plural—into the mainstream. In itself it is not a very exceptional story and can be read as just

---

38. This information was obtained from Ivanir dos Santos, whose CEAP is prominent in the movimento negro and whose administrative manager was supposed to head the office. This grant seems to have had an unhappy ending due to the illness of the manager concerned, as recounted in the relevant file in the foundation archives concerning Grant no. 1000-0467, dated 1 January 2000, and also in my interview with Denise Dora, former human rights officer at Ford's Rio office, March 2016.

another episode of "politics as usual": an interest group comes together, finds an opportunity, and exploits it. The interesting aspect emerges when one notices, as have many others, that a subject that had been either taboo or at least papered over in public discourse, and certainly had not inspired anything approaching mass mobilization, was able to come to the fore and make headway thanks to the efforts of a small number of NGOs, a network of activist academics and a sympathetic but cautiously committed president. In this milieu quotas became something of an obsession: interviewees sometimes enumerated the progress of the cause through the university system like someone with a faultless memory for years of football results. Their success owed much to campaigning in academic fora and penetration of the federal government, with little effort in the legislative branch or at the state level. The shift in subject matter from legal sanctions against acts of discrimination to positive discrimination or quotas encountered far less resistance than efforts elsewhere, notably in the United States post-civil rights.[39]

The next question is how the momentum in favor of quotas for blacks came to focus on entry into university when it is well known that race creates so many other fissures and barriers. Then, within that question, the subject divides into two: a "top-down" and uncontroversial initiative under which the state developed policies to help high-performing low-income and black students go to private universities, most of which are low on the prestige scale; and a host of "bottom-up" initiatives from academics in the more prestigious public universities to create affirmative action in various forms and thus increase the proportion of blacks in their student population. These will be described in the next chapter, after which we will turn to the question of why it was only the latter that generated heated disputes about issues of principle and eventually to broader questions about how all this fits into the evolution of the country's class and race structures.

---

39. In the United States, as we shall see in chapter 4, racial quotas were de facto adopted in employment in the 1970s, but in universities they were struck down by the Supreme Court, though universities continue to circumvent the prohibition in various ways (Skrentny 1996; Sander and Taylor 2012). South Africa has taken a strong quota-based line since the end of legalized apartheid.

TWO

After Durban

Affirmative Action Goes to University

SECAD: A Seedbed of Projects

So far we have seen that Cardoso's government undertook mostly facilitating measures, opening up spaces and legitimizing the identification of
the state with the cause of black advancement. Apart from the programme to support black applicants preparing for the Diplomatic Service entrance exam, the other concrete initiative of Cardoso's tenure in
the affirmative action sphere, limited in scale but highly influential as a
pilot project and experiment, was the Programa Diversidade na Universidade (Diversity in the University Programme—PDU), funded by the
Interamerican Development Bank (IDB) to the tune of US$10 million
(Souza 2005: 181). It arose in the wake of Durban when the then minister
of education, Paulo Renato de Souza, who was in his eighth year in the
post and had previously also been secretary of education in São Paulo, as
well as rector of the state's University of Campinas (UNICAMP), sought
funding for a programme of this kind. This was a response to pressure,
compensating for his previous very public hostility to quotas of any kind
while avoiding investing his own ministry's resources (Almeida 2008).[1]
When I interviewed him in 2008 he was still very sceptical about quotas,
but he was supportive of the initiative of Frei David, the Franciscan who,
besides vociferously promoting the quotas cause in education and public
service, also promoted a more entrepreneurial and self-reliant approach
independent of government (see chapter 5). In spite of Frei David's ex-

---

1. This thesis can be found on the Trilhas de Conhecimentos website, http://www.tril
hasdeconhecimentos.etc.br/

pressed aversion to funding by politicians, Paulo Renato said his Ministry had contributed funding to his EDUCAFRO. As we shall see in chapter 5, EDUCAFRO, closely identified with David's very public persona, is a network of community-based prevestibular courses, which prepare black and low-income students for university entrance examinations, charging only a nominal fee. This was compatible with the minister's resistance to quotas while supporting help for blacks and other disadvantaged people to reach a standard where they could compete on less unequal terms— "leveling the playing field" in the manner of affirmative action in the classic English sense. He also was said to have supported the private initiative establishing in 2002 the Faculdade Zumbi dos Palmares, which enjoyed the support of his party in São Paulo and of the then mayor of the city Gilberto Kassab.[2]

Introduced in the dying months of Cardoso's and Paulo Renato's tenure, the PDU provided the core, and perhaps the justification, for the creation of a whole new secretariat (equivalent to a vice-ministry) within the MEC after Lula's election, SECAD (Secretariat for Continuing Education, Literacy and Diversity), by upgrading the preexisting Coordenação de Diversidade e Inclusão Educacional.[3] Recruiting prominent affirmative action campaigners and professors, such as Eliane Cavalleiro, Jocelio dos Santos, Valter Silvério and Renato Emerson dos Santos,[4] as staff or collaborators, it played a prominent role in promoting the quotas cause through the PDU, seminars, workshops, and collaboration with the Programa Políticas da Cor na Educação Brasileira (Programme on Colour Policies in Brazilian Education—PPCor), based at UERJ, of which also more below. The group worked on the law (no. 10,639) that inaugurated Lula's presidency, introducing the history of Africa as a compulsory element in the school curriculum, and, together with José Jorge de Carvalho, could be called the core agitators of the quotas cause. It is ironic that an initiative which seems to have originated as a device to deflect pressure for quotas should have opened the way, and created the

---

2. The politics became quite convoluted. Kassab was a member of another party but had a de facto alliance with Paulo Renato and Cardoso's party (the PSDB). Paulo Renato, after leaving office, was said to be close to the politically influential educational megaentrepreneur João Carlos Di Genio of the educational conglomerate Grupo Objetivo (of whom more below), which may have supported the Zumbi dos Palmares venture (see chapter 5).

3. The words "e Inclusão" were added after Dilma Roussef's election, making it SECADI.

4. Apart from Cavalleiro, they are, respectively, of UFBA, the Federal University of São Carlos (UFSCar) in São Paulo state, and UERJ and will appear later in this narrative.

funding, for a committed group of academics to travel around addressing meetings on university campuses and to undertake and publish studies in support of the quotas campaign.

Lula's 2002 electoral manifesto only mentioned race and racial disadvantage in combination with other disadvantages linked to gender and disability, as well as the programme of recognition of quilombo communities and their claims to land. Affirmative action was thus only briefly mentioned—eventually receiving detailed treatment in the 2006 manifesto.[5] But this probably counted less than the presence of several PT black activists in Lula's entourage (Paschel 2016: 175). The 2002 manifesto did not mention the teaching of African history in schools, and yet the first legislation of any kind passed by Congress under Lula's presidency was the law making it obligatory in primary and secondary schools, including Brazil's black culture and the role of "o negro" in the shaping of the Brazilian nation.[6] It would take time for this to be implemented since textbooks had to be written, teachers trained, and syllabuses revised, but the symbolism of the gesture was evident and the number of the law—10,639—has been widely quoted ever since. It also created opportunities for people involved in the campaign for recognition of black identity to produce educational materials.

Inclusion became a matter of opening new institutions, staffing them with activists from the movimento negro, and allowing them leeway in promoting affirmative actions. Even then, however, the freestanding resources made available for the implementation (as distinct from the promotion) of programmes of affirmative action were limited: for example, universities and professors received some extra funding to award research internships to black students, broadening a long-standing scheme to give students experience in research (Massi and Queiroz 2010). In addition, the movement, now installed in the federal state apparatus in SEPPIR, SECAD, and also the Ministry of Culture through the Fundação Cultural Palmares (created by former president Sarney in the 1980s for the purpose of promoting black cultural causes), found other means of pressing and implementing its agenda. Apart from funding supportive

---

5. The 2006 programme has a section entitled "Igualdade Racial," which covers affirmative actions to ensure access and continuity in school up to university, continuation of the ProUni programme continued teaching of African history in schools, and general support for the livelihoods of blacks and *quilombolas*.

6. Literally "the black man": the word does not have the same negative connotations as in English. Law 10,639, of January 2003, emphasizes the history of Africa, the black struggle in Brazil, Brazilian black culture, and the role of the black population Brazil's social, political, and economic history.

research, for example on *quilombos*, affirmative action conditionalities or incentives would be attached to tender calls (*editais*) and funding programmes from the federal ministries, notably in education and health, all in the context of booming public expenditure facilitated by rising commodity prices.

It should be explained at this point that there is a difference between what Brazilians mean when they speak of *affirmative actions* and the more familiar English term *affirmative action*. In the United States it has tended to refer to measures that enable people from historically disadvantaged groups to improve their chances either by receiving help to compete, notably for an entrance examination to an educational institution, or by modulating their assessments to take account of the adverse effect of those disadvantages. In principle it is meant to be different from *quotas*, also known as *positive discrimination*, which reserve places in an institution or business for people from a particular disadvantaged group. We shall see in chapter 4, however, that, despite Supreme Court rulings against the principle of race-based quotas, institutions in the United States have found ways to allocate places to people from disadvantaged groups on a racial basis, and even official guidance has amounted in effect to race quotas when applied to business. In Brazil the word is invariably used in the plural and affirmative actions are taken straightforwardly to mean quotas.

SECAD offered a fertile opportunity to activist academics from the *movimento negro* to gain access to resources in the federal government. For example, Renato Emerson dos Santos, had as a student coordinated a *núcleo* attached to Frei David's Prevestibular para Negros e Carentes (Prevestibular Course for Black and Low-Income Students—PVNC) in the Rio favela of Rocinha and later became director of PPCor, the programme funded by the Ford Foundation's worldwide Pathways Programme to promote affirmative actions in universities, and also contributed to SECAD publications: in his view SECAD afforded recognition to people who had not been taken seriously by the "hard line" (campo duro) social scientists—the "analytical hierarchies" (hierarquías analíticas) who did not take race issues seriously, and to illustrate his meaning he quoted Foucault's concept of a "régime d'énonciation" (Interview, March 2013).

The PDU diversity programme's main vehicles were the Núcleos de Estudos Afro-Brasileiros (Afro-Brazilian Studies Centers—NEABs) based in several universities—and the innovative "popular" or "community" prevestibular courses (PICs) similar to EDUCAFRO, which helped potential university applicants prepare for university entrance examinations. These were funded through the MEC's UniAfro Programme to support black students and "black" subjects and received R$6 million in 2003–4 (equivalent to US$2.4 million at the time), and Ford also funded the NEAB at UFSCar and also supported the núcleos generally for the express purpose of promoting affirmative action throughout Brazilian higher education, by funding debates, seminars, speaking tours, and research centres as well as among judges and other professionals—for example by funding a Masters course in Human Rights in the Law Faculty of USP. The Brazilian Black Researchers' Association (ABPN) has a web page listing thirty-six NEABs in state and federal universities across the country, out of a total of eighty-four centres and programmes on African or Afro-Brazilian and race-related subjects.[7]

In some cases (UFSCar and the Federal University of Alagoas in the Northeast) the NEABs provided personnel, stimulus, and sponsorship for the prevestibular initiatives, as well as acting as poles of consciousness-raising for African studies and venues where black and sometimes indigenous students could meet together. Valter Silvério, leading light of the NEAB at UFSCar, told me that indigenous students also congregated there because it was a place where they felt somehow at home. He described the NEABs as an "espaço de convivência," a "meeting point" where people exchange ideas and knowledge and teachers sit down with students and discuss their work: a nexus for the "articulation" (a favorite term in Brazilian political and bureaucratic parlance) of the affirmative action movement inside universities. They also provide support for the implementation of the law requiring schools to teach African history. (Silvério himself oversaw the production of detailed study materials written by academic experts to train São Paulo state teachers on the subject of difference and equality in education, including materials on African history and the absence of blacks in Brazilian literature, and he also directed the Portuguese translation of UNESCO's multi-volume series History of Africa [Secretaria de Estado da Educação—São Paulo, Coordenadoria de Estudos e Normas Pedagógicas, n.d.].) Another prominent advocate of affirmative action who also worked with the SECAD programme Diversidade na Universidade, Wilson Mattos of the State University of Bahia (UNEB), lamented the absence of Africa from his university's history courses, where Europe received twice as many class hours.

---

7. See the ABPN website, http://www.abpn.org.br/neabs/index.php?title=Página_principal

At the Federal University of Minas Gerais (UFMG) in Belo Horizonte, PPCor also funded a NEAB, which undertook numerous activities to link students' academic work to a "positive construction of their racial identity." They operated on campus and in extension programmes, running seminars for students and courses for primary school teachers. The director in 2008, Nilma Lino Gomes, had been prominent in SECAD, did a term as president of the ABPN, and went on to become the first woman rector of a federal university—UNILAB, the International University for students from Brazil and other Portuguese-speaking, or Lusophone, countries, located in the northeastern town of Redenção (Ceará). Later she was appointed by Dilma Roussef as head of SEPPIR and then as minister for women, racial equality, and human rights—the ministry into which SEPPIR was folded but which was first dissolved and later recreated by Temer after Roussef's impeachment.

In one respect the prevestibular courses encouraged by the PDU and funded as partners of the PIC programme, continued in the line of affirmative action strictly interpreted as supported by the previous Minister Paulo Renato, because they aimed to improve the candidates' competitive position in the exam, not to reserve places for which they could compete separately. Figuring as a "popular" response to the for-profit *cursinhos*, which specialize in preparing students for those examinations, they also had a palpable element of social solidarity, being staffed by volunteer students and teachers, and they fed into the growing movement for quotas and university access as a form of social or educational advancement, as well as a platform for black identity politics. SECAD briefly funded the independent Steve Biko Institute in Bahia, which was the original model of a prevestibular course for blacks, as well as others run by NGOs and several with words such as "Conciencia Negra" or "Zumbi" in their titles. Although none of the PVCs, as they came to be called, practiced any sort of racial selection of their students, according to qualitative accounts (dos Santos 2011) their teaching often included consciousness-raising material on the theme of race: this certainly was the case with those inspired and organized by Frei David, but also the descriptions in the SECAD reports on them have an undisguised militant agenda (Lino Gomes 2006). It would be wrong, nonetheless, to see them as narrowly focused or sectarian: this sort of material is not of interest only to black students: on the contrary, in the context of the broadly dissident or left-wing atmosphere of the educational world, most students could recognize themselves in learning about the injustices of Brazil, of which racial discrimination was one dimension. The PICs, PVCs, and

NEABs achieved much approving mention in quota debates, as well as contributing to the sedimentation of affirmative action in universities and the federal state apparatus. Seminars sponsored by SECAD also promoted the agenda of quotas and published their proceedings with UNESCO support in 2006 and 2007 (Lino Gomes 2006; Lopes and Santana Braga 2007) All this activity exemplified the institutional penetration of the bureaucracy by the movimento negro, aptly summed up in by Emerson dos Santos' term "capilarização"—a word that can be translated as "penetration among the hairs of the state."[8]

It seems that SECAD was somewhat at sea in allocating the BID funds and brought in UNESCO as a service provider while also appointing PP-Cor to select which initiatives to support (Almeida 2008). The funding relationships are hard to disentangle: Denise Dora, human rights officer at Ford's Rio office, told me in October 2008 that the foundation had contributed $7 million to SECAD (compared to the IDB's $10 million), but maybe she was referring to PPCor's contribution to the functioning of the secretariat. It funded PIC/PVC projects attached to twenty-seven public universities (Almeida 2008)—twenty-nine institutions according to the person in charge of evaluating them (Fernandes 2007)—but not all necessarily in public universities, since some were in independent PVCs like the Steve Biko Institute. The projects consisted of PVCs established by universities, often after mobilization by staff through established decision-making bodies, including elected university councils, and existed in nine states with 5,370 students (in or around 2007). On average only some 15 percent of their graduates passed the vestibular examination (Fernandes 2007: 29), but the frustration expressed in Fernandes' evaluation derived less from that low success rate than from the lack of attention in the programmes to race-based themes that were meant to be their innovative feature (Silveira 2007). The picture of this programme, then, is a mixed one: the managers at the centre saw it as a highly focused operation intended to raise consciousness among teachers and students in the PVCs while the teachers themselves tended toward what the managers described pejoratively as *conteudismo*—excessive focus on the *content* needed to get their students through their exams (Silveira 2007). Little attention was paid to one very striking feature of Fernandes's report, namely, the predominance of women among the

8. The two edited books referred to were part of a series of thirty-three published between 2006 and 2009 on this and other subjects of interest to SECAD such as teacher training for bilingual and intercultural education and "educação popular" in Brazil and the Americas. Their impact and distribution remain unknown.

PVC students in PIC/PDU projects—67.5 percent according to a survey of 7,200 students in the first year of the programme.

By 2006 SECAD was supporting seminars and publications that promoted and celebrated the agenda of quotas, for example, in a book with the militant title *Tempos de Lutas* (Times of Struggle), edited by Nilma Lino Gomes, with contributions from Renato Emerson dos Santos, Jocelio Teles dos Santos, and Moisés Santana of UFAl (Lino Gomes 2006). But eventually the fashion passed in the ministry: already in 2007 Arsenio Schmidt, head of SECAD's Diversity and Citizenship Department, told Nina Almeida that support for prevestibular courses was a thing of the past. Although they were very good, he implied that they were no longer necessary because now there were other policies to support Afrodescendants, including quotas and the NEABs (Almeida 2008).[9]

The secretariat was not exclusively devoted to identity politics. For a time it ran a programme entitled Conexões de Saberes (Knowledge Connections) to help students from the popular sectors and potential leaders and project managers to remain in their courses and save them from dropping out,[10] to encourage them to do research linked to their university studies in their own communities, and to promote dialogue between universities and those sectors. A few years later it seems to have transmuted into the Programa de Educação Tutorial (Tutorial Guidance Program—PET), which funds study groups of students with specially assigned tutors in federal universities and an apparatus of scholarships, supplementary payments to academic staff, oversight committees, and so on, all contained in a lengthy administrative decree dated June 2010.[11] Like other add-ons to the overall quota policy, these programmes are more selective than first-year quota admissions and reward good academic performance without a race-based criterion. (The awards are hardly princely: $R400 per month or about US$150, according to a call put out at the UFMG in 2014.)[12] Like other similar

9. He said much the same thing to me in November 2008.

10. I interviewed Leonor Araujo, head of diversity (coordenadora-geral da diversidade) in SECAD in November 2008. She spoke of Conexões de Saberes as a "differentiated affirmative action programme" that awarded scholarships whose purpose was to "train community leaders with managerial capacity."

11. Portaria MEC number 976, 27 July 2010. This is an eight-page document; the original Conexões de Saberes document was only two pages long—Portaria number 1, 17 May 2006. The design is very similar to Ford's Pathways Program and may indeed have derived from it, since PPCor was funded through Pathways.

12. See "Núcleo Conexões de Saberes seleciona estudantes para projeto de construção de suas memória," 14 May 2014. https://www.ufmg.br/online/arquivos/033298.shtml

devices, such as the research internships, they operate as springboards for promising or energetic students who through them can begin to stand out from the mass.

The NEABs have not been designed as research centres, but Brazil has for long had two major institutions focused on race research. In the UFBA the Centro de Estudos Afro-Orientais (Center for Asian and Oriental Studies—CEAO), created in 1959, has published the journal *Afro-Asia* since 1965 and has been in the forefront of both Afro-Brazilian studies and the campaign in the university that led to the adoption of quotas. It had tended to focus more on cultural themes and Afro-Brazilian religion, but in the 1990s, under pressure from Ford, the CEAO shifted its emphasis to social justice. The Centro de Estudos Afro-Asiáticos (CEA) was created in Rio in the private nonprofit Universidade Candido Mendes, run by the well-connected figure Candido Mendes with a geopolitical eye to Brazil's African ties and some funding from the Ford Foundation. It was also for a time home to local Rio activists, published the journal *Estudos Afro-Asiáticos* from 1978, and hosted pioneering sociological research by Carlos Hasenbalg, Nelson do Valle Silva, and Livio Sansone.[13]

SECAD made no mystery of its mission, as can be seen from the militant or activist language of the publications supported by it, with the PDU and UNESCO, in its series Educação para Todos.[14] Thus a paper on the UFBA (Reis 2007) on issues concerning both the access of blacks to university and their ability to stay the course in the face of financial constraints, speaks of quotas as a form of reparation, and another on the UFAL in the state of Alagoas speaks regretfully of universalism and the system of academic merit based on examination results as mechanisms that undo the collective identity forged by the quota system at

---

13. In 2010, after many years of financial crisis, IUPERJ and its academic staff were absorbed by UERJ and renamed the Instituto de Estudos Sociais e Políticos (Institute for Social and Political Research—IESP). A few years later, in 2016–17, the UERJ itself was thrown into a disastrous financial crisis by the state government of Rio, which all but ceased paying its bills and began transferring budgeted funds only intermittently. This may have done irreparable damage to the institution. The 2017 vestibular exam was taken by thirty-seven thousand people, fewer than half the number of applicants the year before. Cleaning contractors were not being paid, and in July university staff persons were going to receive one-quarter of their salaries for the month of May (*Folha de São Paulo*, 16 July 2017). Also in July, the 2017 academic year was suspended indefinitely and as of October 2017 the August and September salaries still had to be paid as well as a month's worth of salary from 2016. The state, labouring under multiple fiscal and corruption crises, was only paying the police, schoolteachers, judges, and legislators at the time.

14. These can be can be found on the website of the MEC (portal.mec.gov.br).

entry into university (Santos 2007). The paper contrasts the good fortune of seven white students sampled who did not need to work to pay their way, with the forty-three negros and pardos three-quarters of whom needed to work for an income, and other papers in the same book provide vivid illustrations of the sacrifices students have to make to stay the course of their studies (93). The paper on the UFAL points to the absence of black academics who might strengthen students' confidence and provide the networking that is so important in gaining access to research assistantships and other subsidies (Santos 2007). This confirms what I learned from interviews and is consonant with the widely quoted pattern of Brazilian sociability, whereby personal connections are believed to be essential for any kind of advancement. Hence also the importance of projects like The Colour of Bahia (A Cor da Bahia) which was started in 1993 with Ford funding by Antonio Sergio Guimarães and others at UFBA, and whose graduates included the late Luiza Bairros, future head of SEPPIR under Dilma Roussef.[15] It continues to this day as a thriving research and training programme in race relations, black culture, and identity.[16] At the Institute of Philosophy and Social Sciences (IFCS) of the UFRJ in Rio, a Social Research Laboratory led by Yvonne Maggie undertook a programme funded by the Ford Foundation incorporating students as research interns so that they could avoid dropping out for financial reasons. Established already in 1986 as a response to an alarmingly high student dropout rate, but without an explicit affirmative action component in its selection process, it led to a dramatic improvement in the numbers of students who successfully completed their courses. But interestingly, a survey showed that students attributed their acquisition of a network of contacts and critical understanding of Brazilian society to the "commitment, loyalty and even paternalism" of their teachers more than to their own intellectual prowess, which was taken for granted (Villas Bôas 2003:59). These are not "just" affirmative actions, for they create entitlements for specific groups, and the experience of the Núcleos illustrate how they may sow the seeds of group identity and collective consciousness among their beneficiaries.

Another example of a state-sponsored niche for politicized black students is the Ministry of Health's Afroatitude Programme, run jointly by

---

15. Luiza Bairros had also been head of the Secretaria da Promoção da Igualdade (State Secretariat for the Promotion of Racial Equality—SEPROMI), the equivalent of SEPPIR in Bahia. She died of cancer in 2016.

16. For more on this program, see http://www.acordabahia.ufba.br/?q=frontpage

its AIDS programme, the Higher Education Secretariat of the MEC, the Special Secretariat for Human Rights, and SEPPIR, which provided five hundred research internships to undergraduate *cotistas* (beneficiaries of quota places) to enable them to work on their professors' research projects and prepare them for careers as health assistants. It arose in a context in which various bodies, including NGOs, were alerting black people to health risks of particular interest to them, notably sickle-cell disease. (The programme was not uncontroversial: Peter Fry criticized the concept because of the identification it seemed to project between HIV and black people [2006].) In SECAD's case study of the State University of Matto Grosso do Sul (UEMS) a project funded by Afroatitude paid students nominal monthly amounts (R\$241, less than the minimum wage at the time) to work on projects explicitly geared toward black politics: evaluations or descriptions of quota systems and beneficiaries, the depiction of blacks in Brazilian cinema, race relations in local schools, and so on (Benedito 2007). The health ministry also funded a PVC at the UFAL, presumably through the same programme (interview with Moisés Santana, March 2009).

These initiatives from above and below can be located on an axis from situations in which the race-based collective activity could be called allusive or implicit, mixed with socioeconomic, health, and gender affinities, to others in which it is explicit and emphasizes the separate social, political and even cultural concerns of blacks and others. The case in which affirmative action fed most explicitly into identity politics was the Ford Foundation's two-year project entitled Espaços Afirmados (Spaces of Affirmation—ESAF) at UERJ, described in slightly contrasting terms in two essays in a collection edited by João Feres Jr. and Jonas Zoninsein as we shall see in chapter 3 (Pinto 2006; dos Santos 2006b). But in other examples described by SECAD authors, students' racial identification is often mixed with socioeconomic issues. Quota beneficiaries are not described as an entirely separate racial category of student: they share characteristics such as colour, identity, and neighborhood with others; while career choices emerge as a major differentiating factor that impinges on inequality, cotistas being underrepresented in high-prestige courses (Lopes and Braga 2007).

One of the most effective contributions to these two SECAD volumes is a low-key account of the PVC in Campo Grande, the capital of the state of Matto Grosso do Sul, located a thousand kilometers from the coastal metropolitan centres and possessing a substantial black population— which accounted for 40 percent of the town but only 1 percent of the university's students (Queiroz and Silva 2007). The paper, based on interviews with students at the Milton Santos PVC—named after the world-famous geographer who was also a black Brazilian—was written by its two coordinators and may therefore reflect their own agenda, but nonetheless it provides further indications of how the consciousness-raising programme of SECAD's coordinators and managers could be translated in many ways in the classroom. In this case the emphasis was almost exclusively on the boost to self-confidence that the interviewees experienced simply by attending the PVC: of course they mention their colour and the burden of their history, but, almost naïvely, they express the belief that self-confidence plus study would enable them to reach the same standard as everybody else. This is different from the message put out by harder line activists—but then in Campo Grande the academic barriers may not be as high, and the competition not as tight, as in the metropolitan centres.

FIES and ProUni: The "Zigzag" of Public and Private Provision in Brazilian Education

If the race issue was introduced in the public universities through this array of connections between activist academics and institutions, the Lula government introduced it into private higher education via a race-cum-socioeconomically based scholarship scheme called the University for All Programme, or ProUni, with incomparably larger resources but without the web of academic connections or the consciousness-raising, or for that matter the controversy, surrounding the introduction of race-based schemes in the public sector.[17] The scheme condenses several issues relating to inequality in education. The first is an intellectual puzzle: the private universities are regarded as offering a bad deal educationally, so was it the "elitism" of the intelligentsia that, when ProUni was introduced to help high-achieving black and low-income students, distracted them from engaging in any debate over the implications of the scheme for racial classification and social inequality—the same issues that were raging in relation to public universities? The second is the provision of subsidies to supposedly lower quality institutions, most of which are for-profit businesses, so that they can offer scholarships to negros, pardos, indigenous people, and people from low-income families. The third is

---

17. In the section heading, the term "zigzag" is borrowed from the title of Luiz Antonio Cunha's "Zigue-zague no Ministério de Educação" (2006).

the belief that private fee-paying higher education is mostly for poor and therefore poorly educated people. The fourth is the weakness of the certification arrangements for qualifications offered by the private sector, raising the suspicion that it offers poor quality to poor people—and charges for the service.

In 2010, something of the order of 4,736,000 students were studying in private institutions of higher education, compared with 1,644,000 in the public sector (federal, state, and municipal).[18] For low-income students access to public higher education is difficult, even with quotas. The standard view is that geography, family income, and institution type (public/private, university or nonuniversity) are the primary influences on achievement, and this is borne out by a study conducted on the basis of the 1999 *provão*—an examination taken by students since 1996 throughout the country to assess the quality of their institutions (Sampaio et al. 2000: 49). Overall, the best marks were obtained by students from high-income families in public institutions in the Southeast and the worst by students from low-income families in private ones in the Northeast. However, the widely shared assumption that students with dark skin colour tend to study at the lower prestige private universities was not borne out: the study found that negro and pardo students were a higher proportion in public than in private universities (20 vs. 12 percent) and in any case that students in private universities clearly tended to come from better-off families. It also found a category of poor and very poor people who had managed to overcome barriers throughout their education and also, controlling for all relevant variables, that low-income students in public higher education in the Southeast did better than any other group in private higher education nationwide (Sampaio et al. 2000: 35, 38, 49). Finally, in the background is the harsh reality of the vast numbers who fail to get the minimum pass mark required to be considered even for quotas at public institutions, as documented with large-scale data from UERJ by Mendes and his colleagues (Mendes et al. 2016). Wilson de Almeida quotes another source, which, using data from the national household survey, the Pesquisa Nacional de Amostra por Do-

---

18. See also appendix A. The figures are taken from the Higher Education Census produced by the MEC's own research institute (INEP). Their proper interpretation would require much closer inspection and a detailed knowledge of the ways in which such statistics are assembled. For example, they do not take into account the difference between daytime and nighttime courses or part-time and full-time study, so they are just orders of magnitude and noteworthy only as such. Thus they can only be an indication of the size of the private institutions.

micílio (National Household Sample Survey—PNAD), shows almost exactly the same pattern (de Almeida 2014: 86). However, there are reservations, beginning with the date of the study since so much has happened in Brazilian higher education since 1999. The data do not separate out the "high-end" nonprofit private institutions (mostly Catholic universities), which are likely to attract above-average numbers of students from above-average socioeconomic backgrounds, and they also shed light on an important aspect of higher education that we have frequent occasion to remark upon, namely, the prestige hierarchy of courses—and likewise the different standards of living their graduates can expect. The study shows that, at the extremes, students in the humanities and mathematics,[19] as well as economics, tend to come from substantially lower income families than those in medicine and dentistry—a polarization that is particularly marked in the public universities (Sampaio et al. 2000: 40). A 2005 pamphlet promoting affirmative action at the Federal University of Bahia (UFBA) and written by the Rector and other high authorities, including prominent quotas campaigner Jocélio dos Santos, points out a similar pattern: In a state where 75 percent of the population are self-assigned as black, courses such as Communication, Architecture, Engineering, and Medicine had less than 30 percent self-assigned black students as compared with less competitive ones like Librarianship, Social Sciences, Accounting, and Chemistry, where they numbered 57 percent (Almeida Filho et al. 2005: 13). These differentiations may also cut across the public-private divide. There is scattered evidence of the poor quality of the education provided in the for-profit institutions, as in the extremely low success rate of their law graduates: data from about 2007 reveal that only 10 percent of the law graduates of the very large, multicampus, Anhanguera education business passed the Brazilian bar exam, without which they could not translate their academic degrees into professional qualifications (de Almeida 2014: 70)—but then only 18.5 percent of all candidates passed at the first attempt in the years 2010–2012.[20] Overall,

---

19. Math is a low-prestige subject apparently because it is a teacher-training course, sadly.

20. Data released in 2013 by the company that manages the OAB exams show that the Anhangera success rate, though below average, is not as bad as it looks: of the 361,000 (!) people who sat the exam over eight sittings between 2010 and 2012, only 18.5 percent passed at the first attempt and even after multiple attempts the pass rate was only 58.8 percent. See *O Globo*'s G1 Education supplement, 22 July 2013. De Almeida does not say whether the 10 percent figure refers only to first attempts. http://g1.globo.com/educacao/oab/noticia/2013/08/so-185-passam-de-primeira-no-exame-de-ordem-da-oab-diz-estudo.html

however, the most important points to emerge from this source are the regional contrast and, against the standard narrative of campaigners, the negro and pardo presence in public universities.

Although quotas may help, students still need to qualify on the basis of their marks in the end-of-schooling nationwide Exame Nacional do Ensino Médio (National Secondary School Examination—ENEM), and in addition competition for places is more intense in the more competitive courses like medicine, engineering, and law and in the more prestigious institutions like USP, UERJ, UFMG, and UFRJ. Until recently the vestibular exam has acted in effect as a social filter because people had great difficulty in getting high enough marks in it without attending and paying for a cursinho, but more competitive universities still require applicants who have reached a satisfactory ENEM grade to go through a second-stage vestibular. So the private sector both prepares people for university entrance and provides university degree courses. But the arrangements for supporting and regulating the private sector are far from straightforward and offer an object lesson in the operation of Brazilian corporatism and the way education can resemble a tradable commodity.

Unusually, in Brazil, apart from organizations or businesses that are either "for profit," paying taxes on income or profit, or "not for profit," not subject to those taxes, there is a third category invented for educational establishments that are private but do not pay federal, state, or municipal taxes on their income or profits. This originated in 1934 and was extended in the 1967 Constitution and a constitutional amendment in 1969, being subject to certain conditions that were widely circumvented; attempts during the 1990s to tighten the intermediate "for-profit tax-exempt" category a little by attaching conditions, were largely unraveled by political deals in Congress and by the courts (Cunha 2003, 2006, 2007).[21]

The affirmative action programmes ProUni and Fundo de Financiamento Estudantil (Higher Education Finance Fund—FIES) came to their rescue again in the subsequent decade, leaving them at an advantage compared to nonprofit philanthropic providers (mostly Catholic and Protestant universities) and also to businesses in other sectors. At several stages Cunha explains the political influence of educational en-

---

21. At first Cardoso's government did succeed in establishing the legal recognition of profit in education, requiring providers to choose between for-profit and nonprofit status, which carried conditions of openness in publishing their accounts and also imposed a minimum expenditure on teachers' salaries (rather, by implication, than on dividends), but this was eventually struck down by a court order in 1997.

trepreneurs: after the 1964 coup they were able to cash in on their political support for the mobilizations that had prepared the way for the military takeover, and with the return of elected government in the 1980s they acquired significant influence in Congress. Today the higher education providers among them are organized in the Frente Parlamentar de Apoio ao Ensino Superior Privado (Congressional Private Higher Education Front) composed of no less than 171 deputies and 36 senators from across the political spectrum, which flexed its muscles by proposing 292 amendments to the ProUni law (see below).[22] A sense of the atmosphere is captured in the depiction by a journalist of the influential entrepreneur João Carlos Di Genio, whom we have already encountered, owner of the Universidade Paulista (UNIP) and other establishments and claiming 890,000 students in 2015, depicting carnavalesque parties at his mansion in Brasilia where politicians would turn up "without their wives."[23]

One might imagine that as a counterpart to these tax benefits and other exemptions the private institutions were subject to some kind of accreditation process, but the government, deferring to the said congressional influence, appointed private sector representatives to the body responsible, the National Education Council (CNE), where they blocked this. Despite a brief swing of the pendulum back in favor of state provision after the transition of the 1980s, governments led by both Cardoso and Lula were offering places on the council in exchange for the passage of unrelated legislation in the Congress. In 1996 the private institutions successfully resisted proposals to routinely publish their performance ratings.[24]

Resistance to evaluation is not confined to the private sector: students and rectors in public universities have also resisted, on political grounds—opposition to the neoliberal character of such evaluations—or in the case of rectors because they saw it as an encroachment on their autonomy. Paulo Renato de Souza—Cardoso's minister of education, it will be recalled—has described the pressures: in 1996, soon after he took office, he was visited by a very prominent senator from a big state who

22. How many of these were adopted is unknown. See an interview with Wilson de Almeida in the weekly *Carta Capital*, 19 December 2014, prior to the publication of his book on the subject (de Almeida 2014).

23. Wilson de Almeida quotes a report dated 1 September 1999 in the magazine *Veja* describing what politicians called the "Di Genio circus." The circus closed down when "finally, aged 50, the confirmed bachelor got married" (de Almeida 2014: 65).

24. Performance indicators are based on marks obtained the *provão* (Cunha 2003: 52). The first exercise, in 1996, involved 616 institutions and 55,000 students (50).

asked that the ministry approve the upgrading of a "faculdade" in his state to university status (which is more profitable because it confers far more freedom to create degree courses); eventually it transpired that the institution belonged to the senator himself (Souza 2005: 148). The minister's memoirs do not describe the political concessions he had to make in the recognition process, emphasizing instead the endless judicial guerrilla he faced from student organizations and universities. On one occasion, he ordered the ministry's fax machine to be unplugged at the weekend so judicial decisions could not prevent the *provão* from being halted at the last minute on Monday morning by a surprise judicial injunction (*medida cautelar*) (162).

However, the state is not entirely toothless: the UniverCidade and the Universidade Gama Filho in Rio, both belonging to the Galileo Educational Corporation, were closed in January 2014 (*Globo Educação*, 13 January 2014) on account of multiple financial and educational irregularities and failings. This was not a midnight raid: such procedures can take many years as appeal and counterappeal succeed one another. In May 2016 it was declared bankrupt, and in June 2016 it transpired that the owner of the Universidade Gama Filho was under investigation, together with forty-six other people, for having set up a fraudulent financial scheme whereby investments supposedly made by two pension funds (which they had founded) in the university were diverted to their own bank accounts. Eleven thousand students and two thousand staff were affected, and the Piedade neighbourhood where the university was located "practically became a ghost town." Local inhabitants were reported to fear that the university's deserted swimming pool would become a breeding ground for tropical infections like dengue, zika, and chicungunha (*O Dia*, 24 June 2016).

The affirmative action programmes FIES (2003) and ProUni (2005) were not only a response to student demand. The private sector had become caught up in a fierce competitive war during the late 1990s to which it responded by multiplying courses and setting up teaching spaces ("campuses") in malls, gym halls and the like. The upshot was that barely half their places were filled in 2004, only 52 percent of their students received their degrees (compared to 76 percent in the public sector), and the student default on fee payments was out of control (Andrés 2008: 82). By 2007 the debt owed to the tax authorities and the Social Security system by private institutions of higher education amounted to R$9.6 billion (some say R$12 billion) and was unlikely ever to be repaid (Andrés 2008). Under ProUni this debt would in principle be paid off by reserving 10 percent of student places for high-achieving low-income and disabled students and ethnic-racial groups classified as "pretos, pardos e indígenas"—5 percent on half scholarships and the other 5 percent on full scholarships. In 2005, 112,275 grants were awarded, rising to 163,854 in 2007 (Heringer 2010: 131; see also appendix B). Awards are renewed each semester, subject to satisfactory performance by the *bolsista* (award-holder), so to properly interpret these numbers would require data on renewals. Preto and pardo students accounted for half the beneficiaries, which sounds positive, but would have to be evaluated in the light of the proportions in earlier years and of the criticisms that they were nonetheless being "relegated" to the supposedly poorer quality private sector.

The for-profits ended up having to contribute 8.5 percent of their gross income to the scheme, while the nonprofits contributed 20 percent. Unsurprisingly quite a few nonprofits have changed their status, taking all their assets—which of course had never been taxed—with them. Even the token penalty imposed on private universities who failed to fulfill the conditions for joining ProUni—1 percent of the previous year's turnover—was removed in Congress. In addition to these legal advantages it would appear that "hundreds of thousands" of notional free places are not taken up for ProUni because the number on offer is inflated to enable institutions to remain in the scheme and thus preserve their tax amnesty (Andrés 2008).

These are not small-time concerns: in 2013 the two biggest higher education providers, Kroton (whose major shareholder had been minister of tourism and institutional relations in Lula's first government) and Anhanguera, merged to become the world's largest private education group by market capitalization (*Financial Times*, 30 May 2013), and in July 2016 the enlarged group bought out its biggest rival Estacio de Sá. They have been built through multiple acquisitions and function as nationwide organizations with campuses in many major cities. Wilson de Almeida describes how the Universidade Estacio de Sá, in accordance with the trick mentioned above, by switching its status from nonprofit (filantrópica) to for profit, had reduced its tax liabilities, reduced the number of free places it had to offer through ProUni, and pleaded successfully for a delay in the payment of social insurance dues. The corporations' dependence on these subsidies was illustrated when, after her reelection, President Dilma Rouseff appointed a much more fiscally austere (and therefore short-lived) minister of finance. Shortly afterward a decree appeared in the official gazette prohibiting students in receipt of a full-fees ProUni grant from simultaneously receiving a FIES loan or, if they were on a half-fees grant, from receiving a loan in a separate institution or separate course (*Diario Oficial da União*, 29 December 2014; *Financial Times*, 6 January 2015). The implication was that the programme provided opportunities for students to multiply their access to loans granted on very favorable terms by registering simultaneously for several institutions and courses. The effect of the clampdown on Kroton's share price was immediate: a fall of one-third between December and January.[25]

A second way to expand access to higher education (and fill empty seats in the private sector) was through loans to private sector students, under FIES, whose lending terms were loosened in 2011 with an interest rate of only 3.4 percent (in circumstances where banks would lend, if at all, at a multiple of that). There is no race component in the conditions, the means test is a very generous maximum per capita family income of twenty times the minimum wage, and from 2012 no guarantor was required. As a result 250,000 students were expected to enroll in the scheme in 2012 (*O Estado de São Paulo*, 4 July 2012). But like ProUni, the scheme held quite concrete benefits for the private universities themselves, since fees would not be paid by the student borrowers themselves but directly by FIES, thus avoiding "leakage" to their other expenses and the resulting default (which the article said stood at 9.5 percent in 2011, though whether this was a percentage of debtors or of debts was not stated).

The ProUni grant pays all or half of a student's tuition fee (*matrícula*) depending on their family's per capita income, but it does not pay living expenses. (In any case the overwhelming majority of private university students study part time and can be presumed to be employed at least part time.) The ceiling for qualification, or means test, is a family income of one-and-a-half times the minimum wage per capita for a full grant and three times for a partial grant. This can be quite generous depending on the size of the household, since all members count toward the per capita total, irrespective of age. But that should not be taken as a criticism: if the ceiling is lowered too far there will not be many qualified applicants: it should be remembered that, after introducing quotas in 2001, the UERJ

---

25. For readers interested in such things, the merged Kroton share price had risen 85 percent in 2014, a period during which the São Paulo market rose by only 5 percent. Estacio's share price fell even further, as compared with a 10 percent decline in the Brazilian stock index. (By 2016 they were back at the 2014 level in the post-Dilma market revival.)

had to raise the income ceiling from R$300 to R$500 per capita,[26] because at the lower level it failed to attract enough qualified students to fill the quota (Junqueira 2007). This despite the low average qualifying academic standard for ProUni compared with that for public universities.

According to a government statement, in July 2011 174,500 beneficiaries had graduated since the scheme's inception, and another 464,500 were currently studying with its support, equivalent to almost 10 percent of the private sector's notional 4.7 million students at that time. These figures do not take into account the social and academic differentiation in the private sector itself between institutions of varying quality and reputation, between an elite of mainly Catholic nonprofit universities (Pontifical Catholic universities—PUCs) and the rest, and between a minority of nonprofit and a large number of for-profit institutions. However, a little noticed and undated World Bank paper written around 2012 points out that about half of the more than 1,200 institutions that joined the programme, out of an overall total of 2,022 private higher education institutions, were nonprofit and philanthropic institutions (Salmi and Fèvre n.d.). The paper concludes that "the strong participation of non-profit and philanthropic universities is a clear indication of the program's influence," or, one might add, of the relative disinterest of the for-profit institutions that were participating less than might have been hoped or expected—yet still apparently offering more vacancies than they could fill; another hypothesis, however, is that, although the qualifying academic standard does not appear very demanding, being fixed below the national average of the ENEM examination,[27] ProUni grants were still being obtained more than proportionately by an upper layer of better qualified students gaining entrance to the small number of academically more competitive nonprofit private universities. This would hardly be surprising and is not intended as a criticism: better students are more likely to qualify and more likely to apply to higher-rated institutions.

Under Cardoso and his minister Paulo Renato public universities were starved of funds, while the MEC opened the way for rapid expansion of private higher education. Under Lula, much more ambitious initiatives were undertaken to expand higher education and fill it with students, including the creation of several new federal universities across the country (see appendix A). But the demand for higher education is

---

26. At the time R$500 was roughly one and a half times the minimum wage.

27. The ENEM is the nationwide end-of-schooling exam. The marking system is hard to understand, but 500 is regarded as at least a notional average. See, for example, *O Estado de São Paulo*, 29 January 2010. ProUni applicants must have a mark of 400 on the ENEM.

insatiable and it is understandable that governments encourage private provision. Given the fiscal cost and perhaps also the rigidity of the public sector, in which by constitutional fiat undergraduates pay no fees and all tenured academic staff are civil servants, with the corresponding entitlements and guarantees, including strong pension rights paid by the universities out of their own budgets, the private for-profit sector, where students have to pay fees and most teaching is done by hourly paid staff, offers a tempting alternative despite doubts about the quality of what is offered in some of its institutions and about the real value of the resulting qualifications in the job market.

Some of this is speculative: apart from the World Bank study, there is no publicly available evaluation of the private sector or of ProUni or FIES, or indeed data that would enable an outsider to undertake an evaluation, nor is anything known of the negotiations between private sector institutions and the government. The big players in private higher education are businesses, which are unlikely to open their books to independent scrutiny, something that would call for the skills of an accountant more than a social scientist. None of the painstaking quantitative exercises published about quotas and race differences in universities includes data on the private sector. A social scientist might undertake an ethnography, but once again the institutions would not be open to this sort of research. Their disposition toward the outside is symbolized by the electronically controlled access to their premises. It would seem that students who have fallen behind in their monthly payments find that their card will not open the turnstile.

Rolling Out Affirmative Actions in the Public Sector

Even when affirmative action was in its infancy or barely existed, access to undergraduate university places by black students was growing fast, and faster than that of whites, at least according to broad nationwide data. According to the Laboratório de Análises Econômicas, Históricas, Sociais, e Estatística das Relações Raciais (Laboratory for Economic, Historical, Social, and Statistical Analysis of Race Relations—LAESER), the proportion of the negro and pardo population aged eighteen to twenty-four in undergraduate courses grew from 3.6 to 16.4 percent between 1988 and 2008, while the equivalent proportions for whites were 12.4 and 35.8 percent. Significantly, the proportion of negro and pardo women enrolled in those courses grew fastest of all, from 4.1 to 20 percent. These numbers include a majority of students in private universities, so it might be suspected that a disproportionate number of negros and pardos were likely to go to private institutions. But, on the contrary, in 2008 the proportion of negros and pardos in the relevant age group who were enrolled in public institutions was greater than that of young white people: 38.4 versus 32.7 percent (LAESER 2010: 227). These numbers contrast markedly and positively with data on the poorest strata reported in a 2012 paper, which tells us that in the poorest quintile of the population only 3 percent of children reach higher education (Andrade 2012). Although not strictly comparable, the contrast warns us not to routinely identify "black" and "poor," let alone "black" and "under-achieving."

This background, and the dynamic it reflects, has to be kept in mind as we follow the debates about affirmative action. That dynamic stems from the growth of a black middle class, from the expansion of public higher education during Lula's presidency, and perhaps also from an artifact, namely, the growing popularity of negro self-assignment among young people and especially among the better educated of them. Nonetheless, like the INEP study quoted in the previous section, this shows that even before quotas were established, blacks, and especially black women, were piling in to higher education, but it does not show and is not intended to show that quotas were unnecessary. It is important to know how those black and pardo students were distributed along the prestige hierarchy of subjects and institutions—and in any case the argument of this book is that the justification for their quotas goes beyond the technicalities of social engineering.

Even before ProUni, affirmative actions had begun to be adopted in public universities throughout Brazil. The first ones included four state universities—UERJ, the State University of Northern Rio (UENF), UEMS, and UNEB—and one federal university, UnB. The two state universities of Rio were pushed into an affirmative action programme by the unexpected presentation and rapid approval of a law in the state legislature in 2001. There followed two years of confusion, with the application and replacement of provisions almost incomprehensible to the outsider but meticulously described by Elielma Ayres Machado in her dissertation (Machado 2004). The law started out as a measure meant to set aside places for graduates of the public school system, with vague provisions for blacks and pardos. The entrance exams for students starting their studies in 2003, which took place in 2002, did not properly explain these to the candidates. To begin with, it was announced that 50 percent of places would be reserved for students from the public school system (for the most part), but after the first part of the two-stage examination process candidates learned that 40 percent of the total number of places would be reserved for those from the public (state) school system who declared themselves to be negros or pardos, without saying what would happen with those who met both criteria (135–36). If the number of candidates making this declaration and gaining sufficiently good marks did not reach 40 percent, the remaining reserved places would go to negros and pardos from private schools.[28] The governor of Rio at the time, Anthony Garotinho, was looking to treat public school graduates as a constituency: the state government was funding their schooling, and he apparently believed the universities that the state was also funding should make more space for them. The upshot was (a) confusion, since it looked as if the university's "traditional" (and relatively privileged) clientele could be cut to 10 percent; and (b) not very different for negros and pardos from what it would otherwise have been, as most of those who gained admission did so on their marks as public school students without the need for a quota (149). There followed a rush of lawsuits, mostly brought by students who complained that the quotas had prevented them from gaining admission even though they had better marks than others who did, but all but five out of three hundred failed: Garotinho's motives may be elucidated by the phrase "suspect capitalization" ("capitalização dubia") used in this connection by a prominent movimento negro figure from Rio.

After this UERJ, with the state legislature's overwhelming approval, developed a system that at least made sense arithmetically: the new law (no. 4,151 of 4 October 2003) set aside 45 percent of places on the basis of family income, of which 20 percent would go to "blacks and members of ethnic minorities," 20 percent to public school graduates, and 5 percent to indigenous peoples and those suffering from disabilities. An important change in this law was the primary qualifying criterion of family income, which was set by the university itself. As always, to qualify for the race-based affirmative action, candidates were required only to declare themselves negro (in the broad sense to include pardos) on the application form, but they also had to say on what grounds (173). The answers given by applicants to that question would make fascinating reading.

Thereafter two state universities, UNEB, UEMS, and the federal UnB, followed in quick succession: the first used a mixed approach, while the

---

28. The categories "public" and "private" school are a simplification based on the two exams mentioned. The apparently highly oversimplified outcome, on the assumption that all blacks and pardos were educated in public schools, might mean that there would be only 10 or even 5 percent of places "left over" for the private school graduates.

other two allocated quota places only by racial self-assignment. The UnB, on account of its high profile, gained national notoriety for its "pure" race-based policy of allocating 20 percent to blacks. But at the same time, almost unnoticed, 6 municipalities (admittedly out of 5,565), 5 major ministries, and one or two large private companies were adopting quotas for filling vacancies, mainly for blacks and women (Heringer 2004). By August 2009, 51 state and federal universities had affirmative action programmes or reserved places, and of these 42 were designed to favour public school graduates and 33 to favour blacks (Heringer 2010: 44). The public school qualification may have been intended as a proxy for income, and many used a combination of these two criteria. Very few used directly the income criterion—which was to become a qualifying criterion in addition to the public school criterion in the 2012 law. By 2010, 12.1 percent (41,000) of the 341,000 new students at public universities were admitted through a reserved places or quotas scheme. Of those 41,000, the vast majority (76 percent) benefited from the quotas for public school graduates and 13,000 (32 percent) from race-based quotas (LAESER 2012: 2).[29] All this occurred in a context of massive university expansion—with the number of registrations (not just admissions) almost doubling from 0.57 million to 1.03 million between 2003 and 2010.[30] Negros and pardos together had increased from 34.2 to 40.8 percent, which may seem little at first sight but not when placed in the context of a doubling of the total student numbers (Feres et al. 2013).

The two most prominent state universities in São Paulo, UNICAMP and USP, resisted. Eventually UNICAMP instituted a device to raise the vestibular marks of public school applicants that was dismissed at first as ineffective but, after a redesign of the scheme, had a significant impact on the social profile of its admissions.[31] The most resistant institution was USP. In 2006 USP turned its attention officially to the low representation of public school graduates among its students. In tune with the position long associated with its professoriate, the university made no special mention of race except as part of a list of socioeconomic exclusions that called for the university to act, as can be seen in its Pró-Reitoría's 2009

---

29. Figures rounded to the nearest thousand (see below, pp. 132–33).

30. The figures in this paragraph are all rounded. Divided among fifty-nine universities, this gives a (slightly misleading) average of 17,500 students per institution in the federal university sector. The figures are "misleading" because the newer institutions have smaller intakes. Note that in 2011 the entire public university system, federal and state, had 1.6 million students. See appendix B.

31. See section entitled "Race versus Income Quotas and Their Evaluation" in chapter 3.

report on the subject and the article summarizing it by Matos and others in 2012 (Pimenta et al. 2009; Matos et al. 2012). USP's response was an outreach programme, INCLUSP, that enrolled public secondary school (ensino médio) students in monitoring or continuous assessment and dispatched 565 USP students as "ambassadors" in 700 schools to encourage pupils to think about applying to the university (Pimenta et al. 2009: 21). USP also gave public school applicants an allowance of 3 percent extra marks in the vestibular exam, subsequently increased by various parameters (Matos et al. 2012: 722), which reversed a decline in admissions of students from public schools and made a difference of almost one thousand. In a long telephone conversation in April 2010, Quirino Augusto Camargo, one of the authors of the report and also a Pró-Reitor, described it as giving those pupils a "nudge" (*um empurraõzinho*). Between 2006 and 2009 there was in fact a decline in the number of applicants overall (for which there were many explanations) but there was also a rise in the proportion of public school students who entered, reaching the 30 percent target for public school students admissions. The report did give a nod to race issues, providing data showing that while self-assigned black students declined as a proportion of applicants (perhaps in tune with the decline of public school applicants in general) there was a small increase in their admission: from 12.3 percent to 14.3 percent between 2006 and 2009 (738), denoting an improvement in their performance.

However, public school graduates continued to be concentrated in the less competitive Human Sciences, which received half of them in 2009; also, the rise in their representation was mostly in evening courses, reflecting these students' need to earn an income during the day. But the trend is not uniform: public school students accounted for only 4 percent of daytime law students in 2006, rising to 17 percent in 2009, while in the evening courses they rose from 14 to 37 percent; in engineering they rose from 14 to 18 percent, but in medicine, which is taught only as a full-time course, they rose, impressively, from 5 to 39 percent (41). Overall, students from public schools increased significantly in Human and Biological Sciences, but not in Natural Sciences (Ciências Exatas, including Engineering) (734).[32]

We see that USP set itself this task and went about it systematically and purposively with little accompanying fanfare, but we also see that al-

32. USP also paid attention to the important question of "permanência," that is, measures to prevent midcourse dropouts, providing modestly paid research internships to students in need financially, of which 800 were awarded in 2006–9 (Pimenta et al. 2009: 26).

though the results achieved were real they were fairly marginal and un-likely to impress the movimento negro, which, like much of the coun-try's opinion-forming elites, regarded that university as a law unto itself. Insofar as they are comparable, the numbers also reflect a much lower level of inclusion of either public school students or blacks compared with LAESER's national figures, especially when it is recalled that overall student admissions at USP remained stable.

Later, in 2016, USP gave in to growing pressure from students and some staff, and even from the "centre-right" São Paulo state govern-ment, by deciding that 30 percent of admissions would be reserved for applicants who instead of taking the university's own vestibular exam had taken the nationwide Sistema de Seleção Unificada (Unified Selec-tion System—SISU) exam. (The SISU is additional to the end-of-schooling ENEM exam and is designed as a university entrance exam or filter.) It then left individual units to decide whether within that 30 per-cent to stipulate proportions of public school graduates or of particular racial groups. Thus, as an example, quotas were adopted in the Institute of Geosciences according to which half of the 30 percent would be re-served for public school graduates and half for applicants self-designated as blacks, browns, or indigenous,[33] but none of the most competitive courses adopted race-based affirmative action. If the purpose of these measures is to increase the representation of blacks and low-income stu-dents, USP's policy cannot be judged a success: they reached 9 percent of undergraduate admissions in 2015, but most depressing is that the INCLUSP scheme was still not achieving significant results: of almost 40,000 enrolled, only 3,800 were admitted in 2015, and indeed, while the number of pretos, pardos, and indigenous in the scheme rose from 11,202 to 12,070 in 2015–16, the number of those admitted actually fell from 903 to 729 (de Fiori et al. 2017: 62–65). A broader perspective would require an analysis of students going to other public universities in the state of São Paulo, which were expanding and proliferating at the time, but USP remains, like Oxford and Cambridge or Harvard and Yale, the prestige destination, serving as a cynosure of the inequality of op-portunity in society.

One little noticed element in the promotion of affirmative actions has been the role of university administrators. Already in 2010 Angela Paiva published a study of the managers of student admissions inside universities, which showed a broad sympathy for the cause, and around

---

33. I am grateful to Veridiana de Souza Martins for providing this information.

the same time Luisa Schwartzman and Graziella de Moraes Silva conducted interviews with samples of students and administrators, respectively. The most striking feature of the latter article was the activist stance of managers, some of whom had a "connection to the Black Movement" and took the view that the purpose of affirmative actions was to strengthen black identities in order to counter the racial democracy ideology—whereas the student respondents were more nuanced in their emphasis on both race-based and class-based justifications (Paiva 2010; Schwartzman and da Silva 2012: 137). The samples are obviously not representative, but this leads me to wonder whether the *movimento negro*, in an extension of the (unenunciated) strategy of penetrating the federal bureaucracy, has not penetrated university administrations even more, perhaps, than the academic community itself, where, as we shall see, polemics have raged.

The Denouement

The coexistence of different schemata of affirmative action may not be harmful in itself, but the incessant drip-drip of lawsuits brought by disappointed applicants placed public universities under a permanent cloud of uncertainty. Therefore a pronouncement was awaited from the Supreme Court, which would decide once and for all the legality of racial classification and quota places. Eventually, in 2009, the court received an "Argüição de Descumprimento de Preceito Fundamental" (an alleged case of noncompliance with a fundamental precept, or ADPF) calling on it to declare the UnB's quotas admissions policy unconstitutional. The grounds were wide ranging, revolving around the well-rehearsed issue of the legality of racial classification but also evoking memories of Nazi Germany and brandishing the spectre of future racial violence in Brazil. The drafting of the submission was highly tendentious, and it was done in the name of a political party, which did not even pay a lawyer for the purpose, relying rather on a pro bono volunteer—and in the end the party's congressmen voted for the quotas law anyhow (Maggie 2013). But there was a need for a Supreme Court decision among politicians, who over more than a decade had had before them various legislative proposals to regulate affirmative action, and universities needed some clarity if only for legal reasons. Only very few student appeals were granted, but the judicial system was waiting for the Supreme Court to issue a ruling, which would be binding on judges at all levels. The justices waited three years before ruling on the appeal, perhaps because they wanted their decision on this very sensitive matter to be unanimous and leave no room for further appeals (which can happen if a decision is not unanimous, even if it is approved by a majority on the highest court). Also it was perhaps important that their decision fasten on the constitutionality of the principle of racial classification and affirmative actions based on it because that was the only way to orient decisions in lower courts throughout the country. Until the enactment of a new Código Procesal Civil (Civil Procedure Code—CPC) in 2015, Brazilian judges were at best only weakly bound by precedent: according to a paper written by a judge in the São Paulo courts, judges would customarily contradict precedents from their own and higher courts, leading to interminable appeals. Only with the new code was a clear concept of precedent introduced into Brazilian law, thus mixing this feature of the common law with the country's civil law tradition (Becho 2017), so the Supreme Court's decision in this case had to have this special status, afforded presumably by the explicitly constitutional nature of the request for a ruling: it was more than a mere decision on an appeal against a lower court's judgment.

Their rapporteur, Minister Lewandowski, produced a forty-page report.[34] It dealt with a whole range of matters, mostly sociological rather than legal, and did not address the question contained in the appeal itself, namely, the legality of racial classification.[35] Comments by the other judges were brief, but the one point several of them mentioned was the gap between formal and real equality in Brazilian society. The only other extensive contribution was from Minister Marco Aurelio, who said that "meritocracy without equality at the point of departure is but aristocracy in disguise." It is not acceptable, they said, to treat blacks as if they were equal when patently they are not: such superficial equality may be in conformity with the formal constitutional text but not with its substance. They also added, however, that "[A]ffirmative action policies based on reverse discrimination are only legitimate if the pattern of social exclusion that gave rise to them persists through time. Otherwise these policies could be considered permanent benefits in favor of a specific social group to the detriment of the popula-

---

34. See the report on the UOL news website: http://educacao.uol.com.br/noti cias/2012/04/26/por-unanimidade-stf-diz-que-cotas-raciais-em-universidades-publicas-sao-validas.htm

35. The report of a rapporteur does not carry judicial weight, and the votes are just that: votes. That is to say that the accompanying comments do not have judicial weight, unlike the opinions or verdicts of Justices of the US and UK Supreme Courts. The Supreme Court has to decide some nine thousand cases a year (Kapiszewski 2010), but according to my conversations with Brecho in 2017 this is a serious underestimate.

tion as a whole"—something that in their view would be incompatible with any democratic constitution.

Soon after the Supreme Court opened the way for racial classification in its April 2012 decision, the Senate passed the Lei de Cotas (Quotas Law, no. 12,711, August 2012) with only one dissenting vote, from a senator concerned with the implications for university autonomy (*O Globo*, 7 August 2012). The law stipulated that 50 percent of places at federal universities should be reserved for graduates of public schools who must have undertaken their entire primary and secondary education ("ensino fundamental" and "ensino medio") in the public sector.[36] The criteria repeated those in ProUni—whose success was said to have influenced the Supreme Court justices in their decision. To be sure it was a compromise, and although for some critics the dilution of the race criterion with socioeconomic ones was a means of minimizing the racial explanation of social injustice, their view did not seem to gain much vocal support in the months and years that followed. It also required an evaluation after ten years, perhaps in deference to the proviso of the justices just mentioned, but it did not place a ten-year limit on the law's applicability.

Within this 50 percent, half the quota places are set aside for people from families with a per capita income of less than 1.5 minimum wages.[37] However, within the entire 50 percent, places are set aside for "pretos, pardos, e indígenas" in accordance with their demographic proportion in the state where they are applying for university. These allocations are by subject or discipline. That is to say, an institution cannot fill its less competitive courses with cotistas and then say it has fulfilled its obligations. The implementation must be quite complicated: some states, for example Bahia, have an extremely high proportion of negros and pardos, who might squeeze out the white graduates of the public school system. Since all public universities must be open to applicants from across the whole country, it is also conceivable that applicants will respond to opportunities opened up by variations in the colour composition of different populations.

The headlong overall growth in federal universities' student popula-

---

36. This is a rather demanding condition, and in fact a decree published on the day the law went into effect states that surplus, unfilled quota places could go to applicants who had only done their "ensino medio" (secondary schooling) in public schools—having, for example, received their prior "ensino fundamental" in a private school (Decree 7,824, 29 August 2012).

37. The prominent advocate of and expert on quotas, João Feres Jr., told me that the income criterion was inserted by congressmen or senators who did not want the public school places to be monopolized by students from a minority of "selective and traditional" public schools that are known for their high levels of achievement.

tion continued. In a single year, 2013, the total number of undergraduate university places on offer in federal universities grew by 34 percent to 189,000, after which it stabilized, growing by only another 10,000 in 2014. Within that total the number of reserved places doubled in the first year to 59,400, as universities responded to the 2012 law, and then increased a further 18 percent to 77,400 in the 2014 entrance competition. In a context of overall expansion, quota places for the racial groups almost tripled to 37,000. To accommodate the percentages prescribed by the 2012 law, the places in open competition logically had to decline, which they did by 12 percent (Feres et al. 2014). By 2014, 40 percent of places in federal universities were set aside for quotas, on track, apparently, to reach the stipulated 50 percent figure by the deadline of 2015. And it must not be forgotten that the large number of state universities, which had been active pioneers of affirmative actions, mostly followed suit.

Conclusion

This chapter has presented the early stages of the quotas campaign side by side with the efforts by the Brazilian state to legislate against racial discrimination, to recognize that the country had a race problem, and then to attack that problem through executive actions, above all in higher education. The narrative is a little different from others because of the emphasis on the state rather than civil society and also because it points out the penetration of the state by campaigners, especially from the academic world. Although there may be an element of co-optation here, I avoid using that word because of its pejorative connotation. There is no point in moralizing about co-optation in Brazil because that is the way politics happens in that country, in particular when new demands and emerging contentious movements raise their heads, and even before they raise their heads. This is illustrated by the quotas campaign, by the quilombo campaign (French 2009; Boyer 2014, 2016; Lehmann 2016b), and historically by the response of the state to the nascent working class in the early twentieth century (Malloy 1979).

The chapter has also devoted some attention to the (partly nonprofit and partly for-profit) private sector of higher education, a subject that hardly ever appears in the context of affirmative action. Clearly on account of its enormous size and the material benefits it has received from the ProUni affirmative action programme, the existence of the for-profit private sector affects the degree and pattern of inequality in Brazilian education and the prospects for reducing that inequality, but the extent and direction of such causality are at present hard to estimate. The INEP study of 1999 and the more recent research of Wilson de Almeida nevertheless do give reason to doubt the quality of the education they offer. There is, though, a puzzle concerning the asymmetry between the ways in which intellectuals treated (or not) a range of issues in public as opposed to private universities. The very substantial sums allocated to the private sector through ProUni and the other tax advantages enjoyed by the private sector passed without comment, save the little-known articles by Cunha, and even when Wilson de Almeida published his work in 2014, it only generated limited comment. The heavy focus on public universities further strengthens my argument that the driving force behind the quotas campaign is access to the elite rather than reduced social inequality, though it is not an objective to be belittled.

The other pattern that emerges is the diverse—though by no means ineffective—character of the state's response. We have seen the establishment of a bureaucracy (SECAD) created within the MEC with external funding and open to a range of extra-bureaucratic alliances and resources deployed with little oversight (or interest) from the core policymakers of the ministry; another bureaucracy (SEPPIR), with a consciousness-raising mission across state agencies on race issues; the (materially) far more substantial investment in affirmative action in the private sector of higher education, but an investment that consisted of tax and social security income foregone by the Finance Ministry rather than allocations of budgetary resources from the MEC itself; federal government investment in a massive expansion of higher education generally; and finally the adoption of a quotas law in which the government invested little in the way of resources or political capital, leaving it to the universities to implement. Later the federal government also adopted a more wide-ranging affirmative action system that would set aside quotas for negros and pardos in positions filled by competition in the federal public service (Law 12,990, 9 June 2014). Future interpretations will have to take all these initiatives into account rather than focusing exclusively on quotas and universities.

Once again we see how the quotas campaign brought to the fore a wide range of issues related not only to race but also to the nature of the Brazilian state. Brazilian political-intellectual discourse, whose opinion-forming elite mostly think of themselves as left wing, frames the subject of equality in such a way as to blank out the biases introduced by the state itself through the enormous range of its wage and salary hierarchy and through the subsidies provided to big business in the private sector by the BNDES and, for example, through the affirmative action and student loan programmes described here. It was not always thus: during the military government a whole theory of dependent development was developed, notably by Fernando Henrique Cardoso and Peter Evans, in which the state was an active agent of inequality and class formation (Cardoso 1973; Bacha and Taylor 1978; Evans 1979), but this dynamic seems to have been forgotten in today's debates, and as a result there is excess faith in the ability of policy to make a difference to equality through the state, unreformed as it is today.

THREE

Classification Wars

A Brazilian Dispute

It is by no means new to say that naming and the power to name are constituent elements of ethnicity and race relations, and as the word "power" indicates, naming is itself asymmetric, a product of power relations as it is of movements to change power relations. Hegemonic cultures, though, need none of this: they just "are," and they "just" reproduce. As Pierre Bourdieu tells it, they have no need to define themselves or to be named. History passes down and reinforces the way the world is perceived, the frameworks of thought and action, which "more surely than any formal rules or explicit norms" ensure that practices "will conform and will remain stable over time." Habitus contains mechanisms that filter out and remove to the background information that might question the inherited or accumulated order of things.

> [*H*]*abitus* possesses a built-in defense mechanism against change that guarantees its survival intact, by undertaking a selection of new information and by rejecting and belittling, and above all sidelining anything that might lay open to question the information on which habitus itself is founded. (Bourdieu 1989: 101–2)[1]

---

1. My translation. Bourdieu is hard to translate because of his wordy and even labyrinthine style, but the "official" English version, by an unnamed translator, which is to be found on pages 60–61 of *The Logic of Practice* (Bourdieu 1990), is worse. Here is the original: "[L]'habitus tend à assurer sa propre constance et sa propre défense contre le changement à travers la sélection qu'il opère entre les informations nouvelles, en rejetant, en cas d'exposition fortuite ou forcée, les informations capables de mettre en question l'information accumulée et surtout en défavorisant l'exposition à de telles informations."

The habitus in this view ensures the control and circulation of knowledge. The elite, ruling class, or hegemon, stands, so to speak, above the need to be named, yet it controls the naming of the subordinate, the subaltern, and the voiceless.

At the core of citizenship in liberal democracies there lies a pared-down individualist and market-based outlook, which operates as both dominant player and umpire: it fixes and manages the "rules of the game." It "holds the ring" and is the arbiter of taste, ethics, and proper behaviour in public. Understandably, this state of affairs infuriates many opponents, especially those supporting multiculturalism, for whom liberalism and the market are, to varying degrees, an unjust and authoritarian imposition.[2] They may exaggerate the dominance of this outlook, its consistency, and its invincibility, but the cultural dimension and racial dimensions of the dominant habitus do cut deep, especially because, unlike the legal, the economic, and the political, they are intangible and ill-articulated, and not susceptible of open challenge. This is what exasperates Brazilian advocates of black causes when they complain of the "subtlety" of racial discrimination in their country, often in implicit contrast to the United States: it is intangible and most certainly unspoken and inflicts deep psychological damage. In the words of Elisabete Pinto, a psychologist working in the Office for the Health of the Black Population in São Paulo and later a professor at UFBA in Salvador, "Brazilian racism makes people feel it is their fault . . . you introject the racism and it makes you see yourself as others see you, transforming victims into perpetrators." In saying this she was echoing one of many widely recognized and enduring tragic effects of racism and anti-Semitism.

Liberalism and social democracy do not deny differentiated rights to their citizens, but there is a difference between those that operate within the liberal-democratic or social-democratic framework and those demanded by multicultural arguments. For liberals and social democrats differential rights are allocated by criteria that, at least in principle, can be impersonally established, most commonly age, sex, income, occupation, or disability. Multiculturalists, and also those looking for an end to systematic racial exclusion, are looking for the naming of differences and exclusions that are undeniably real and observable in their effects but whose identification nonetheless involves subjective judgments. If they are to gain equality of esteem and compete on a "level playing

---

2. Of course there are others, notably Žižek, who have mockingly described multiculturalism as the handmaiden of neoliberalism (1997); "neoliberal multiculturalism" is a stock phrase in Latin American studies (Hale 2005).

field," as the very English metaphor puts it, their culture, their racial identity, and sometimes their religion have to be named, whereas the dominant culture and its habitus need not be named and indeed their naming is deflected by unarticulated but powerful social mechanisms. The movimento negro in Brazil is not precisely a movement in favour of multiculturalism, although its spokespeople do sometimes mention the claim to a valorization of Brazil's African-originating cultures. Their main demand is the reduction of racial inequality, but this still means empowering blacks to name themselves.

How then do you name a person's colour, or their religion, or their language? You know well that skin colour cannot be taken literally because it is the product of conscious and above all tacit or even unconscious negotiation between the individual and his or her interlocutors, and between different "others," and you also know that the vocabulary of skin colour in any particular context is the product of a combination of socioeconomic status, phenotype, residence, ancestry, grooming, accent, and dress, among other things (see below, p. 145). You know well that a person may fashion his or her religious affiliation in many ways so that attaching an abbreviated label like "Jewish" or "Muslim" does violence to individual or local practices and affiliations. And when language arises as a marker, you know well that a minority or groups affected by stigma or exclusion may have but a patchy command of a minority language that they—or others—may call "their own," even though it is the language of their forebears and their representatives claim it as a heritage lost through social exclusion. Yet when there are conflicts over recognition, when there are demands for an end to racial discrimination and exclusion or religious marginalization, the simplification of naming, the reduction of complexity, the homogenization of variety, become sensitive. Think of colonial reclassifications—the invention of "Hinduism" as an "-ism" and its refashioning outside Asia as a western-style but nonwestern religion (Jaffrelot 1996; Altglas 2005, 2014; Iqtidar 2012) or the naming and invention of tribes across Africa; think of Brazilians who when they reach the United States are surprised to learn that they are "latinos." Sometimes this may be of little importance, but often it amounts to symbolic violence, as in the dicing and slicing (physical and symbolic) of the population of the former Yugoslavia, or the ever-changing fashions that describe the nonwhite, latino, and Hispanic populations of the United States and other countries, none of which ever commands complete consensus among either the subjects or their others (Brubaker 2016: 54).

Yet when it comes to making demands, when the leaders of excluded populations present their grievances, they must name themselves, and they are likely to simplify: they will not get very far by saying, as social scientists in moments of frustration are wont to do, "It is all terribly complex." No wonder, then, that anthropologists are heard to mutter about the "essentialism" and reification contained in the discourse of insurgent primordial identities, even if they are sometimes reluctant to say such things in print (an example among many of the dilemmas that arise for a discipline in which activism has become intertwined with academic convention in tension with its relativist roots). But no wonder also that the preface to a book of papers from the second national meeting of Brazilian Black Researchers' Association (ABPN), written by the leading black academic activist Valter Silvério, contained the following passage:

> [T]he blacks, within the university and beyond, have begun to question the power of naming, classification, and hierarchical ordering wielded over them by their other . . . in "denying" the imposed names of "preto" and claiming for themselves the name of negro, afro-brasileiro, or, more recently, afro-descendent, the blacks have sought through their intellectuals within the universities and without to review, re-create, and resignify their *participation* in the past and present history of Brazil. (Silvério 2003: 11; italics in the original)[3]

The language of this one sentence is itself instructive: first, Silvério talks of challenging the imposed name "preto," which traditionally has evoked "deep black," as well as a certain inferiority, but despite continued use in official documents and by the official statistical agency, has fallen out of favor in popular usage. Then he quickly lists the sequence "negro," "afro-brasileiro," and, more recently, "afro-descendente," revealing the uncertainty of the new names or revealing that there is a search without conclusion for a new name, placing the word "denying" in ironic quotes. The literal and nonliteral connotations of the words "negro," "afro-brasileiro," and "afro-descendente" could be the subject of endless debate, but surely the point is that the blacks, or at least black intellectuals, are claiming and gaining the power to name themselves,

3. "os negros, dentro e fora da universidade, passam a questioner o poder de nomeação, classificação e hierarquização do seu outro ao "negarem" a nomeação imposta de preto e ao se auto-nomearem como negro, afro-brasileiro ou mais recentemente como afro-descendente, têm os negros, buscado, por meio de seus inteletuais dentro e fora das Universidades, rever, recriar, ressiginificar sua *participação* na história passada e presente do Brasil."

and that is why naming is a subject for continuous doubt and debate. The habitus is not as all-powerful as Bourdieu sought to convince us, as testified by this example and many other contemporary public disputes and doubts relating to race, indigeneity and gender.

This chapter, then, is about the tension between the exigencies of identity and Brazil's particular version of universalist bureaucracy as students, professors, and other publics adopt new and alternative strategies of naming, and the state adapts to them, or draws them into its own classificatory orbit.

The Bureaucracy of Naming

If there is sensitivity around the question of naming, the politics of racial justice face serious problems of consistency of approach, especially when real resources—like affirmative action—are at stake. (In contrast, symbolic recognition, in the arts and on the street, could be said to thrive on inconsistency.) In the United States colour classification is standard practice. In the United Kingdom it seems to face little resistance, even though there is ever more métissage, and the state does not impose ethnic or racial classification on individuals or require them to identify themselves by skin colour or ethnic origin. That is to say, although there is political and even legal pressure on businesses, but especially on state institutions and civil service bureaucracies, to become more diverse and document their diversity (meaning almost always gender and racial diversity), objections are not raised in Britain on the grounds that this would entail labeling their staff or members or students in terms of skin colour or origin. In Brazil, however, where racial mixture and a more chromatic race relations regime are long established, naming has become the subject of bitter controversy at least among the intelligentsia. In Britain and the United States the essentialist practice—as some might call it—of naming by colour, or describing collective identities by colour, has not been displaced even by the prevailing ideological distaste for essentialism itself. In Brazil, by contrast, when naming by colour began to appear in a formal bureaucratic context, and in connection with resource allocation, it became highly controversial. Eventually, though, after several years of bitter polemics and numerous personal fallings out, the controversies died down as the practice became institutionalized and resistance failed to take hold.

This point is nicely illustrated by a polemic that arose over the establishment in 2003 by the UnB of an Evaluating Committee (Comissão

Avaliadora) to rule on the validity of applicants' claims to qualify for admission through a black quota.[4] The commission, composed, inter alia, of anonymous "experts in race issues, anthropologists and people with a history of involvement in the Movimento Negro," met in secret and inspected photographs (which all applicants for a quota place had to submit) in those cases where the administration had some doubt about the authenticity of a claim to be qualified as black (Chor Maio and Ventura 2005). If turned down, applicants had a further opportunity to appeal. This aroused a wave of mockery and protest and the commission inevitably came to be known as the "Tribunal Racial da UnB." And who indeed could not but be shocked by a procedure reminiscent of nazism and apartheid, plus the co-option of the discipline of anthropology in seeming contradiction of its aversion to official recognition of race or (at that time) the very notion of race? The commission's proceedings in its first year were contested in the press and by some candidates themselves. Members of the commission stated on various occasions that their job was to verify the physical characteristics of applicants, and the university provided the camera and photographer so as to avoid inconsistencies. One candidate who appealed was interviewed by the commission and asked if he had ever dated a black person or if he had been involved in the black movement. In the end, in that year, of thirty-four appeals, twenty-one were upheld (195). In 2007 the photos were replaced with a compulsory interview for all applicants to the quota competition. Years later the dean of undergraduate studies said that some 15 percent of applications had been disqualified over the period when the procedure was followed.[5] The procedure was discontinued in 2012 with the introduction of the quotas law, which applied to all federal universities and enshrined the principle of self-assignment, yet issues over authenticity or "fraud," which had died down, later returned to the public square.

But listen now to Paulo Vinicius da Silva, professor at the Federal University of Paraná and author of books and articles on the subject of racism in the media and schoolbooks. For da Silva the protests against the commission were disingenuous because they overlooked the real issue, which is not the colour of a person's skin but that person's status as a victim of racialization (da Silva et al. 2007: 199). Furthermore, in a reference to another controversy, this one surrounding the separation of quota and nonquota applicants into different queues when handing in

4. The UnB was following a precedent set by UEMS (Alves Cordeiro 2007).
5. "Comissão Federal para avaliar cotistas é questionada por advogados," *Folha de São Paulo*, 3 August 2016.

their documentation at the UnB (this was before the advent of online applications), which had also aroused criticism, he notes that in security checks at shopping centres, which are supposedly "'generic, impersonal, and non-racialized' black people are in fact victims of explicit discrimination—for example when they are removed from shopping malls—aggression, exclusion, and humiliation, i.e., what is also known as racial profiling" (198). The implication is that since impersonality or colour-blind selection often acts as a cover for racist ill-treatment, why cannot a commission such as this be a means of combating racism? Since the commission has to include experienced representatives of the groups that are subject to discrimination and have had "personal and political experience of the effects of processes of racialization," its members, he argues, are surely best placed to identify the victims of racism. In this perspective the purpose of the selection process, in terms reminiscent of coming out for gay people, is consciousness-raising, and the require-ment that people seeking to benefit from affirmative action should de-clare themselves is part of their awakening to their status as the products of discrimination going back to the times of slavery. "Activists have never said that a black person is one who makes the corresponding self-description, but rather that it was the duty of victims of racism to declare themselves black" (Chor Maio and Ventura 2005: 193). The argument may sound outrageous to some, but uncomfortable and all too often vio-lent encounters with police and private security personnel are dispro-portionately frequent for black people in Brazilian cities (among others) (Fry 1995; French 2007; Waiselfisz 2012). The underlying point is coher-ent in the light of the well-known pattern of coexistence between imper-sonal, colour-blind, or difference-blind meritocracy and the contextual reality of exclusion that is statistically obvious yet sometimes hard to pin down in everyday life. In this context, da Silva is arguing for a committed bureaucratic process that will correct the underlying biases of imper-sonal bureaucracy and undertake classification in the name of changing the pattern of exclusion, not of some sort of fascist triage, and he is ridi-culing those who in his view preach equality before the law while ignor-ing the unequal capabilities that make a mockery of the concept.

The observation that formal equality before the law or bureaucracy is a mere facade for maintaining or accentuating inequality is not new, of course, going back at least to Marx: it was mentioned, in less direct terms, by the Supreme Court Minister Marco Aurelio, and it figures in the essay that introduces the collection from which da Silva's text is taken, pub-lished by PPCor. Written by Raquel César, a law professor, the essay speaks sarcastically of the "meritocracy that always has produced power and priv-ilege" (2007: 14) and gives many good reasons why the quotas for black students are legally justified, but it does not consider the procedural bi-ases inherent in bureaucracy, which concerns some others, like da Silva. She does, however, discuss an issue that figured very prominently in the campaign for quotas and the concomitant racial classification, namely, the removal of the somewhat archaic intermediate category "pardo"—relevant because its use by the census agency, IBGE, confers on it an aura of objectivity and also because so many voices were being raised in favour of binary classification using the single category of negro. So she wrote that leaving only the category of "negro" as a qualification for quota places introduced a "more political connotation," bringing into play a person's racial awareness and not just his or her phenotype (23).[6] Her phrase is rather elliptical, but it seems to mean that use of the term "ne-gro" by those who do not think of themselves as "white" signals their willingness to "stand up and be counted," and that the binary classifica-tion represents political pressure on those who might hesitate—especially those who would define themselves as somewhere "in between"—to com-mit and recognize themselves as black and therefore as belonging to a population of victims, heirs to generations of exclusion.

In theory, one might try to separate the bureaucratic and legal di-mensions of an affirmative action policy from its symbolic dimensions, but in practice the two are bound to become enmeshed, and the sym-bolic dimensions play an indispensable part in motivating support and resistance. Symbolic dimensions can be thought of as self-naming, or performative: hairstyles, modes of dress and speech, musical tastes, the prevalent skin colour among a circle of friends, and neighbourhoods to live or "hang out" in. The list is more or less endless, and merely to men-tion it is to point to the ways in which affirmative action may bring shifts in the modes of social interaction within an institution or field. For ex-ample, with the arrival of cotistas, classroom dynamics can change, as Cicaló's ethnography of an UERJ law course describes in striking detail (2012b). But in that case they did not change in the direction of a firm colour-based division among the students. Gradually the changing face and colour of bureaucracy and decision-making will have an impact on

---

6. It may also be relevant that, although it is still used in the Census and its meaning is universally understood, the word "pardo" has largely been supplanted in daily speech by "moreno" (Telles 2002: 422, Telles 2004), but moreno is almost a neutral word that does not fit into a formal scheme of racial classification in the way "pardo" does after decades and more of official use.

day-to-day dealings in an institution, as affirmative action procedures creep into the different activities and departments. So arguments like that of da Silva reflect a fear that the affirmative action movement may be bought off or co-opted. To some extent, of course, this is what is meant by diversity, but diversity sounds tame: advocates of diversity in universities focus on the benefits of a diverse student population with different views and backgrounds, whereas the symbolic dimension at issue here also brings the bearers or beneficiaries of a movement into the decision-making of an institution, and it may bring tensions as well. The newcomers, bearers of the much-heralded diversity, are themselves likely to be aware that they have arrived because of a movement of some kind, as are the "incumbents" at whose side they will sit. That at least is what the law professor's remarks about the political signal emitted in removing the intermediate category of "pardo" seem to imply, and it is explicit in the stated purposes of some campaigners.[7]

As a firsthand characterization of this push to make quotas a vehicle of consciousness-raising, witness my conversation at UERJ with a highly committed black woman professor. I mentioned the "problem" (if such it is) of students who entered via the quota route and were labeled "cotistas" yet whose high marks in admissions exams would have enabled them to enter by the open competition.[8] Her reaction was "so what?" or "all the better" because they had opted to recognize themselves as black. She had no time for an attitude said to exist among black candidates and students who refused to take the quota route for entrance to university because they wanted to compete exclusively on their merits, unaided by the race-based quota system. For her a university admissions system should force people to choose their racial affiliation, or at least make it advantageous to do so. Subsequent acquaintance with the same person

---

7. In the *Bakke* case (1978) the US Supreme Court ruled against racial quotas on the grounds that, although the racial classification of individuals was acceptable, it could not be the only criterion of student admission. The point here is further illustrated by the criticism of the effects of US judicial decisions, which, since the high tide of affirmative action in the form of quotas began to recede in the wake of *Bakke*, have shifted the balance toward diversity and away from remedies dealing directly with racial inequality (Lipson 2008; Oliven 2008: 147).

8. The "problem" could be one of the following: (a) the candidate was occupying a quota place that could have been occupied by someone else, since he or she would have been accepted anyway; or (b) the candidate would be forever "marked" as a cotista whereas that might not have been necessary. Cicaló's research indicated that cotistas do not feel discriminated or set apart—save that they tend to be from different parts of the city and to have a much lower standard of living, so they can't always go to parties in chic areas, and so on.

makes me doubt whether the statements she made at that time should be interpreted as very "hard line" let alone some sort of racial separatism, but this attitude had penetrated some student circles and opened up a debate. The university had set aside a room for the black cotista students' organization (itself linked to the "Espaços Afirmados" venture);[9] but I heard the opinion that it was a tiny group and some black students did not want to join because its members practiced an inverted racism (racismo às avessas).[10] I was told they did not allow people with straightened hair to join, and although that may sound surprising or even shocking (and may or may not have been true), women have spoken to me of unstraightened hair as a political statement of black identity that sets them apart from the prevailing fashion—or, rather, sets them up as pioneers of a different, more race-affirming style (in a manner familiar of course in other parts of the world).[11]

The deployment of such body language pits the symbolic against the bureaucratic and surely gives voice to a sentiment that bringing more blacks into the university, or opening a path to social mobility for them, is not just a matter of tweaked admissions procedures or technocratic improvement, but should somehow administer a shock, at least a small shock, to society. Other women, however, may just like the style, and after the initial phase it may have become more a fashion statement than a political statement.

The UERJ is a large, elite university but not a mass university on the scale of some in Latin America: in 2011 it had 20,467 undergraduates. Of the students admitted to a first-year undergraduate course in 2011, 32 percent were cotistas educated at state schools, and within that category 14 percent had entered through a "race quota." To put these numbers into perspective, total student numbers had only increased very slowly in the previous fifteen years, from 17,994 undergraduates in 1996 (UERJ, *Anuários Estatísticos*, available online). Thus, assuming that only a few cotistas would have gained admission without the availability of the quota channel, the quotas represented a genuine redistribution of opportunities within a very slowly growing student population, likely to produce palpable changes in the "complexion" of the student body and in many other symbolic aspects. (If overall student numbers had grown the quo-

---

9. Literally this translates as "Affirmed Spaces."

10. I did visit this room and was given a contact number or e-mail address, but the students did not respond to my request for an interview.

11. According to *The Economist* of 28 September 2013, Brazil is the world's second-largest market for hair care products and Brazilian women spend as much as UK women on them.

tas would have brought less redistribution of scarce resources.) It will take much longer, of course, for these changes to filter through to the point where the complexion of the academic staff changes—and with this in view voices were beginning to advocate affirmative actions in postgraduate admissions, something already implemented in UNEB and announced in 2014 for federal universities generally. Meanwhile, it should be remembered that the changes under way are not only seen in the colour of the undergraduate population at UERJ: students admitted under the state-school quota live in different parts of the city, have different commuting patterns and are accustomed to different leisure time activities, and if they have low incomes they reveal it in dress codes, body language, time allocation, and the use of facilities. (The university library suddenly became overcrowded when the cotistas arrived; nonquota students, it is assumed, can afford to buy their own textbooks.) Cicaló's ethnography (2012) also shows multiple tendencies emerging in the affirmative action atmosphere, the varied ways in which individuals signal their class, colour, neighbourhood, and other markers and affiliations, and also how they manage the signals and their own and others' awareness of the signals and the reality behind them. But overall social distance among the cohort he accompanied was reduced over the year thanks to the close contact, which undermined prejudices, and also to professors who encouraged or even imposed mixed study or research groups. The mere observation that in his cohort study the two groups nicknamed each other and themselves as "nerds" (*cones*) and "barbarians" reflects the transformation of the social life of a university in which students from state schools, or from the lower-income suburbs of Rio, whose populations are assumed to be darker skinned than others, had previously little chance of gaining admission to prestige courses like law in a prestige university.[12]

So on the one hand we read a politicized version of affirmative action that seeks to accentuate the symbolic dimension by encouraging students to identify themselves as black (even if they have spent their lives thinking of themselves as brown—"moreno," "pardo," etc.—or indeed white) with a view toward accentuating separateness and awareness, while on the other hand we have "real-life" observations of students who by reshaping the culture of the institution in daily life in so many ways, may accentuate visibility or pride but, on the whole, not separateness.

---

12. *Cones* was an expression coined by this cohort, in student banter, referring to the cones used to mark road works and so on. The *cones* are the cotistas because they were labeled more studious, while the barbarians were more frivolous.

And we also see indications of a possibly uniquely Brazilian phenom-enon—the bifurcation of colour assignment and racial identity—to which we shall return.

These remarks cannot pass without mentioning that at the time of writ-ing, late 2017, the UERJ has for a year been deprived of significant portions of the funding it needs to pay salaries and maintain its infrastructure, due to the chaotic finances of Rio de Janeiro state and to the way its governor has chosen to inflict cuts in public expenditure. In July 2017 the rector an-nounced that the second 2017 semester would not begin on schedule; in-deed the second 2016 semester, delayed and interrupted by strikes and non-payment of salaries, was only finishing at that time (*O Globo*, 6 July 2017). Obviously this crisis places the quota debates in another perspective.

Defense of Binary Classification as Consciousness-Raising

Another defense of the consciousness-raising role of affirmative action came from José Jorge de Carvalho, an anthropology professor at UnB who, with Rita Segato,[13] had drafted the proposals on which the university based its 2003 Target Plan (Plano de Metas) to change its racial complex-ion. The UnB, as we saw, adopted a binary system, excluding intermediate categories like pardo and moreno. Carvalho's views clearly had influenced his own university, and he joined the nationwide campaign for quotas, traveling to speak at universities around the country. His written contribu-tion is not often quoted, but it is worthy of attention less because of its radicalism than because of the ways in which he argues around the subjec-tive dimension of race that he attributes to potential students.

As one who saw race quotas as above all a vehicle for black consciousness-raising, Carvalho regarded them as an encouragement to candidates to understand that by opting for the black quota they were making a political statement and implicitly declaring themselves to be victims of discrimination (Carvalho 2005). In his view, referring to the notorious "Race Tribunal," if the responsibility for deciding who is and who is not black is entrusted to a bureaucratic or even anonymous com-mission, then it removes the responsibility from the applicant and "de-politicizes the process of affirming black identity in Brazilian academia" (188). In this reasoning the category pardo offers an opportunity for both deception and self-deception: on the one hand it could allow many

---

13. Segato is a prominent anthropologist who has taught and acted as a consultant in numerous projects and initiatives concerning gender, violence, and indigenous rights throughout Latin America.

people who are not true victims of discrimination to qualify, while on the other it offers an escape for others who, in Carvalho's view, do not want to recognize their blackness and victim status and are thus sidestepping the political challenge of standing up and saying, or admitting, that they are black. The objection that such policies are designed to equalize opportunity, not to raise consciousness, let alone punish "false consciousness," and that to proceed thus may create bias and a new sort of injustice by nudging people in a particular direction, is dismissed, like universalism and meritocracy, as a cover for perpetuating the deep roots of racial exclusion.

Carvalho would have preferred to rely on real confrontation, unmediated by evaluating commissions. In response to the criticism of the separate queues formed by quota-based and open competition applicants to UnB, he remarks that a light-coloured person standing in the "wrong" queue would certainly be called to account "by word, gesture, or a sideways look" from "phenotypically black" fellow applicants, leading to an incident, an inquiry, and possibly exclusion of the applicant from the entire process. This would be much more severe than the procedure in place at the time, which merely obliged the applicant to renounce the quota and join in the general competition with no other sanction, but nonetheless it would be justified (Carvalho 2005).

Carvalho is not concerned here with conscious deceit or pretense by racists stealing a place from people who are truly victims of discrimination (2005: 189), which would have been punished with removal by the Evaluating Committee. Rather he is concerned that people might misassign themselves. The language used—and the absence of quotation marks—shows that he sets aside as irrelevant the vast area of doubt represented by mestiços, morenos, and pardos. But this world of affirmative action is replete with genuinely ambiguous cases: can one simply dismiss the case of the young man who, having been turned down by the commission, exclaimed, "But my grandfather was as black as the night"? The university's reply was that the quota system is designed to combat discrimination based on colour, not on origin (*Estado de São Paulo*, 26 May 2004). The exchange illustrates one aspect of the contemporary salience of the zone of mixedness and the dialectic between a sense of who one "really" is, who one's ancestors were, whether one is "truly disadvantaged." This knot has been the subject of a three-way comparison of France, the United States, and Brazil by Sarah Abel (2018) and was eloquently disentangled by Rogers Brubaker in his *Trans* (2016)—a book that confines itself exclusively to the United States but has far wider relevance.

Skin Colour versus Identity

In their study of academic achievements of affirmative action beneficiaries, Rubia Valente and Brian Berry drop an intriguing aside referring to admissions to private universities: "About 13.86 percent of students admitted through racial affirmative action claimed to be white." They then explain that "this is due to the complex and amorphous Brazilian definition of race: many African descendants who are of mixed heritage, and might be on the border of whiteness, claim to be white" (Valente and Berry 2017: 26). Although their remark should not be surprising for most Brazilians, it does need some elucidation, for where some suspect deception or mistaken assignment others see genuine doubt or shifting circumstances. This can be seen if we separate skin colour, which is chromatic and flexible but becomes fixed when inscribed in official documents, from identity, which normally has to fit into a widely shared set of categories such as branco-pardo/moreno-negro-preto. The contrast is similar to that conventionally ascribed to the distinction between race and ethnicity, though the latter is increasingly in doubt when self-assignment is the norm. (Rogers Brubaker uses them interchangeably, as does Tianna Paschel.) Hence the limited relevance of comments that Brazilians use more than a hundred colour categories: that is true, but it does not mean that when asked how they identify themselves racially they will choose among more than a hundred terms, as confirmed by Telles, quoting a 1975 survey (Silva 1987, quoted in Telles 2002: 422). It does mean, though, that they might use different terms to describe their colour and (separately) their identities as they grow older, as they move through the life cycle and as they shift between different social milieux. When racial identity becomes an official category, then doubts can set in about motivations even among the self-assigning individuals themselves, and while some may respond by taking a tactical approach, others may have genuine doubts and hesitations. Explanations of one's own successes, failures or disappointments may also change with circumstances—as we shall discuss later.

These issues are the subject of an analysis by two economists of survey data comparing *self-described skin colour* and stated *identity* of students before and after admission, as well as introducing skin-colour classification ("ratings") of their photos—not of the individuals in person—by a panel (Francis and Tannuri-Pianto 2012). Researchers had access to surveys completed by students before and after their admission, some from before and some after the introduction of the race quotas. The surveys did show discrepancies between students' self-classification before and after their admission, but the pattern of the discrepancies changed after quotas were introduced. For example, when quotas had not yet been established, 10.8 percent of those who described their *skin colour* in the post-admission survey with the word "pardo" had counted their *identity* as "negro" preadmission "but then changed their minds and counted themselves as non-negro once they were admitted and established as students."[14] (Note that "identity" refers to a binary choice between negro and non-negro, whereas self-description, or self-assignment, refers to a three-way choice among branco, pardo, and preto—omitting "negro.") But once quotas had been introduced the percentage making this change shot up to 31.8 percent, although among those describing their *skin colour* with the polar categories "branco" or "preto" there was barely any change. In other words, those who had taken the darker identity option of negro were now, after the introduction of quotas, tending more often to veer toward the lighter skin-colour option of pardo. Or, to adopt a more tactical interpretation, people who felt more brown than black tended more often to veer toward black when applying to university after the quotas had been introduced, but they did not change their self-description as pardos.

The surveys do point to the growing attraction of these students to negro identity. The proportion of those describing their skin colour as pardo while reporting their identity as negro on both pre- and postadmission surveys also rose after the adoption of quotas from 11 to 24 percent. Furthermore, the "third-party" assessment of skin colour by the panel shows that among the darkest quintile those counting themselves as negro rose from 57.1 percent among those applying before quotas were introduced to 77.1 percent afterward (Francis and Tannuri-Pianto 2012: Table 10). Put another way, before quotas were introduced as many as 33 percent of those who would have been intuitively assigned to the darkest fifth of the population in skin colour terms by a notional average member of the public were not describing themselves as black, but this proportion declined to 23 percent afterward. The authors summarize the findings in a subsequent article as follows: "[T]he evidence suggests that after the implementation of racial quotas, one group of students—pardos with a lighter skin tone—were more likely to identify as negro [before admission] when applying to college

---

14. This form of words was provided by Andrew Francis in a very instructive email, July 2013, for which I am most grateful.

but as non-negro [after admission] when attending college, while another group of students—pardos with darker skin tone—were more likely to identify as a "negro" both when applying and attending" (Francis and Tannuri-Pianto 2015: 2774).

In this subsequent article the authors published a follow-up study based on a survey of almost one thousand conducted five years after the respondents had left the university. By then the percentage who *identified* as non-negro on both surveys had decreased from 86 to 77.9 percent, and the percentage who *described themselves* as pardo increased from 28.9 to 34.3 percent. (Francis-Tan and Tannuri-Pianto 2015: 2785). A small but clear "darkening" of identity and skin colour assignment is repeated for people who shifted from "non-negro" while they were studying to "negro" five years after leaving the university: their proportion was almost negligible among people who went to university before the institution of quotas (1.2 percent), but among those who went after quotas were instituted it rose to 4.6 percent. A possible impact of quotas, however, could be observed in the change of identity, which, because of the availability of the intermediate category of pardo as racial self-assignment, offers an insight into the people "in between," who are of most interest to the movimento negro and intellectuals like José Jorge de Carvalho: people who described their race as pardo after quotas were established were "about 10 percentage points more likely to identify as negro" five years after graduating than they would have been if they had joined the university before quotas. To this is added the external assessment of a person's skin colour, and here again the people in the darkest quartile "were about 20 percentage points more likely to self identify as negro in 2012 than they would have if racial quotas had not been implemented" (2786). The authors conclude that the pattern of switching one's race or colour assignment from pardo to branco as people graduated from college has been counteracted by the quotas policy. It would seem that the Carvalho and Segato's, and the movimento negro's, campaign of consciousness-raising has had a measure of success.

The material is complex, but two points emerge: (a) there is a consistent tendency among people who are studying or have studied at the UnB, for those in the intermediate categories to shift in the direction of both negro identity and negro self-assignment, but (b) although the tendency is in many of the indicators statistically significant, it is not large. This would imply that the quotas policy provoked reflection rather than dramatic change among students. Overall, however, the authors may be too hasty in attributing causal efficacy to the introduction of quotas, save in a very broad sense, since so much else was going on in the background, including the political activity of the movimento negro, no doubt extensive discussion of the quota issue among students, and the polemics in the public sphere about the issue, in which the UnB featured prominently.

The UnB study's findings accord to some extent with Luisa Schwartzman's account from Rio, Brasilia, and Bahia: using large-scale "before and after" data from surveys conducted at the time of university entrance and then in the students' third year, and surveys of students later in their careers, she found growth in the proportion self-assigning as negro but, unlike the Brasilia survey, found few who by their third year had redesignated themselves with the intermediate category pardo (2008). It also fits in with cultural trends identified in the 2010 Census, which shows a growth in the proportion of nonwhites in the population as a whole. (The "preto" population rose from 6.2 to 7.6 percent of the population, while the pardos rose from 38.5 to 43.1 percent. This kind of data has led some people to say the negros, meaning pretos plus pardos, are half the Brazilian population.)

But the ambiguities—or at least apparent ambiguities—do not go away. In a separate paper Schwartzman (2009b) describes data that show how young people can identify subjectively as moreno and yet, without any inconsistency, register as negro when undertaking official procedures like applying for a university place *because that is what they think the form is expecting of them*. (At the time UERJ was only using branco and negro, omitting both preto and pardo, as race/colour categories.) The second part of her observation takes into account the variability and context dependence of colour designation: among a cohort of pardos in the period after the introduction of quotas, 69 percent described their colour as negro in a socioeconomic survey while 84 percent of them did so on the quotas application form (231)—a pattern also reflected in the UnB study. But she goes on to explain that the colour terminology developed by the authorities was propounded by activists from the movimento negro, who tended to push for a binary classification system, and that her interviews show that students may have been puzzled by these categories, which did not fit with those they used in everyday life: hence her title "Seeing Like Citizens" that alludes to a contrast with "seeing like a state"as in James Scott's book of that title (1998). She describes the background to her surveys as "the increasing involvement of the new racial project with state bureaucracy and quantitative social science [which] leads policy designers to 'see like a state,' that is, through categorical and statistical simplifications of social reality, taking into account only a limited set of criteria that fits the goals of doing social policy from a distance." And she then goes on to describe how, to some extent at least, those simplifications shape the outlook of the students who may or may not benefit from the policies.

After all, it is not surprising that a person self-designates in different ways in formal and informal situations or when offered only certain categories and not others, especially when the categories on offer are not glaringly incompatible. So the campaign to expand the scope of the negro category to encompass as many nonwhites as possible has encouraged people who regard themselves normally as moreno to write themselves down as negros without renouncing their sense of themselves (their identity) as morenos.

The incongruence between ancestry and colour also returns: thus Schwartzman quotes an interviewee who opted out of the colour quota because she did not feel discriminated against on account of her colour (2009b: 39). She identified as black, mentioning that her crinkly hair was not "good hair" and referring to her grandmother as "negra," but this did not undermine her belief that she was too well-off to apply for the quota. Policymakers and activists insist on colour as the vector of discrimination, and respondents themselves make the distinction between colour and ancestry quite easily when speaking of or interrogating themselves. However, when it comes to filling in a form to apply for the quota competition, there is much second-guessing about the quotas and their purpose, encapsulated in the question "Are quotas for me?"; in deciding which box to tick, they ask themselves what the purpose of the quotas is. They second-guess the formal language in the light of what they hear and see on the street, in the media, and at home, and they may also be influenced by the race-conscious preparatory courses they may have attended to prepare for the vestibular examination, such as EDUCAFRO.

Further evidence (in case more was needed) of the multidimensionality of colour assignment emerges from the national attitude survey conducted by Stanley Bailey with the Universidade Federal Fluminense in 2002, pointing, once again, to the disconnect between the binary classification and popular concepts of skin colour—what Bailey describes aptly as "racially ambiguous common sense" (2008: 605). Respondents were presented with a set of photographs of men along a spectrum of skin colour and when forced to choose between "branco" and "negro" tended to reclassify people in the middle of the spectrum as white; he also found that the prospect of qualifying for a quota place under a binary scheme only stimulated about 56 percent of the "mulatos" (pardos) to switch their self-designation in a darker direction—though one might put it the other way round, saying that 44 percent of "mulatos" chose "branco" despite the attractions of qualifying for a quota place (600). This leads Bailey to worry that the binary scheme would not capture many people who ought to qualify for quotas. In the event, of course, the 2012 law applied the race quota to "pretos, pardos, e indígenas," which ought to make it clear to pardos (or mulatos) that it is for them. In the light of the common usage "afro-descendentes," it is also striking that Bailey found much scepticism or even puzzlement when asking about African origins: people would say, even indignantly, "I am Brazilian," implying that they had nothing to do with Africa (593–94).

Leading advocates of quotas, however, were uncomfortable with these ambiguities: they pressed to replace the three-way colour classification with a binary one, and they opposed the socioeconomic criteria of qualification as a dilution of the principle of quotas as a programme of reparation for blacks. A close collaborator of the rector of UNEB and prominent campaigner for quotas even described it, in 2010, as a denial of the existence of racism that accorded with the views of "most intellectuals in humanities and social sciences". In Rio de Janeiro, when a socioeconomic criterion was imposed in 2003, some, like Renato Emerson dos Santos, took the view that as a result the "positive connotations of blackness could be undermined" in the daily life of students (2006b: 121). That is, the students who were excluded from the black quota by the means test would not develop a consciousness of their black identity because of their exclusion from the benefits of affirmative action, even though they themselves may have suffered discrimination on account of their colour. As coordinator of PPCor, he gives a very positive account of the Espaços Afirmados (ESAF) support programme for selected black cotistas, which provided a space set aside for them, mentoring, funding for books, theatre and film workshops, and the like. The ESAF programme also encouraged political initiatives like a statewide gathering of black students: Encontro Estadual de Estudantes Negros. Unsurprisingly, with this support, the beneficiaries—themselves the result of a process that selected 156 out of 396 applicants—achieved good academic results. Dos Santos extends the discussion beyond the question of equal opportunities and black empowerment to the "reconstruction of the structure of knowledge which goes to make up the university" (127), thus invoking a multicultural argument that is quite unusual in Brazil outside the Amazonian context, contesting the established canon of knowledge imparted. Such a "desracialização" would be to the detriment of the teaching of the historical and social experience of the groups benefited by the quota system. In this perspective, those who have suffered or have merely been at risk of racial discrimination are deserving of affirmative action irrespective of their socioeconomic situation. Dos Santos complains, in tune with the adviser to the UNEB rector quoted above, that opponents in the university have developed a cunning strategy of resistance by shifting the issue to one of income and making (nonracialized) low-income students into a "new identity group" (127). This is described, pejoratively, as an *assistencialista* policy based on universalist (i.e., income-based) criteria that prevent the adoption of differential race-based affirmative actions in place of the universalist approach. ("Universalist" here also has a specific and pejorative connotation, referring to the purportedly neutral—but in practice discriminatory—consequences of nonracial and nongendered criteria in social or educational policies.)

This discussion raises several difficult questions of principle. One is the acceptability of self-assignment in the assignation of state resources; another is whether any consideration is given to where the burden of the cost will fall; and a third is the convergence of different agendas on the definition of quotas. The discussion of self-assignment in terms of the risk of dishonesty, or *fraude* in Portuguese, is contradictory at its core because skin colour is a subjective matter: the suspicion of dishonesty makes little sense if colour is self-assigned. Since one of the main issues at hand is the campaign to dispel racial prejudice, to change the atmosphere surrounding race, the application of strict criteria is an illusion. At best one can hope that extreme cases in which self-assignment defies popular common sense will be discouraged by a person's social milieu. In the United States this notion of "fraud" has arisen in the wake of the 2014 "Dolezal affair" (Brubaker 2015, 2016) and from time to time judges in Brazil have been called on to resolve disagreements and imposed a racial classification on candidates for quota places (Guimarães 2017: 5).[15] I discussed the question of "fraud" in an interview with a public prosecutor (Procurador da República) in Recife in April 2010, and he used the

---

15. This is a technical field into which nonexperts venture at their peril. A Google search revealed two instances in which Brazilian judges received appeals by job applicants who had been excluded from quotas in a civil service competition on the basis that they were not qualified for a quota despite their own self-assignment as black or pardo. See *JusBrasil*, 14 July 2017, and the other two, years earlier: https://qualconcurso.jusbrasil.com.br/noticias/255113877/justica-decide-que-candidato-precisa-parecer-negro-para-entrar-em-cota and https://trf-1.jusbrasil.com.br/noticias/457776280/decisao-candidato-a-vaga-em-concurso-publico-pelo-sistema-de-cotas-tem-pedido-acolhido-pelo-trf1

word "reasonable" several times, saying that when called upon to pronounce on the issue legal officials had to use their own judgment.

The Bailey survey did detect an awareness of the cost of quotas for students displaced from university admission by quota places: the question gave rise to a decline in previously expressed support from whites, browns, and blacks (Bailey et al. 2016).[16] Support was also affected negatively by levels of education, independent of colour assignment, but even then it remained positive overall. Nonetheless, an Americas Barometer survey analyzed by Bailey and his colleagues, did reveal a pattern whereby support for affirmative action was infinitely higher than in the United States.[17]

The contrast with the United States, at least at this moment, is striking: in a recent paper Arlie Hochschild describes the deep bitterness among people who resent being asked to extend their sympathy to those who have "cut in line" ahead of them thanks, among other things, to affirmative action, while they themselves are being called "insulting names: 'Crazy redneck!' 'White trash!' 'Ignorant southern Bible-thumper!'" (Hochschild 2016a: 6). The very title of her book describes people feeling like strangers in their own land (Hochschild 2016b). This does not chime with Bailey's findings—or at least not yet. In recent years the rhetoric against the PT has grown very bitter, and I have heard its administrations described as a communist takeover, but this has not come from people who feel disadvantaged by affirmative actions. In fact, no sociological hypothesis has been advanced to explain the viciousness of the anti-PT rhetoric. The sectors from which it emanates did well out of the Lula years of high commodity prices and relatively high economic growth, and they could hardly be said to have lost out because of the cash transfer programme (Bolsa Família) for the extremely poor, which, although some brand it a massive vote-buying operation targeted at the poor and ignorant, is a low-cost operation costing less than 2.5 percent of government expenditure. As we have seen, the survey evidence, limited as it is, shows broad support for affirmative action in Brazil compared to the United States, and in fact there has been little if any hostility toward affirmative action based on conventionally right-wing thinking,

---

16. Support was high among whites (47.0 percent) in 2010, but declined to 19.7 percent when the "zero-sum question was put, reminding respondents that quotas for some meant less places for others. The declines in percentage support among "browns" and "blacks" in response to this question were from 69.7 to 32.4 and 60.6 to 34.3 percent, respectively (Bailey et al. 2016: 16).

17. The US figure for support among whites was only 3.5 percent.

and certainly not from racially inspired ideas. Rather the rhetoric seems to be one of class contempt directed against Lula, seen as an upstart working-class leader. Such critics have concentrated their fire on the PT as a political operation to gain power, and on land rights for indigenous peoples, which are said to limit the expansion of large-scale agro-industry—yet Lula and Dilma were quite partial to those interests, to such an extent that Dilma appointed the leader of the agro-industry (ruralista) lobby, Senator Katia Abreu, as her minister of agriculture.

Some politicians have tried to ignite the fire of race, notably Deputy Jair Bolsonaro, who says things that have not been heard almost anywhere in the western world for decades, even in the United States, advocating the death penalty for young offenders, opposing women's rights and affirmative action, putting an end to Indian lands, and defending and advocating military rule, torture, and so on. Bolsonaro gained more votes than anyone else in the Rio de Janeiro elections for federal deputy of 2014 (almost half a million out of 4.3 million shared between 46 successful candidates), and in mid-2017 he was rising in nationwide opinion polls. Occasionally some evangelical members of the Congress, whose caucus comprises 16 percent of the Chamber of Deputies (87 out of 513 are said to be in the *bancada evangélica*), have made racist remarks, but they should not be regarded as representative of the country's highly diverse evangelical churches and their more than 40 million followers.

Despite these rhetorical excesses, the evidence repeatedly tells us that, whatever Brazil's other problems, including the racial bias in police violence (Waiselfisz 2012), race shows little sign of achieving the combustible political potential it has in the United States. The description of the surveys offered here may have been somewhat prolix, but they do point to a degree of bifurcation of colour self-assignment and identity, and they connect that bifurcation to a presence of affirmative action in public debate. The conclusion to be drawn is that racial categorization has many facets, even in a social environment where racial disadvantage is widely acknowledged, because it can be deployed in different contexts. Sometimes it is identity, sometimes it is colour assignment for some sort of official or formal purpose, sometimes—though rarely—it is for political mobilization, and sometimes it is related to music or religion. Again, unlike the United States, these spheres are not superimposed on one another, despite an obvious degree of overlap. For example, religion pulls pardos, negros, morenos, mulatos and mestiços and others in many different directions: it attracts them to evangelical churches of different sorts, to church music of different styles (Burdick 2013), to different sorts of possession cults (which also attract large numbers of nonblacks), to Catholic churches, and sometimes to more than one of the above. "Black churches," in the sense of churches that are a refuge for historically excluded black populations, are unknown. There are certain musical genres that seem to attract a following composed almost exclusively of people of colour (rap, funk, Afro-reggae), as likewise do certain carnival *blocos* in Bahia (Agier 2000: 197–201), but these are hardly broad-based phenomena among the black population, appealing rather to a particular age group or a particular cultural scene in Rio and Salvador.

These examples point to a dispersal of the fields and modes in which people can, so to speak, mobilize the colour of their skin. They also point to the danger of misusing the category "identity," not only because official deployment of race encourages instrumental or simply pragmatic self-assignment, but also because identity is such a treacherous word to use sociologically. Discussions about race carry an undercurrent of a subaltern or oppressed identity that cannot be cast off, which many experience as something like a life sentence, yet when we observe the deployment of blackness in the symbolic sphere we can appreciate its multiplicity and the positive charges it brings for many people.

It therefore becomes impossible to make the slightly judgmental distinction that lies behind some debates between individuals' authentic and opportunistic choices of race, colour, and identity in formal or informal contexts. Brazilians, or at least those who are lucky enough to circulate in more than one or two social milieux, are forever choosing, and doubtless they do so based on what they feel about themselves and others what they think might advantage them in their personal or professional lives. We shall return to the theme in the next chapter in the section entitled "Am I Black after All?"

Affirmative Action Schemes and Outcomes

Affirmative action in Brazil in the early years of the century can be thought of as a host of small-scale initiatives carried forward by committed professors and administrators and attracting like-minded black students. The UERJ ran several bursary programs, including Espaços Afirmados (Batista 2007). Another was sponsored by SECAD's program in support of innovative courses (PIC) and a third by Afroatitude, the Health Ministry programme that chose its beneficiaries on the basis of an interview and "group dynamics." A fourth was an internal programme, ProIniciar. The SECAD-supported programme was run by a group of

committed black professors grouped under the moniker SEMPRE NE-
GRO (Forever Black) at the UERJ. It organized courses and seminars, as
well as providing grants to allow students to join in research and extension activities between 2003 and 2007.[18] But overall, compared to the
number of cotistas, the beneficiaries were few, and the most materially
advantageous programme, Espaços Afirmados, bore the hallmark of the
Ford Foundation's strategy of focusing substantial funds on a carefully
selected number of people and areas in order to achieve an effective
impact. ProIniciar was described by a vice-rector, as a strategy to reduce
dropout rates: this involved upgrading basic skills, workshops on a wide
range of subjects (foreign languages, drug issues, teenage pregnancy),
and cultural activities. Its broad purpose was to open up to them cultural
experiences of whose existence they were scarcely aware: some of the
students had never been to a cinema before coming to university (Villardi 2007).

Students at UnB could access "an array of programmes that support
their academic and social development, including tutoring services, public seminars on the value of blacks in society, and a campus meeting
space to study and interact" (Francis and Tannuri-Pianto 2012). The NE-
ABs were, as we have seen, fashioned on similar lines. But as far as the
UERJ is concerned, the grant schemes only met the needs of a handful
of low-income students and there is no mention of the criteria governing
the award of these small subsidies.

These studies indicate that students arriving under quota schemes
were likely to engage in a bureaucratic guerrilla action in search of resources that would enable them to stay the course. In fact, it was the high
dropout rate that had moved Yvonne Maggie to persuade the Ford Foundation (where Peter Fry was an officer), UFRJ, and CNPq to fund the
Laboratório de Pesquisa Social (Social Research Laboratory—LPS),
which provided research internships at the UFRJ. Under this programme,
which lasted ten years (1988 to 1997), undergraduates worked on race-
related projects to enable them to avoid dropping out of their course. In
this it was highly successful: between 1988 and 1993, 604 students enrolled in the social sciences course, but only 35 percent (215) completed
it; yet of those 215, 146 had scholarships/internships from the programme.
A third of those had a parent with a university qualification (a figure far
above the national urban average), but 16 percent came from families in
which neither parent had even completed primary schooling. Twelve per-

---

18. For more on this programme, see http://www.neab.uerj.br/semprenegro.htm

cent of the beneficiaries declared themselves negro and 22 percent pardo. Access to the programme was by interview or invitation, but after 130 interviews for her study of the programme Glaucia Villas Bôas concluded that, at least for the interviewees, the main way of getting in was through good relations with their teachers, who, they said, did not always apply the qualifying criteria rigorously (2003: 58)—the "bureaucratic guerrilla" again. It was an affirmative action programme in the strict sense, not a quota programme, for it was using incentives and changed structures to equalize opportunity. These "Brazilian" refinements should be interpreted in a Brazilian way, that is, they should be seen in a context in which it is generally assumed that personal relationships are part of the stuff of life at this microlevel and do not necessarily lead to corrupt or unfair outcomes. It is ironic that Fry and Maggie later became reviled as enemies of affirmative action in circumstances to which we shall return.

A vivid and highly readable account of such a bureaucratic guerrilla—as well as of the provocations of everyday racism—is provided by a black doctoral student in anthropology at the Museu Nacional in Rio de Janeiro in a contribution to a special issue on affirmative action of the USP anthropology journal. Anderson Pereira came from a low-income neighbourhood of the Amazonian city of Belem and after many false starts and with the unfailing support of a family of extremely limited means found his way into a private university in Belem where, as a ProUni beneficiary, he was the only black student in his class: when he announced where he lived, along with everyone else, someone murmured, "He's going to rob me"; for five months no one spoke to him, but eventually he made friends with a new black student and also obtained a prize. Years later he recounts other classic encounters in Rio—for example, with the police, who stopped him at the gates of the Museu in Rio, where he was studying—a "black man out of place." But in the context of the "bureaucratic guerrilla" what is interesting is the succession of favours he received from his professors, who offered him lodging on his trips to Rio to be interviewed for a scholarship and a place, paid his fare, found a place for him on a short course, and lent him money for his first month's rent in Rio. The story is exceptional, but the role of these favours is not (Pereira 2017). (Although the title of the article mentions that he is gay, the subject does not receive special attention in the text.)

Another barrier to be overcome was the vestibular entrance exam to public universities. It has been very difficult to do well in the vestibular entrance exam without attending a for-profit *cursinho*. But the pattern and the system are changing in response to public debates about elitism and exclusion: universities opened up quota places, "comunitario" cursinhos, or PVCs (of which more in chapter 5) provided a channel, and the initially quite tight requirements to qualify for a quota place were relaxed; the means test ceiling was raised, and the rules about state school attendance qualifying people for quotas have been relaxed somewhat, thus opening the universities up to people who have attended both private and state schools (Cicaló 2008). The at least partial replacement of the vestibular by the national end-of-schooling exam (the ENEM) as the basis for university admissions has undermined the gatekeeping monopoly of the cursinhos, and it means that a student does not, at least in the first round, have to travel to the university to sit an exam: the universities have begun to introduce multiple choice tests, which are (unfortunately) more suited to the education received in public schools, in the place of or in addition to a discursive Portuguese writing test. Faced with very large numbers of applicants and having to select among them, many universities still require those applicants who get through the first round to attend a vestibular exam. This should, nonetheless, make it a little easier for less well-off applicants to apply to universities far from their homes and should reduce the social selection effect of the vestibular. There are also some provisions from the universities to waive examination fees, but these are not race-based exemptions.

The difficulty public school graduates have in dealing with a discursive text is just one of many signs of a shocking educational divide. In their study using 2010 admissions data from UERJ, Alvaro Mendes Jr. and his colleagues concluded that without the quotas the cotistas had hardly any chance in prestige courses, but they also found that quotas made a big difference even in less competitive courses (Mendes et al. 2016: 312)—although Valente and Berry cast some doubt on these conclusions, especially since they are based only on one university (Valente and Berry 2017). In their nationwide analysis of a very different data set, they find that if students admitted on a "pure" socioeconomic quota (i.e., public school graduates) are set aside cotistas "perform better than students admitted through traditional methods" (21). This in turn undermines the assumption that blackness (self-assigned as usual) is a proxy for low income and poor educational achievement, while confirming that low income (for which public school attendance is a rough proxy) does affect grades. (We return to these questions in the next chapter.)

André Cicaló's research provides further confirmation of the inequality at the school level but then points in an altogether more encouraging direction. In the final vestibular exam for the UERJ law course in 2007, quota students generally placed between the thousandth and the eighteen hundredth position, all the higher positions being taken by non-quota applicants, suggesting an enormous gap since only some thirty students were admitted (Cicaló 2008). Yet their subsequent academic performance did not replicate such a massive difference. Cicaló describes students who had entered via the quota route having initially greater difficulty with studying, not least because they had such a poor background education in reading, summarizing, and writing continuous prose in Portuguese, yet they managed to at least narrow the gap by the end of their first year.

The prestige hierarchy among courses is paralleled by differences in the culture of students in different disciplines. Ethnographic observation at UERJ by Paulo Pinto noticed the difference between medicine, where quotas were regarded among students as little more than a tactic to get admitted, and the social sciences, where the beneficiaries were much more politicized and more likely to regard their cotista status as a mark of identity (2006).

Social Dynamics in the Classroom

Amid the evidence of race-based inequality and campaigns of racial consciousness-raising, are there indications of repercussions among students themselves? The two available qualitative studies of students under the quota regime at UERJ are not strictly comparable, but they do show the pitfalls of hasty statements about life at the university under the quota regime. Cicaló does not understate the shadow that race can cast over relationships between different groups, nor the stubbornness of stereotypical assumptions even in the face of the internal heterogeneity of colour or income groups, but at the same time he is loathe to label social distance in the university as racial, let alone racist.

> Although many students had felt discriminated against or uncomfortable in certain situations during their academic life, as in society, there is no doubt that most of my quota interviewees had expected more confrontational and racist attitudes from the wealthier students at university than they actually experienced, especially considering the alarmist information spread by the mass media and fomented by some literature in this regard. (2012b: 257)

He also points to the difficulty of interpreting statements or actions in isolation, citing, for example, the contrast between statements in which students seemed to deny intimate socializing and accounts of them staying at each others' homes. In fact, much social distance seemed to arise from mutual ignorance on the part of people who, but for quotas bringing them together at university, would never have encountered one another socially in a city divided by socioeconomic segregation. And so, as students neared their final year, attitudes changed: middle-class/white students expressed their satisfaction at coming into contact with this other Rio and at discovering how misleading were some of the scare stories that had circulated when they first applied to the university. Cicaló also observed that the social boundaries had become more blurred, as, for example, when he saw quota students socializing with their teachers in the bars of the expensive Zona Sul (Ipanema, etc.) (2012: 258). (He does not mention romantic attachments.)

Yet at the same time we should listen to the more polemical responses heard by Paulo Pinto, who describes the varied, sometimes ambivalent, student responses to the efforts of various interests to shape student identities at UERJ (including the Espaços Afirmados programme). Pinto relates the attitudes of students to the culture of different disciplines—that is, the political proclivities of the academic staff and their transmission to students. Medical students were largely indifferent to the substantive rationale of quotas, and he quotes one who remarked of a colleague who was party to the conversation, "Ela é cotista, e agora que ela voltou da praia ela e mais cotista ainda" (She is a cotista, and now after spending her holidays on the beach [getting tanned] she is even more of a cotista). To this the colleague responded, "Mas eu acho que sou parda" (But I think I am parda) (Pinto 2006: 151). (Only readers unfamiliar with Brazil will be surprised that this exchange did not provoke a violent argument.)

Pinto also found pragmatic attitudes among medical students, like one who was against the quota system in principle but applied successfully through that route, reasoning that otherwise someone else, with lower marks, would have got the place (2006: 153). It is in his exchanges with students in the social sciences that we find the sharper side of these issues: data published in the newspaper *O Globo* purporting to show quota students getting lower marks than others provoked an outburst in which a student asked how they could be expected to do as well as others when they had no library, no money to get to classes or for photocopying, and she goes on, "If you don't want to help us, then stop throwing shit at the fan and leave us alone. . . . Are we the dregs of the university?"

The prevalent culture in the education and social science courses encourages the affirmation of black identity and the recognition of a heritage of struggle and victimhood: "If you want to know who is black in Brazil, set up a committee with doormen and policemen"; "Being black is a political question." But also, to illustrate the socialization that he sees among students in these courses, Pinto quotes another student saying he/she is "learning to be black" (158–60).[19] It would be wrong to take these phrases, or the contrasting findings of Cicaló, as definitive. As Pinto says, the responses of students from some courses do parrot jargon learned in class, so one does not know the extent to which such attitudes translate into a long-term feature of social interaction. Also, in this world in which the courses themselves occupy a social hierarchy, and in which politicization is more prevalent in the lower-prestige courses, the cotistas in the more prestigious law course studied by Cicaló would be likely to view their own situation in a more favourable light than others whose career prospects are less rosy. Finally, Cicaló was not asking such directly political questions as Pinto, so he got different sorts of answers.

Binary Classification in the Public Square

Among the professors, debates about quotas became so bitter that people of different views avoided attending the same academic meetings on the subject, and there were some bad-tempered confrontations on television.[20] Thus the literature quoted here is largely divided into edited books in favour and edited books against. Although the reality of racial disadvantage and discrimination is not in dispute, this consensus did not smooth matters at all.

The tone of speech around the theme of race is not a purely academic matter. A distinct shift was marked already in the later years of the military regime when the MNU emerged in Rio and Bahia. Founded in 1978 and consisting largely of intellectuals, the MNU's rhetoric was a more polarized version of Brazil's race division than anything that had gone before. It engineered a shift in the image of Zumbi dos Palmares from hero of national resistance—as it had been in the 1930s—to hero

---

19. Here are the quotes in the original: "Se você não vai ajudar, vai ficar jogando merda no ventilador? Então deixa quieto. Será que nos somos o cocó da universidade?"; "Para se saber quem é negro no Brasil basta fazer uma comissão composta de porteiros o policias"; "Ser negro é uma questão política"; "Eu estou aprendendo a ser negro."

20. See, for example, the "debate" in 2009 between Frei David and the USP professor Demetrio Magnoli on YouTube: http://www.youtube.com/watch?v=LoFFn8ZXXQ4

of black and slave resistance, as it has remained since. At the 1995 Zumbi March in Brasilia, a leading MNU figure, Luis Alberto, who twenty years later was still a PT deputy for Bahia, proclaimed that other heroes were "*their* heroes, Zumbi is *ours*" (Hofbauer 2006: 388), and since the call in 1978 for a Dia Nacional da Consciência Negra to coincide with the date of Zumbi's execution it has become a national day of commemoration and celebration of black identity and an official holiday in many municipalities and five states. The MNU explicitly joined race to culture and religion to conform a black civilization, and in a move to recover and recognize the African and proudly pagan authenticity of the possession cults, it belittled supposedly Catholic syncretic elements in the candomblé pantheon (such as St. George and St. Barbara) as mere devices used to conceal their paganism from the whites (396–97). For MNU spokesmen Brazilian misery as well as Brazilian wealth were fundamentally rooted in race, so both the political left and right were foreign to the black cause because they were part of white civilization (399). Claiming cultural and religious authenticity in the 1980s and early 1990s, they prefigured the advocacy of a binary model in the later quotas campaign.

This sharpness of tone continues in the polemics surrounding the question "Who is black?" (or "Who is *really* black?"), which was used as an argument against quotas for blacks. Thus an article already quoted in a volume published by PPCor, accuses the media and "certain intellectuals" of making an issue of this by reifying the "ideological arguments produced by the culture industry" (da Silva et al. 2007: 180–81). The author goes on:

> The Brazilian intelligentsia, sheltered in the country's universities, is made up mainly of white intellectuals, many of whom have furthered their research (and their careers) with state funding of research on the black population. These "negrologists" expect the objects of their research to behave like objects, passive and silent. That is to say, Brazilian science has specialized, since the nineteenth century, in the disciplining of black identity, building it up into an observation field framed by silence and fragmentation. . . . In this case a thin line connects science policy, devoted to sustaining studies, writers, and theoretical positions in defense of a myth of racial integration, placing blacks and indigenous people in a subaltern position, and of the political project of the intellectuals seeking to prevent the rise of social movements in support of the demands of the black population. (180)

Later on the text says that Brazilian academics have cloaked themselves in an "essentialist" identity as researchers, critics, social scientists, and so on, which they use to question the authenticity of the identities promoted by social movements, thus legitimizing "racist practices," though without appearing to be racist themselves, and criticizing social movements for their nonobservance of the niceties of academic life. The passage, which expresses similar views to those of Renato Emerson dos Santos, Wilson Mattos, and Valter Silverio quoted earlier in this and the previous chapter, concludes by quoting José Jorge de Carvalho saying that the Brazilian university was built on the exclusion of blacks and non-European theoretical perspectives.

Although some of the vocabulary is unusual—"negrólogo" is clearly derisive but not a commonly used expression—and although the bald statement about the "white intelligentsia" is also unusual, at least in print (though not without foundation, as few will deny), the passage nevertheless well expresses one underlying tension in these polemics, which casts a suspicion of self-interest over the arguments and not infrequently is tainted with awareness of the differing colours of the participants. It is not a ubiquitous tension, but it is awkward.

We can already see how the promotion of a binary scheme of racial identity, together with the foregrounding of race in spheres of life where it had previously been silent, though by no means absent, has caused the most bitter polemics. Opponents of race-based quotas frequently objected that the allocation of university places by race might place lower-income whites at a disadvantage and higher-income blacks at an advantage. This missed the point about naming: the advocates saw quotas as dealing primarily with racial exclusion and only secondarily with inequality in general. But a significant ethical issue arises when it comes to colour classification by self-assignment: the state is looking to help a disadvantaged category but is forcing the beneficiaries to make a decision that for some may just involve ticking a box, but for others involves a commitment to a label, and in some cases perhaps a label they had never thought about, least of all in legal terms.

The applicants for quota places were being asked to resolve on their own, individually, the practically and ethically complex problem that the policy, in its various guises, was failing to resolve for them, namely, the classification of individuals in one or another racial group and the very decision of whether to apply for a quota place. We saw in the last chapter how the first UERJ application form asked students to explain why they believed themselves to be black. In the new form they had to declare their race "sob as penas da lei"—at the risk of legal proceedings if they made a false declaration. Given the subjective nature of the declaration, the "threat" seems surreal, but there have been reports of applicants being put off applying when faced with that forbidding phrase, even though there has been no report of a resulting prosecution.[21] There are also students who, in advance of entering university, may anticipate a stigma attached to quota students.[22] The quota system imposes often complex second-guessing about which courses will have more or fewer of their peers applying and which might be the courses, or institutions, for which they would be better advised not to take the quota path, while they or their families have to decide whether to invest in private schooling, which may well improve their performance in the national or university entrance examinations but will possibly exclude them from any quota.

Peter Fry, in one of his writings against racial classification, attributes the rise of the binomial usage in place of the triple formula "branco-pardo-negro" to Carlos Hasenbalg, the Argentine sociologist whose doctoral dissertation in the United States was the first attempt to quantify racial inequality in Brazil on the basis of publicly available data using the binary "black/nonblack" formula. Nonetheless, the Brazilian social scientists who wrote on the subject in the period leading up to the 1990s, even Hasenbalg,[23] did not reach the levels of simplification that then became standard, as in the statement by Sueli Carneiro, quoted indignantly by Fry, that blacks comprise 45 percent of the country's population but only 2 percent of them gain access to university (Fry 2005, 2009).[24]

21. The "Instruções específicas para os candidatos às vagas do sistema de cotas" for 2008, in accordance with Rio de Janeiro State Law (Lei Estadual) number 4151/2003, requires applicants for the "cota para alunos negros" to state as follows: "eu (nome completo), inscrito no Vestibular Estadual 2009, sob o n° (inscrição), declaro, sob as penas da lei, identificar-me como negro."

22. See the remarks by Amy Jaffa quoted in chapter 5.

23. Hasenbalg's University of California, Berkeley 1978 doctoral dissertation was translated into Portuese in 2005 (Hasenbalg 2005 [1978]).

24. Sueli Carneiro's comment was posted on a site called "Caros Amigos" in July 2002. The historian Murilo de Carvalho, in a widely noticed newspaper article, described this as "statistical genocide" ("Genocídio racial estatistico," *O Globo*, 27 December 2004). But Carvalho's fiercest criticism of the binary scheme is that it excludes the vast population of mixed indigenous descent—as distinct from the indigenous peoples in Amazonia—who are simply wiped out by the removal of the "pardo" category, as in the "race tribunal" at UnB, which for him is a device employed to "pick out" the "afro-descendentes" among the pardos. He remarks that this is particularly important in the north of the country where slavery was barely introduced and the descendants of slaves are far less prominent than

In the late 1990s racial statistics and their simplification became a mass industry, producing data largely in support of the *movimento negro* and the quotas campaign. The data were produced by various institutions and programmes, including LAESER; the Grupo de Estudos Multidisciplinar da Ação Afirmativa (Multidisciplinary Research Group on Affirmative Actions—GEMAA), led by João Feres in the former IUPERJ, now the IESP attached to UERJ; IPEA, the government economic think tank; and Edward Telles's research. The first two of these were or are funded by the Ford Foundation while Telles was an officer in the Foundation's Rio office in the 1990s, and some of the race research at IPEA was funded by United Nations Development Programme (UNDP) office in Brasilia. The quantitative work that has been most influential among students and activists, produced by IPEA under a project funded by the UNDP, is a working paper written by an economist not specialized in the field of race. Quoted as authoritative in conversation by campaigners and in the activist literature, it was originally prepared for the Durban Conference and is still available without charge from IPEA's website (Henriques 2001). It is a highly condensed (forty-eight-page) account that focuses exclusively on the role of race in shaping inequalities in income, education, and labour markets. The document is careful to state at the outset that it is not offering an explanation or even a description of inequality in general but rather a description of the disadvantages suffered by blacks in comparison with whites. Nonetheless the tone and content cannot but draw the reader to the view that race is the only determinant of social inequality in Brazil, simply because other variables, like education, region, gender, and housing, are brought in not as possible intervening variables but to illustrate the thesis further. Note that Edward Telles's book, which has been translated into Portuguese, does undertake precisely such more sophisticated exercises and gives very strong and more convincing reasons to believe that race or colour, however construed, does have a significant independent effect on inequality (2004).[25]

The Henriques paper has several features that place it in the category

those of Indians. And indeed the *caboclos, cafuzos,* and similar categories describing people of mixed Indian descent simply do not appear in all the polemics about race and affirmative actions. They have only appeared in a secondary guise with the introduction of "traditional populations" into the list of potential beneficiaries of land redistribution, principally in the Amazon, referring to populations of rubber tappers (*seringueiros*), riverside villagers (*ribeirinhos*), and Brazil nut gatherers (Boyer 2015, 2016).

25. The Portuguese translation of Telles's *Race in Another America* is available in Portuguese from his website, http://www.soc.ucsb.edu/faculty/telles/

of state-sponsored activist literature like the material from SECAD. It starts out with the threefold categorization including "pardos," as in standard IBGE usage, but suddenly on page 15 switches to the binary classification. It also repeatedly describes Brazil's race relations regime, unusually, in terms of *raças* rather than colour or ethnic groups, downplaying métissage. Brazilian usage, even in activist literature, tends to use "racial" as an adjective and to avoid depicting the society baldly as composed of two or three races. The working paper uses the word *race* not as an analytical construct, an abstract word denoting differences based on colour and ethnic belonging and their mobilization, but rather to divide a population according to genetics or origin. The text also uses the word *discriminação* very frequently, thus giving the impression that racial disadvantage is the result of purposeful discriminatory actions and policies, as against the received wisdom among antiracists, that a major problem of the Brazilian race relations regime is its "subtlety" (o nosso racismo sutil). It is also silent on the gender dimensions of inequality in general and of racial inequality specifically.

Curiously, some of the tabulated material presented seems to show that skin colour is not precisely correlated with disadvantage—for example, the incidence of poverty in southern Brazil appears to be greater among "pardos" than among "pretos" (Henriques 2001: 12). Another intriguing passage states that it is the black-white gap among the wealthiest 5 percent that seems to be responsible for the average income gap between whites and blacks overall, so that if the top 5 percent were removed income would be more unequal among blacks than among whites. A similar interpretation is found in a much more careful study based on wage data of the same period in the IBGE's PNAD survey. This study estimates the disadvantage (or penalty) arising from sex and race once the effects of education and age have been eliminated, and it finds, first, that black women are the most affected by specifically racial discrimination, but also, and importantly for us in the present context, that specifically racial disadvantage "kicks in" in the upper half of the distribution and becomes particularly acute in the top decile, outweighing disadvantages of education and age (Biderman and Guimarães 2004: 191). This offers a statistical counterpart to (though not exactly an explanation of) my contention that the campaigns for affirmative action aim primarily to get more blacks into these elite strata. My purpose, though, is mainly to note that the usage and tone found in Henriques's working paper is that of an activist document written for and published by a government research agency. It was not followed by further published research on the subject but remains a much-quoted source. Later IPEA established a Racial Equality Unit, which posts very useful information on its website, as well as publishing a regular item in the annual *Boletim de Políticas Sociais* providing updates on government policy with respect to race issues, charting the creation of committees, the passage of legislation, and so on.[26]

Gender: The Absent Universal

Movimento negro activist discourse reserves a particular bitterness for what it calls "universalism." In one sense this refers to the existing (pre-quotas) system of admissions to universities and also to the ubiquitous competitions for government employment in Brazil, whose difference-blind anonymity is regarded as a facade for the perpetuation of existing privilege. In another sense universalism has been pejoratively attached to feminism, or a certain feminism, by black women leaders, such as Sueli Carneiro, who accuse it of ignoring race. But those criticisms seem rather dated now, not least thanks to her own efforts: her main achievement has been as founder and leader since 1989 of GELEDES, one of the most frequently mentioned institutions in conversations about the *movimento negro*, whose name derives from the Yoruba term for a secret religious society of women. GELEDES is an NGO active in the pursuit of legal cases involving racial discrimination and in promoting affirmative action and the inclusion of blacks in business and government. It has received significant funding from the Ford Foundation ($1.3 million between 2006 and 2011 and substantial sums in previous years) and to a smaller extent from the MacArthur Foundation and the Brazilian government. In an interview in November 2008, Carneiro told me that the organization gained its first break from a black executive who, arriving to head the Bank of Boston's operations in Brazil, asked "Where are the blacks in this bank?" Working with him and the bank gave GELEDES a start in promoting affirmative action in business. The irony of the group's debt to a US company as its first supporter was not lost on her, but, as we shall see when we come to describe the Faculdade Zumbi, it was not a unique circumstance.

In the early 1990s Carneiro had written about the double exclusions of black women on account of gender and colour; the *machista* attitudes

---

26. For more on the Racial Equality Unit (Coordenação de Igualdade Racial), see http://www.ipea.gov.br/igualdaderacial/

she attributed to black men; and the complex of powerlessness, desire, and ambition that in her view governed their tortured relationships with both white and black women (1999).[27] In our conversation she grounded her criticism both of feminism and of the movimento negro in their shared "universalizing" conception, which excludes the "specificity" of black women's condition. (The movimento negro, for its part, also criticizes universalism but in terms of its race blindness, not its gender blindness—see chapter 4.) It is worth adding, though, that women, like her, are now highly visible among leaders and militants for the defense of black causes in Brazil, not only in the organization she founded but in others such as CRIOLA and ABPN, while women seem to predominate among black university professors.[28] In 2017 all the members of the council of the ABPN were women. At the first National Conference for the Promotion of Racial Equality (CONAPIR), organized by SEPPIR in June 2005, slightly more than half (52 percent) of the delegates, who had been nominated at twenty-seven state-level meetings in the lead-up to the meeting, were women—an exceptional proportion in officially organized events in Brazil.[29] SEPPIR itself has been led by women since its inception—and even after its demotion by Temer was led by one of his few female appointees, though some might interpret this less as a victory for women than as an indication of the low priority of race issues in the eyes of this president. In a study of prevestibular courses for blacks and people of low income supported by SECAD's Educação na Diversidade programme it was found that 67.5 percent of the students were women and 51.5 percent of these were black women (Braga and Silveira 2007). Trends among the population as a whole still reveal a pattern of disadvantage, but it is changing: black women since the 1980s and even before have overtaken black men at all levels of education. In addition they show that the race gap in higher education, although it is narrowing, is now wider among men than among women (Carneiro 1999; Rosemberg and Madsen 2011).[30] And yet my GELEDES interviews were the only ones

---

27. Though published in 1999 in an edited volume, the paper states that it was written in 1993. The volume's editor, Rebecca Reichmann, was a Program Officer with the Ford Foundation in Rio de Janeiro from 1988 to 1993.

28. This is an impression, of course. The distribution between institutions, subjects and salary levels would have to be analyzed for a complete interpretation.

29. See SEPPIR Informe Anual (Annual Report), 2005. The proportion might be similar in events relating to health and education.

30. The LAESER data show that net participation (i.e. per cent of the 18–24 age-group) in higher education rose as follows between 1988 and 2008: White men: from 7.2% to 19.2%; white women: 8.1% to 22.7%; black men ("pretos" and "pardos"): 1.6% to 6.2%;

that mentioned women's issues: in public talk about affirmative actions gender receives little mention, and much the same is true for the published material. We must, however, beware of drawing over-optimistic conclusions from educational performance of women or historically excluded racial and ethnic groups: quite often they leave the education system and then run into a brick wall in the labour market (for the French case, see Brinbaum et al. 2012, Beauchemin et al. 2016). There is wide recognition that women have moved ahead of men in education in many Latin American countries, but this superior educational performance does not necessarily extend into the labour market let alone into wages and salaries.

Conclusion

This chapter has tied together the core themes at stake in Brazil's impassioned debates about affirmative action and shows both their interconnectedness and their complexity. We began by asking "Who names whom?" and we then explored the disputes about what the names should be and the arena (the university) where the names (black, white, brown—branco, pardo, moreno, preto, negro) were deployed. We found that the same name is deployed in different ways in different contexts—in bureaucratic contexts and everyday interaction, for example—and can also be wrenched away from the control of the named by the cut and thrust of political debate, intellectual polemics, and academic tribalisms. Those tribalisms were ideological, pitting liberals and social democrats (and occasional self-styled conservatives) against people who identified more squarely with the Left, but they were also tinged with generational and class-based animosity, as we shall see in chapter 4.

The debates about naming were deeply interwoven with bureaucracy and the law. Nowhere else in Latin America has such a debate arisen even though all the region's countries have a five-hundred-year history of racial mixture intertwined with racial exclusion in many forms, and almost all the countries now have laws and programmes—often called multicultural or more usually intercultural—designed to remedy that exclusion (Lehmann 2016a). In Spanish America there is widespread recognition of mestizaje as a cultural phenomenon and extensive aca-

---

black women: 2.0% to 9.2%. For a proper interpretation, these numbers should at least separate pretos and pardos, be divided into public and private institutions and broken down by course etc. but the sources do not provide that information.

demic discussion about what it means for the empowerment or otherwise of indigenous populations (Wade 2005)—an ideology of mestizaje is often blamed for playing a role similar to that of racial democracy in Brazil, engendering a type of false consciousness whereby indigenous people have been despoiled of their heritage. Yet in Spanish America the question of where to draw the line between, say, "indios" and "mestizos" or "indios" and "blancos,"[31] is studiously avoided; even when land is at stake one hardly ever hears of people's entitlement being challenged on the grounds that they are not "indio" enough. The idea of enshrining a person's race in a bureaucratic or legal document, even on the basis of self-assignment, is unheard of. The same can be said of intercultural education programmes in which there is no question of restricting participation on ethnic grounds (Lehmann 2013a). But Brazil is different, so much so that it is often asked whether it is "really" part of Latin America at all (Bethell 2010). When black exclusion is at stake the cultural dimension is scarcely present and is not the subject of government largesse: social inequality is at the forefront, and the resources on offer—tens of thousands of university places plus modest student financial support—are not negligible. But we can also see that there is more: a sense of bitterness among some black intellectuals and their most widely heeded spokespeople that those who deny the racial dividing line are denying their history and the heavy inheritance of exclusion that has materially and psychologically affected black people in very large numbers. Hence the politics of naming.

---

31. It is gradually becoming clear that the Anglo-Saxon assumption that mestizo means 'mixed race' and is somehow inserted in a hierarchy between indigenous and white is a misreading of everyday usage: mestizo is a reference of superiority and often social equivalence to blanco (see notably, for the case of Mexico, Martinez Casas et al. 2014).

FOUR

Race, Class, and Education in the Search for Social Justice

Universalism and Modernism under Fire

The previous chapter ended with a discussion of gender, describing it as the "absent universal" in the advocacy of affirmative actions. But criticism of universalism is by no means limited to gender: the words "universalista" or "meritocracia" are widely used pejoratively, even derisively, in the denunciation of racial exclusion. In this discourse difference-blind universalism is embodied in examinations (notably the vestibular) and *concursos*, which open competition to all on the same formal terms but make no allowances for structural disadvantages arising from people's racial and social backgrounds, schooling, neighbourhood and so on.

Opponents of quotas (the dissidents as I will call them) have readily recognized the injustices of the country's application of unalloyed bureaucratic methods to selection. For example, Simon Schwartzman, a prominent sociologist of the 1960s generation and an expert on education, began a highly critical article on quotas in 2008 by asserting the principle that people who have had fewer life chances should be given more opportunities than others and also that once they have gained access to universities they should be properly supported and not left to fend for themselves.[1] Schwartzman, Maggie, Fry, and others would say that, far from excessively universalist, the country's social policies are insufficiently so, that its educational and social policies have long borne the mark of inequality in provision and implementation, and that the

---

1. S. Schwartzman 2008. This text, entitled "A medida da lei de cotas para o ensino superior," though published only on the Web, has been widely quoted.

proper response to the underachievement and discrimination suffered by blacks and other disadvantaged groups is a consistently universalist one that would aim to reduce glaring inequalities in the state's provision, as well as punishing acts of discrimination. They would not, however, allow for racial criteria to be taken into account in such policies, and Schwartzman's paper in fact argued that race quotas would change little and might even be harmful to the cause of equality by driving students from wealthier classes out of public universities and into the high-cost end of the private sector (as happens in Mexico but has not yet happened on a noticeable scale in Brazil). In principle, I think this conflates affirmative action applied on an individual basis with the collective criterion: the collective approach "simply" reserves quotas for a racial (or other) category; the individual approach looks painstakingly at applicants case by case and works out their disadvantage, weighing it with their potential, their grades, and so on. One frequent device is to give preferential consideration to applicants whose performance is well above the average for their school. This individualized approach may seem to be challenging given the numbers involved, but it is precisely what colleges have done in the United States in order to circumvent the restriction on racial selection decreed by the famous *Bakke* case of 1978 (Sander and Taylor 2012). However, the effect on the culture of the institution would be small, and there is above all reason to doubt the efficacy of such a purist interpretation of universalism with respect to the equalizing of opportunity on a broad front. The approach that might satisfy the dissidents' objections, because it privileges the leveling of the playing field over large-scale inclusion, is unlikely to achieve the desired objective on anything like the scale required. In any case, the results in the United States are mixed as we shall see.

Since a rival policy has not been produced to deal with the specifically racial dimension of social exclusion, the dissidents are exposed to being labeled as naysayers or rejectionists without an apposite alternative response to the problem. Alternatives, such as that proposed by former minister of education and later federal deputy Paulo Renato de Souza in late 2008, did without racial criteria entirely, relying on the standard alternatives of income and state school education. In a speech whose text he passed to me, Paulo Renato also only grudgingly recognized the role of race in contributing to inequality, speaking of "algum grau de discriminação racial" (a certain degree of racial discrimination) in Brazilian society, and he regretted the multiplication of organizations fighting for the rights of ethnic minorities, leaving the poorest income groups with only "direitos difusos" (poorly defined rights) and without the seasoned spokespeople who are attracted to ethnic causes. "Enough," he cried, (Ora!): the best way to defend those minorities was through income-based rather than race-based quotas. Another standard response—on which few would disagree in principle and which is echoed in many countries—was that the real problem lay in the very poor quality of public primary and secondary schooling. But this is a very long-term project requiring massive investment in money and people, and above all it is not apposite: that is, it does not "answer the question" and this sort of down-to-earth pragmatic response is insensitive and almost offensive to black campaigners. By this I mean that it does not respond to their demand for recognition and for representation in prestige universities with all the symbolic capital that brings.

Nonetheless, even if they did not produce a genuine policy alternative, opponents of quotas have themselves undertaken initiatives aimed at improving the chances of black people in university. In addition to the Laboratório de Pesquisa Social, Yvonne Maggie was involved in a Programa Cor e Educação (Colour and Education Programme), which studied the community-based previstibular courses for black and low-income students founded by the Franciscan Frei David (pronounced Daví) in the suburban parish of São João de Meriti in Rio. She also was more concerned with racial inequality than racialized cultural representation: her study of the celebrations of the centenary of Abolition in 1988 lamented the paucity of protests—violently repressed in one instance—against the persistent inequality and discrimination faced by black Brazilians (Maggie 1994).

But the mood changed once the campaign for quotas got under way a decade later: Maggie was shocked by what she saw as an attack on Brazil's modernism, born in the historic cultural festival the São Paulo Semana de Arte Moderna, of 1922. The modernist school produced, among others, the writer Mário de Andrade, whose *Macunaíma* describes the fantasmagorical life of a personage who is successively transformed from black to white and into a French woman, is put under a spell by a candomblé priestess (*mãe de santo*), and eventually materializes as "the beautiful (albeit useless) starburst of the Ursa Major constellation" (Maggie 2008). *Macunaíma*'s author, like others of his generation, was looking to encapsulate Brazilian distinctiveness, defining the country as a civilization on its own terms in contrast, in Maggie's words, to the then prevailing comparisons with "so-called civilized societies," which found in Brazil only "lack, absence and emptiness" (41). Barbara Weinstein, in a masterly study, delineates the modernists' awkward combination of a hyper-valuation of Brazil's distinctiveness and its racially mixed population with an equally high evaluation of the promise of industry and technology embodied by São Paulo as the country's most advanced region and con-trasted with the dilettantishness and backwardness of the rest of the country (Weinstein 2015: 149). Mario de Andrade's rebuff of approaches from Abdias do Nascimento and the Experimental Black Theatre can be seen in this context.

Brazilian modernism found expression notably in art and literature and in the architecture heavily influenced by Le Corbusier. It also in-cluded the figure, alternately untouchable and unmentionable, of Gil-berto Freyre, today reviled by some as the false prophet of an illusory racial democracy and respected by others as the writer who "made Brazil Brazil." Freyre initially developed his idea of Brazil as a "social and eth-nic democracy" in the 1930s in opposition to European and Portuguese fascism and Brazilian *integrismo*—to which, it will be recalled, the embry-onic black organization FNB was, for mysterious reasons, not opposed. He was referring not to democracy in a political sense but to the culture of a society characterized by social and sexual interaction among racial groups. This concept had little to with the political conception of de-mocracy based on citizenship and rights, although in his middle age he was prominent in the opposition to authoritarianism and the extreme Right and was exiled by Vargas. His first use of the term *racial democracy* was only in 1962, in a lecture in Portugal, when he deployed it to express his opposition to exclusivist (and of course essentialist) racial identities such as "négritude," which were coming into vogue in the period of Af-rican decolonization and were gaining an audience among Brazil's black intelligentsia (Hanchard 1994; Guimarães 2001, 2005b; Lehmann 2008).[2] His notion of democracy in the context of race was based on culture and social interaction, and he spoke of racial democracy as an ideal, distant from reality. As he grew old and came to enjoy his guru

---

2. Guimarães' articles mostly mirror one another; my own makes similar points about Freyre's use of "democracia racial" but was written without knowledge of his earlier paper, which has the virtue of placing Freyre in his historical context and attempting to put paid to the labeling of him as a reactionary intellectual (at least up to the 1960s). This labeling goes back to battles for influence and prestige between Freyre and members of the so-called São Paulo school in the 1950s and 1960s, led by Florestan Fernandes, which held to a more *marxisant* interpretation, according to which even if Brazilians lacked prejudice, this was to be explained in the context of a class society; they tended to portray Freyre, patronizingly, as a reactionary and provincial figure ensconced in the northeastern city of Recife (Falcão and de Araujo 2001; Pallares-Burke 2005).

status, Freyre did not object when his phrase was deployed for propaganda reasons by a Brazilian diplomatic service looking to curry favour in Africa during the military regime that he now supported. So it could be said that Fry and Maggie and others were following in the path first traced by Freyre in that they held to a modernism that does not equate itself with the idea of a unified global modernity but, prefiguring Eisenstadt, envisages "multiple modernities" (Eisenstadt 2000). For them, the institutionalization of binary classifications would be both illiberal and a way to undo Brazil's modernity.

The dissidents sometimes criticized quota supporters for importing foreign models into Brazil, and in this they received unsolicited support from the notoriously polemical sociologist Loïc Wacquant, who spent a brief period in Brazil on a Rockefeller programme (Telles 2003: 37) and, together with his mentor Pierre Bourdieu, wrote one of the most intemperate papers ever to be published in a learned journal. They denounced US-based foundations, notably Ford and Rockefeller, for exporting both neoliberalism and multiculturalism to the rest of the world as a cover for "downsizing and denigration of the state, the reduction of social protection," and so on, and also for imposing on their Brazilian associates the "white/black dichotomy" prevalent in the United States (Bourdieu and Wacquant 1999: 42, 46). They saw in Brazilian agitation for affirmative action a reduction of social inequalities to race and regarded this as part of a far-reaching US-based neoliberal conspiracy against class-based interpretations. The article would no doubt have been even more forceful had the authors realized the full extent of the involvement of the Ford Foundation in the campaign for racial quotas in subsequent years.

So scandalous was the publication of the article that one of the *Theory and Society* journal's own editors published a note in the same issue "challenging a number of assumptions and generalizations" contained in it and seeking "to encourage a debate towards establishing a more fruitful agenda for understanding the complex relays between identity, power, governance, globalization, capitalism" (Venn 1999: 59). Somehow, the editors managed both to publish and simultaneously to be embarrassed by it. Its "factual" claims were rebutted by Telles (2003) and others (French 2000; Hanchard 2003), although none has openly complained about the shocking manner in which the authors referred to Michael Hanchard, a pioneer in the post-1990 wave of race studies in Brazil, as an "Afro-American political scientist" (Bourdieu and Wacquant 1999: 44).

Polemics aside, the implication of these criticisms is that a binary system of racial classification, especially if inscribed in official documents and practices, is an alien transplant (from Brazil's eternal Other, the United States) into a culture shaped and pervaded by race mixture and, importantly, by cultural traits or habits that are not constrained by racial frontiers. The implication infuriated Jocelio Teles dos Santos of UFBA's CEAO, who, in an interview with me, said that Brazil has been allocating quotas since the colonial period and "anthropologists and sociologists" were guilty of "unforgiveable analytical simplification" (um simplismo analítico imperdoável). The fact that people who spent their professional lives writing about "the poor, blacks, women and peasants" were opposed to quotas was not at all paradoxical and revealed their attachment to the conscious and unconscious structures of power. Another interviewee, who had been closely involved in the PPCor programme, as well as acting as Frei David's lawyer, spoke of the "cynicism" of "the Left," which had "never proposed egalitarian policies for universities." This theme illustrates—as do the arguments about universalism—how these questions of identity have cut across assumptions about what is "left" and what is "right" as well as what is Brazilian and what is not. It was not so long ago that hostility toward imported models—especially economic models and those identified with the United States—was thought to be a hallmark of "the Left," but now these words cannot easily be applied to the different "sides" in the quotas debate in which opposition to quotas and racial classification is variously denounced as "Marxist" or "liberal" depending on the speaker's preferences. For Paulo Sergio Pinheiro the country's academy was "very white and very racist" and his own university—USP—"the most Marxist university," deserved much criticism in this regard. But Bernardo Sorj, a professor of sociology at UFRJ, agrees with Bourdieu and Wacquant, and Slavoj Žižek for that matter, that the pressures for affirmative action and the politics of recognition in general are part of a worldwide fashion for victimization in which universal ideas are giving way to the narratives of victimhood, which inspire claims by disparate groups: in Sorj's view the people agitating in the name of the black population, the NGOs, and the Ford Foundation are spinners of a fabricated version of Brazilian history in which a new actor is created, namely, the "Afro-Brazilians with their own memory of themselves as victims of history in the image of the United States model"—a model that, "setting aside the economic benefits of affirmative actions, bears no relation to the country's historical and cultural realities or its patterns of sociability" (Sorj 2008: 28). In an interview with me in 2008, when the polemics were particularly intense, Sorj took up the anti-American theme, denouncing the transmission of these ideas as "colonialism of the Left" and as such part of a "Washington consensus of the Left."[3] In his opinion the movimento negro was pushing for "a racist society" and for "the state to define who belongs to what race." Now that several years have passed and Brazil is consumed by other crises, the language around the subject has become softer.

Similar criss-crossing associations came through in other interviews. One recipient of Ford grants and a prominent defender of the black cause told me that he was worried that now that the Foundation's Rio office was no longer staffed with Americans, but rather with white Brazilians, his cause might lose support (his fears were misplaced). As we have seen, the movimento negro has found US-based multinationals to be more sympathetic to the cause of affirmative action, and more open to hiring blacks, than Brazilian corporations are, while the Steve Biko Institute in Salvador and the Faculdade Zumbi in São Paulo have strong relationships with historically black colleges in the United States. The movimento negro may not proclaim the United States to be a model for Brazil, but instinctive anti-Americanism seems not to bring forth the same sympathy among its adherents as it has done for many decades among Brazilians who identify as left wing.

The United States: A Pure Liberal Model?

The mismatch in the meaning of "universalist" deployed by opposing camps parallels the mismatch in the usage of the term "affirmative" by defenders of quotas in the plural—"affirmative actions"—as opposed to the singular usage "affirmative action" in English. In both cases a substantive concept of fairness is opposed to a procedural concept. But that distinction is not so straightforward, and the experience of the United States is not as purely procedural as one might assume. In his exhaustive account of the translation, in the United States, of affirmative action in the workplace and labour markets (not universities) from the statute books into bureaucratic and regulatory practice, with additional contributions from the Supreme Court, John David Skrentny argues that the pure "classical liberal" abstract individual in the "colour-blind" ap-

---

3. An allusion to the package of orthodox economic policies promoted by the IMF and the World Bank and the US government in the wake of Latin America's 1980s debt crises—also known as the "Washington consensus." It should be added that distrust of the United States, mixed in with a degree of envy and rivalry, has for very long been the hallmark of Brazil's highly elitist diplomatic service—so it is hardly a monopoly of the "left" (Bethell 2010).

proach, the notional beneficiary of the original affirmative action without racial preferences (the famous Title VII of the 1964 Civil Rights Act), is a chimera. This idea summarized the approach not only of liberals like John Rawls (of whom more later) or of the Supreme Court justices of that time who interpreted the act, but also of the leading lights of the civil rights movement itself, who for a long time resisted fiercely any slippage from absolute equal treatment for all to special treatment based on skin colour: Martin Luther King in particular was highly resistant until he made some concessions when under attack by Black Power and related movements (Skrentny 1996: 32, 74). Couching his argument in as little ideology as possible, Skrentny shows that bureaucrats and policymakers found it impossible to create a path to equal opportunity in the workplace without fixing targets (i.e., quotas) for companies: by the late 1960s policymakers were giving up the premise that affirmative action did not involve colour-conscious decision-making and policy: this was the "only meaning" which could be given to the language of affirmative action (Skrentny 1996: 165). To follow their advice involved some tortuous legal-semantic manipulation, as when the secretary of labor during the Nixon administration, defending measures requiring government contractors to implement affirmative action, had to make a distinction at a Senate hearing between a "quota" (not allowed) and a "goal" (allowed) (200).

Skrentny's resulting view that the prohibition on racial classification had to be circumvented if affirmative action was to proceed finds confirmation in a polemical, though well documented, book by Sander and Taylor. They are severely critical of the way affirmative action has been applied in US universities, and find that, in order to increase the number of black students in them, administrators bend every rule in sight. Their main method is something like numerical levitation, raising applicants' marks in admissions examinations by making allowances for all kinds of disadvantage.

Sander and Taylor argue that the consequence of this manipulation is a higher than average rate of failure among the "beneficiaries." They find that students who are admitted through affirmative action are disproportionately likely to drop out, to shift from tougher to less demanding courses, and to fall behind later in their careers (the profession in question was the law) (Sander and Taylor 2012). They also present qualitative evidence of students who find themselves ill-prepared for the highly competitive atmosphere of prestige colleges and as a result become depressed or lose motivation and fall behind. But perhaps their most striking or even shocking finding is that those who go to historically black institutions, like Howard University, where the student population is overwhelmingly black, end up doing better on average than those who are admitted to prestige schools via affirmative action. They are less likely to drop out, and they are more likely to succeed later on (41–48). There still remain troubling questions, however: maybe this pattern reflects tacit or silent racial prejudice against those isolated blacks who make it to prestige schools and into prestige law firms, or maybe the graduates of historical black universities are doing better because they later join firms or bureaucracies where blacks are not so unusual, so they do not (once again) feel exposed as a minority.

These conclusions coincide with some of the views of the dissidents in Brazil, who predicted that poorly prepared students benefited (or not) by quota places would be set up to fail. The difference, though, is that while affirmative action in the United States, at least in prestige institutions, is a carefully targeted exercise in which the small number of beneficiaries are likely to feel exposed once they join their university, the Brazilian quotas are intended as a broad-based and poorly calibrated exercise in which successes and failures are more likely to be randomly distributed and the beneficiaries are less likely to feel exposed. (The examples from Cicaló and Pinto in the previous chapter show the advantage of a sizable numerical presence for the beneficiaries of affirmative action, as reflected in their performance in one case and their self-confidence in both.)

The implications of the Sander and Taylor argument are, again, that the distinction between procedural and substantive fairness, which underpins the classic notion of affirmative action ("leveling the playing field") is in practice a fiction because administrators "honour the rules in the breach" by finding ways to circumvent the prohibition on racial selection, and, second, in any case even when the rules have been stretched in various ways, the system is unlikely to substantially improve the lot of the racially disadvantaged—even of the minority among them who gain access to prestige universities. For some this means abandoning racial preferences in favour of purely socioeconomic ones, but for movement activists and those who want to increase the representation of racially disadvantaged groups *in the elite*, it means that collective, substantive measures are even more justified, for two reasons. The first derives from the nonacademic benefits of attendance at elite institutions for advancement in later life, notably the networks one creates and the self-promotional skills one acquires. The second is that larger numbers of beneficiaries counteract the disadvantage of being an isolated, identifiable, relatively low achiever competing with high achievers in the same classroom and likely therefore to underperform (Sander and Taylor 2012: 46).

Further support for this skepticism comes from a book by William Bok and Derek Bowen, respectively former presidents of Harvard and Princeton universities (with a supporting technical team), even though it is regarded as the best advertisement for the benefits of affirmative action in US prestige universities. The reason for this claim is that amid the statistical trends of broadly good results for black students in terms of graduation rates, they still show clear racial differences in those rates and above all they show that when grades (as distinct from mere graduation rates) are examined there emerges a clear and consistent underperformance by black students in relation not only to white students but also to their own scores in admission exams (the Scholastic Aptitude Tests, or SATs), which would, on average, have predicted that they would do better (Bowen and Bok 1998: 74–77). These results hold even when all the standard controlling variables are taken into account. The authors—whose work, it must be recalled, dates from the 1990s—were at a loss to offer a general explanation of this. They do, however, mention better grades for black students at a tiny number of well-endowed institutions that instituted tutorial arrangements for them—thus counterbalancing possible feelings of inadequacy and isolation. But this merely casts doubt on how affirmative action could help black or low-income students to reach high levels of achievement in higher education on the large scale that is required in the United States, let alone Brazil, where even the prestige institutions are mass universities with tens of thousands of students operating under permanent budgetary stress.

For our purposes, however, when taken together with the more recent claims by Sander and Taylor, such findings need not support a retreat: they could also provide the basis for radical social engineering by increasing the proportion of disadvantaged groups represented in elite institutions *without increasing overall student numbers* so that they can both realize their potential without the psychological costs and also gain access to the elite. This may well happen in the current Brazilian context of economic downturn and fiscal austerity: it could leave a certain proportion of students from wealthier backgrounds deprived of the university education that they and their parents have regarded as their birthright, encouraging the expansion of what might be called the "high-end" sector of fee-paying institutions, as Simon Schwartzman predicted. But it could also increase the chances of cotistas gaining access to the elite, even though many will not fulfill all their ambitions. It is precisely those costs that strengthen the argument for a large scale, broad-brush approach to affirmative action.

Thus we can see that the question of the acceptability of official racial classification—excluded by the difference-blind requirements of a classic liberal approach—is intimately tied up with the acceptability of a collective approach to affirmative action: if you reject the latter, the policy will not succeed save in isolated individual cases. The collective ("sledge-hammer," "broad brush," or "rough justice") approach will produce more high-performing black and low-income students, but in the absence of special tuition and the like it will also likely leave a disproportionate number of them underperforming. The advocates are obliged to admit that there will be "collateral damage."

It should be added that there is some established federal support for individuals: students who study at federal universities do have access to supplementary financial support on application: one type is the "programa de educação tutorial" (PET), which encourages them to study in groups under the supervision of a professor and pays R$ 400 a month; the other, which can be in addition to the PET, is the "bolsa permanência" that is worth the same but can be supplemented up to at least twice that amount for indigenous and quilombola students, who are accorded priority on the grounds that they have to study a long way from their home base. R$ 400 is but a token amount though—less than half the 2017 minimum wage of R$ 937—and the method of selection, if any, is unknown. In addition, there are various schemes and niche opportunities (like research internships) that committed students can pursue. The "bureaucratic guerrilla" once again.

Ideological Battle Lines: Liberalism and Social Democracy on the Back Foot

For Peter Fry and Yvonne Maggie, the quotas campaign had as its purpose to undermine Brazil's race relations regime, in which mixture and métissage dominate, so as to shift it in the direction of a bipolar system. Fry, like most social scientists educated in the marxisant atmosphere of the 1960s and 1970s, had once upon a time been a critic of Gilberto Freyre, but now he and Maggie invoked Freyre positively (Fry and Maggie 2005). They did not invoke racial democracy, and they did not deny for one moment the reality of racial discrimination, but they did oppose fiercely the implantation of official recognition of a binary system. Fry was convinced, having done research and work in Zimbabwe, as well as Mozambique,[4] that official sanction produces polarization and does not simply reflect it. For them Brazil's 1996 National Human Rights Programme was a denial of the long-standing ideology of a "racially mixed Brazil" in favour of a "classification prevalent in other parts of the world, notably South Africa and the United States" (Fry 2002: 99). In Maggie's view even to use the prefix "multi-" in describing the country was to deny its hybrid character (Maggie 2005, 2008).

This dissident posture is hard to argue in the public square, however coherent it may be, for if these scholars are agreeing that racism is endemic in the society why are they arguing against policies and benefits designed specifically to improve the opportunities of racially discriminated groups and declaring that race "does not exist"? For them, and social anthropologists generally, race is indeed a "construction," but the point is too rarefied for use in political disputes even when academics are the leading protagonists. How could they gain the support of the black intelligentsia when, in the heat of argument, their leaders could accuse them of telling they do not exist? In the place of quotas they argue for the punishment of acts of discrimination under existing laws, but this, too, gains little traction in public debate and also does not deal with racial exclusion as a statistically patterned, structural phenomenon. Fry, in a phrase similar to Cardoso's allusion to "Brazil's ambiguity and non-Cartesian characteristics," defended the "Brazilian model" or "Brazilian sociological intelligence" and lamented the personalization of some of these disputes (2000: 111). His support of affirmative action in the strict liberal sense, and of the provision of low or zero cost prevestibular courses to "negros e carentes" (blacks and people of low income), such as those run by Frei David, and the undoubted affirmative action character of the Cor e Educação project which he ran with Yvonne Maggie, went unnoticed in the highly polarized atmosphere.

Battle lines were drawn even more fiercely by the book *Divisões Perigo-*

---

4. Peter Fry earned his PhD at University College London based on his fieldwork in Zimbabwe. He has lived and worked in Brazil since the early 1970s and has been a very prominent figure in social anthropology there, also holding leading positions in the Associação Brasileira de Antropologia (Brazilian Anthropological Association—ABA). He also worked for the Ford Foundation in southern Africa, as well as in the Rio office. It is worth stating that although I have heard extremely fierce criticisms of his views on the issues discussed here, I have never, ever heard anyone refer to him as a foreigner. Yvonne Maggie has spent her entire life and career in Brazil.

sas (Fry et al. 2007), to which many prominent opponents of racial classification and quotas contributed.[5] There is a patronizing tone, and an element of "talking down," in some of its essays, which seem to say, "*We* know the classical philosophers, and *we* know the history of Rwanda, Liberia, and the USA." Several of its authors criticize the oversimplification of history that ignores the vast diversity of Africa and reinterprets the Zumbi episode as a modern-style revolt (a representation described as a "sequestro intelectual"—an intellectual kidnapping); there are allusions to the importation of alien notions and practices of race division modeled on those of the United States; and there are some irate references to nazism, the Holocaust, and a science mockingly named "raciologia." This sort of language only appeals to the converted.

In a lengthy critique of *Divisões Perigosas*, João Feres, who has published a succession of opinion pieces and papers in English and Portuguese on the subject, responded in detail. He criticized the authors for defending racial democracy (as if this were a crime) and questioned the fears expressed in the book about the impending "racialization" of Brazilian society and the prediction that the binary system of racial classification brought by a quota system would cause a crisis in Brazil's national identity (Feres 2008: 67–68).[6] Indeed, neither such outcome has occurred or looks like occurring: Brazil's crisis as of 2017 is of political economy and institutions, not identity.

The most important issue taken up by Feres is the dissidents' view that racial classification and the distribution of benefits to particular racial groups violates the principle of liberal republican citizenship and equality before the law (of which he is skeptical). We have seen, in our discussion of civil rights in the United States, that in any case this view can barely be sustained in practice. But can it even be sustained in theory? Feres argues that if this were the case the same criticism could be made of benefits for people of low income, for graduates of state schools, and so on, in which case, one might add, republican citizenship would be incompatible with any kind of welfare state. But of course republican citizenship is perfectly compatible with a welfare state: that is not the point at issue. The point at issue is the "difference blindness" built into the impersonal processes known as proceduralism, for strictly

5. Many of the essays had previously been published as opinion pieces in *O Globo*, the Rio daily regarded by supporters of progressive causes as a mouthpiece of reactionary opinion and big business.

6. The text is available on the GEMAA website, Grupo de Estudos Multidisciplinar da Ação Afirmativa, http://gemaa.iesp.uerj.br

speaking that principle would not allow the state to take account of subjective (mutable) differences like religion and self-assigned race. Disability, income, age, gender, and the like are, for the most part,[7] impersonal attributes that even the most extreme version of the "difference-blind" approach would accept for the purposes of social policy—and such factors are fully incorporated in Rawls's schema, which we can take as the standard formulation of republican liberalism. But the question is whether his schema can accommodate these more subjective characteristics. Stated another way: we can agree that racial background is a serious source of disadvantage, but can it be used in allocating resources if race is assigned without an impersonal or codified procedure, let alone if assignment is undertaken by the individuals standing to benefit from it?

Sometimes state racial classification is a project of domination or exclusion or worse. But not necessarily: we saw that at the UnB, for a time, the attempt to bureaucratize racial affiliation came from those who wanted to prevent "fraudulent" applications for racially defined quota places. "Conversely" there was an outcry from certain supporters of the black cause in August 2016 when the Ministry of Planning said it would institute a commission to check for fraud in applications for race quotas in federal government *concursos*. Others however, notably Frei David, supported the measure: he said that whereas in earlier years the problem had been to persuade people to recognize themselves as black, it had now been noticed that "cunning whites" (brancos espertos) had been quicker to wake up to the opportunities on offer. At the same time SEP-PIR put out a statement about frequent denunciations of fraud and "the appropriation of a prerogative that belongs to black individuals" (*Folha de São Paulo*, 3 August 2016). In June 2017, a row broke out in São Paulo when 138 people who had taken part in a concurso for schoolteachers as self-declared negros qualifying for a 20 percent black quota were summoned without warning to appear before a commission established by the city's Secretary for Human Rights: the commission, inevitably described by one of them as a "race tribunal," canceled their self-assignment. The procedure was in line with a decree published by the mayor in 2016 but they had not been warned of its existence. Frei David and EDU-CAFRO for their part issued a declaration in support of the principle but recommending improvements in the procedure. They pointed to the

---

7. I say "for the most part" because the statement is no longer straightforward as far as gender is concerned.

Facebook page of one of the people involved as evidence that she was not really black at all and had used makeup and other devices to appear so. But the woman in question retorted that she felt like a slave queuing up to be sold: she had spent her whole life affirming herself as a black woman and suffered racist attacks and now she felt as if her identity had been stolen from her (*Folha de São Paulo*, 26 June 2017).

So, in addition to the paradox of self-assignment in deciding eligibility for valued resources, which is not compatible with strict bureaucratic impersonality, we have an enduring question mark over the practice of racial classification for official purposes of resource allocation to individuals in a society pervaded by race mixture. Even the most enthusiastic proponents of official recognition of racial identity do not want the state to decide the racial category in which an individual belongs—although they may in the end be driven to resort to that, and we have seen that judges sometimes are already taking, or being asked to take, that power. So the paradox remains of self-assignment in deciding eligibility for valued resources, which is not compatible with a liberal concept of equality before the law. This has been much more of a concern in Brazil than in the United States, where even judicial decisions do not seem to express any doubts about the consistency of assigning individuals to a racial category—although the categories in censuses and educational documentation have for some time been multiplying as the métissage and diverse origins of the country's population are increasingly recognized and as newly vocal subgroups demand official recognition.[8] How, then, can impartiality and legitimacy be achieved in the midst of this maelstrom of subjectivities? Does John Rawls help us to find an answer?

Rawls's ideal society—and that is mostly what he wrote about—requires "substantive equality of opportunity": "all citizens must be guaranteed a fair chance to compete for offices and positions in the basic

---

8. See, for example, the "Final Guidance on Maintaining, Collecting, and Reporting Racial and Ethnic Data to the U.S. Department of Education," which states, "Educational institutions and other recipients will be required to collect racial and ethnic data using a two-part question. The first question is whether the respondent is Hispanic/Latino. The second question is whether the respondent is from one or more races using the following five racial groups: American Indian or Alaska Native, Asian, Black or African American, Native Hawaiian or Other Pacific Islander, and White. Respondents will not be offered the choice of selecting a 'two or more races' category . . . [and] elementary and secondary institutions and other recipients are required to use observer identification when a respondent, typically a student's parent or guardian, leaves blank or refuses to self-identify the student's race and/or ethnicity." "Refused to reply" is not an admissible answer. *Federal Register*, vol. 72, no. 202, 19 October 2007. There are further rules about the classification of mixed categories.

structure of society, regardless of social circumstances (e.g., class status or family background)" (Taylor 2009: 480); and "those with similar skills and talents should have similar life chances." By "talents" he must mean an individual's innate potential as it would be without disadvantages stemming from background or socioeconomic circumstances. He argues that because "a system of natural liberty . . . permits distributive shares to be improperly influenced by . . . social circumstances and such chance contingencies as accident and good fortune," the state must prevent "excessive accumulations of property and wealth" and sustain "equal opportunities of education for all." In this way "those who are at the same level of talent and ability and have the same willingness to use them, should have the same prospects of success regardless of their place in the social system" (Rawls 1972: 72–73). It is a model of the purest meritocracy, and one that relies on unbounded faith in the potential of education as a tool of individual and social improvement.

Strange as it may seem in the light of this very radical critique of inherited advantage, combined with his support for a competitive social system, Rawls seems to have avoided public and written statements on the subject of affirmative action for racially disadvantaged groups, and his egalitarian agenda is limited by the rigorous conditions he imposes on measures meant to remedy inherited inequality: such measures must be *to the benefit of the least advantaged, not only of those directly targeted,* and must also conform to his individualist and proceduralist requirements. But more perhaps than equality, Rawls looks for balance, as when he says an efficient structure (not an egalitarian one) is reached "when there is no way to change the distribution [of expectations] so as to raise the prospect of some without lowering the prospect of others" (1972: 70).

For Rawls blanket allocations based exclusively on racial identity are, by implication, problematic, as they would be for other philosophers such as Amartya Sen and Anthony Appiah. Their views are thus not compatible with those associated with the politics of recognition as outlined by Charles Taylor (1992). Yet none of these would accept that the mere existence of differences in cultural habits, language, religion, or racial identity should *in themselves* form part of a schema for the allocation of resources by the state. The implications of Sen's capabilities approach in Brazil would be much more radical than race-based affirmative action because they would go far beyond university admissions or access to government jobs, they would go much deeper than education reforms, they would expand the range of choices open to all by energetic state intervention, with less sensitivity to the "transcendental institutionalism" for which Sen criticizes Rawls's theory (Sen 2009), or to careful procedural-ism; and they would aspire to go well beyond the subsistence levels guar-anteed by *Bolsa Família.*

Robert Taylor's exposition of the implications of Rawls's model for affirmative action concludes that it does not allow for any kind of quotas, although it does allow for many other initiatives such as supplementary courses, tutoring, mentoring, and targeted programmes like Head Start,[9] with no limitations on resources or any time horizon. The reason for the exclusion of quotas from the Rawlsian schema has to do with the proce-duralist condition that excludes any prejudging of the outcome: that is, there should be no preset percentage of black students or, for example, women judges. At best this interpretation of Rawls allows, in extreme situations, for very small quotas to "open the door."

Rawls, as the classic modern exponent of a liberal concept of justice, is highly relevant because in their denigration of universalism and the concept of equal treatment of all citizens before the law, quota advo-cates are attacking liberalism in general, not just the neoliberalism which builds a political model on free and unregulated markets and is routinely branded in so many quarters as the root of all contemporary evils. In an interview in *O Globo* (21 April 2002) Ricardo Henriques (au-thor of the IPEA study described in the previous chapter) reiterated the hostility to formal equality that we have already encountered, say-ing that it was time to "break with that great French republican matrix" according to which "the imperative of equality is the best matrix for any intervention, treating everyone as equal." "This," he went on, "is the most cynical strategy for dealing with the problem" (quoted in Maggie [2005] 2008: 45–46).[10]

The Rawls scheme, and indeed any modern welfare state, assumes that there are circumstances in which it is cynical and therefore unfair to treat someone "equally." Even if there should be an underlying assump-

---

9. Head Start is a programme that "promotes school readiness of children under 5 from low-income families through education, health, social and other services," associated with the Great Society initiatives of the 1960s and 1970s, but still in operation under the auspices of the US Federal Department of Health and Human Services and replicated in the United Kingdom.

10. Another way of formulating the same position is to call for unequals to be treated unequally, but the use of the word "unequal" to describe this differential treatment is mis-leading because normally when someone is described as being treated unequally it is as-sumed that it is to that person's *disadvantage*, whereas the quotas and affirmative actions are meant to be to the person's *advantage*. We shall come back to this puzzle when discussing the ideas on this subject of Antonio Sergio Guimarães.

tion that fairness requires equal treatment, there are others in which fairness requires a person to receive different, or special, treatment. In any case, one should not confuse the positive entitlement to equal treatment before the law with two things that are quite different: on the one hand the privation of a right as a result of a state ignoring a person's disadvantage, leading to maltreatment or neglect; and on the other the consolidation of privilege by a self-reproducing class that can gain extra benefits from universal rights because of its superior material means and privileged access to the state's decision-making. It is a distortion to say that the dissenters' commitment to equality before the law commits them to either of these positions.

It is impossible to offer an absolute, timeless, and universal definition of the individual as a pure impersonal bearer of rights such as that which might be imagined by strict proceduralism. The definition is context dependent and likely to change over time, thus blurring the distinction between the formal and the substantive, or between human, civil, and social rights. The welfare state in Europe was inspired by a concept of citizenship classically summarized in T. H. Marshall's optimistic three-stage evolutionary model from civil through political to social rights. In a classic social democratic welfare state social rights were designed, among other things, to enable people to translate their entitlements to equal treatment under civil and political rights into effective exercise of those rights. The circumstances in which such support can occur have evolved and expanded, allowing for low income, disability, social disadvantage, old age, and other factors. The list of characteristics that should be taken into account when individuals claim special treatment or an exception to formal equality before the law, gets longer and longer, with time and with social mobilization, as new groups gain political consciousness and a voice in the public sphere, but the purpose of the exceptions is to enable both equal treatment and equal exercise of rights, even while remaining faithful to proceduralism and the bureaucratic impersonality it entails. The inclusion of race poses a special sort of problem for the demand for impersonality in a difference-blind procedural regime because it cannot be classified in a bureaucratic way and attempts to do so are often controversial. In future they will become more so as countries (like the United States) accustomed to everyday clarity in race boundaries become increasingly *métissés*.

Robert Taylor's account of Rawls rules out quotas on the grounds that they prejudge the outcome but leads to the conclusion that affirmative action may be a requirement of justice, so long as it is affirmative action in the strict sense, without quotas. This may be a faithful interpretation of Rawls, and may make sense in theory, but in practice it is unrealistic because, as Skrentny showed, the purpose of affirmative action can hardly be anything but the inclusion of a particular excluded group. If the affirmative action does not produce the desired outcome, then its design will have to change. In addition, it can be argued that there are two sorts of grounds for engineering an increased presence in the elite of excluded groups: first, that systematic exclusion of a group is harmful to social cohesion; and, second, that there will be a benefit to all if the potential or unrealized talents of people from excluded groups are fulfilled—as Helio Santos said right at the start of the Brazilian story, though the argument has not been heard of much since then. It will never be a popular argument among antiracist movements because it carries an assumption that they and their followers are in some sense mere auxiliaries in the pursuit of general prosperity. The concern for social cohesion seemed to be in the mind of the "boss of all the bosses" who ruled for decades in Bahia, Antonio Carlos Magalhães, and, despite his right-wing label, mobilized his associates in support of the Estatuto de Igualdade Racial (Racial Equality Statute), the precursor to the quotas law (Sales et al. 2011). In accordance with this reasoning, it could also be argued that, while the quota system, by setting up a separate competition for university admission, does ensure that a certain proportion of students will be from the groups specified, the outcome envisaged is not for them individually but for society as a whole: that is, the quotas can be seen as a procedural device aiming to achieve a societal good, namely, an increase in black and moreno or pardo representation among university graduates and then in the upper echelons of society. The micro-unfairnesses and disappointments of cotistas who fall by the wayside as well as others who fail to be admitted in the general competitions, are then mere details, or a cost worth paying. In these circumstances the Rawls condition of benefit to the most disadvantaged probably is not satisfied because the criterion is race not socioeconomic status.

The movimento negro's rhetoric focused more on recognition and a proportional notion of equality, but although its spokespeople rarely referred explicitly to access to the elite, it is my interpretation that their emphasis on the prestige institutions, and on higher as opposed to lower levels of education, and their lack of interest in ProUni meant that access to the elite was a major underlying, perhaps even unconscious, priority. This is understandable since it is at the elite level that racial exclusion is most visible in Brazil (Biderman and Guimarães 2004) and queries about whether one can distinguish between people of different colour in that monochrome world melt into irrelevance. For example, more than once I have heard from or read of people of an earlier generation—in particular Frei David—being advised in a supposedly "friendly" sort of way that because of their colour they were wasting their time applying to the notoriously elitist Diplomatic Service—a reputation the service itself is trying to undo with its own affirmative action programme. Aspiration to Brazil's Diplomatic Service is a classic expression of high ambition and one that can be achieved in theory by talent and hard work because the path is only through exams and *concursos*. The same can be said of the higher judiciary, finance, and industry and even of the professoriate in the most prestigious universities. In these areas a big push into universities might make a difference to the colour of the elite, so long as the unspoken, "subtle" forms of exclusion can be overcome. Further statistical support for the claim that inequality widens in the upper deciles is provided by Stanley Bailey and his colleagues in an article that was mainly designed to explore the implications of using six different (binary and ternary and multiple) racial classification schemas. Applied to 2,330 people from the 2002 PESB (Pesquisa Social Brasileira—Brazilian Social Survey, also funded in its first two rounds by the Ford Foundation[11]) the six schemas coincide on one point: after controlling for many nonrace factors influencing wage levels, they found that the racial wage gap increases in the "top 10–20%" on all six classification schemes, whereas at the lower levels of the income distribution race-based wage differences can disappear altogether, depending on which classification is used (Bailey et al. 2013: 114–15).

It is in the context of that aspiration that one can understand the irritation of advocates of black recognition and advancement when they are told that it is hard to draw a line between racial groups or that Brazil is a mestiço country. They are not looking to be bank managers or school principals, and they are not satisfied with black prominence in sport and music—they are looking to be movers and shakers, to wield true power.

The demand for proportional representation in universities and the civil service, with major institutions recruiting hundreds of thousands of students or officials, is not compatible with Rawls, who focuses on education as preparation for the labour market in a well-ordered society rather than on outcomes. Furthermore, Rawls had no time—and probably no

---

11. PESB covers much more than race: it s a wide-ranging nationwide survey organized by the Fluminense University in Rio modeled on the US General Social Survey carried out by the National Opinion Research Center.

feel—for the politics of recognition. That politics takes innumerable forms, but here the demand is for visibility (literally) and voice. The demand is also for recognition of past wrongs as entitlement to present benefits, which can hardly be calibrated in the precise way that a Rawlsian approach would require, as in "If your great-grandmother was a slave then you are entitled to so much, but if you had three great-grandparents in the same condition, you get more."

Charles Taylor speaks critically of the "Eurocentered intellectuals" who would make "positive judgments of the worth of cultures that they have not intensively studied" (1992: 70). But here we speak of a recognition that allows people to name themselves and invert the symbolic violence against which many of their intellectual leaders rebel: the violence of silencing and invisibility. This is a qualitative, emotional, and collective demand that is hard to satisfy definitively and is easy to discredit with arguments about genetics, numbers, or colour lines: easy, that is, to discredit in the eyes of some, and impossible to discredit in the eyes of those spokespeople. But the difficulty of satisfying the demand definitively is not a reason to reject it, for even if it will not be satisfied with today's response, resentment will only get more bitter in the face of no response. To be sure we can never claim that the demands of a movement represent a unanimous or even majority view among its constituency, but again, to question its representativeness does not silence it, and as we see in the polemics surrounding quotas and the movimento negro, it can further inflame the rhetoric.

This is why poorly calibrated but wide-ranging remedies are justifiable. The argument conforms to some extent to Sen's critique of Rawls's "transcendental institutionalism," which concentrates on "perfect justice" rather than "relative comparisons of justice and injustice" (Sen 2009: 5). Sen contrasts a focus on arrangements—as in Rawls's proceduralism—with a realization-focused conception of justice (7), a "deontology" that is to be valued in and of itself (23). He therefore disagrees totally with Rawls's rejection of a focus on outcomes. Stated in terms of the demands of the movimento negro, the broad-based promotion of blacks into universities and the civil service is a step toward enhancing their capabilities, to use Sen's favoured concept, and as such can be welcomed independently of the qualifications of each individual candidate. Access for negros and morenos to given university places in proportion to their numbers in the population should take some of them nearer to the elite out of sheer force of numbers, even with the current mixed racial and socioeconomic criteria for quota allocation, since, as the next section shows, the two criteria are somewhat correlated and thus the two sorts of quota should be mutually reinforcing. The Brazilian state walked into this massive experiment absentmindedly (perhaps because it did not require much in the way of resources), and, although the consequences over ten years are largely unforeseeable, they are unlikely to be disastrous.

Race versus Income Quotas and Their Evaluation

When the assessment of eligibility for reparatory justice or scarce state-held resources is based on self-assignment, and when many people may be genuinely uncertain about where they fall on the colour spectrum, then doubts arise concerning the legitimacy or reliability of criteria of eligibility. The alternatives are either a socioeconomic "proxy" that circumvents the dilemmas of racial classification or a mix of race and socioeconomic criteria, as eventually emerged in the 2012 quotas law. But it is worth stating here that the socioeconomic "cut" ("recorte" as policymakers call it, in parallel with the "recorte etnico-racial") plays an ambiguous role in these discussions. Many commentators and several institutions advocated and implemented proxy versions: in order to respond to the pressure for race-based affirmative action, they proceeded on the basis that blacks are on average poor and attend state schools because they cannot afford a private education, so universities could avoid the prickly decision about racial classification by creating quotas for public school graduates or else applying a means test on the assumption that the socioeconomic criterion would replicate symmetrically the notional racial quota. These devices were not universally welcomed, and some criticized them as at best an attempt to deflect race-based and identity-driven demands for recognition and reparation and at worst a denial that there is a problem of racial exclusion.

One effort in this direction was undertaken by UNICAMP. Initially the policy used was to award thirty extra vestibular marks to public school pupils and ten extra marks to negros and pardos. Given that this was out of a total of five hundred, it is not surprising that the proportion of low-income students admitted barely shifted from the starting point of 30 per cent in 2003 (Feres et al. 2013). However, after years of similarly disappointing results, in 2015 the university adopted more generous allowances with the intention that by 2017 half its entrants would be from state schools and 30 percent of them *pretos, pardos,* or *indigenas.* In 2016 it announced that it had achieved the goal one year ahead of time, with 51.9

percent of the 1,714 students admitted having been educated in public schools and 43 percent from those racial groups. Surprisingly, more than 80 percent of those admitted even to the highly competitive medicine course were from public schools.[12]

That figure of 43 percent is striking, and this sort of approach, based exclusively on a socioeconomic criterion (state school education) but applied generously, receives some support from Mendes and his colleagues (2016)—but the support needs qualification. On the basis of 27,415 applicants to the UERJ 2010 vestibular, they find (a) that without the racial quotas young people who are both black and from low-income families would hardly have any chance of admission to prestige courses, and applicants from low-income groups too often do not even achieve the minimum grades required for admission (Mendes et al. 2016: 312); (b) that "in all regressions whites perform better than the other groups," but "the progressive inclusion of control factors leads to a reduction in all the coefficients related to skin colour and, with the exception of the 'indigenous' category, statistical significance remained at the 1 percent level"; and (c) this apparent irrelevance of colour is then strengthened by a simulation in which the allocation of "just 20 per cent of the quota places to deprived applicants from public schools with no racial criterion would raise the proportion of self-declared blacks from 8.6 per cent to 10.5 per cent," bringing the proportion of black students at UERJ "close to the proportion of blacks in the population of Rio de Janeiro state (11.1 per cent)" (Mendes et al. 2016: 321–22). The meaning of the phrase "20 per cent of the quota places" is unclear: presumably the authors mean a 20 percent quota, that is, 20 percent of total places. The "11.1 percent" black population of Rio excludes pardos, but the authors argue that the black-brown division is "neither clear nor stable," so they regard a benefit that shows fairness toward the self-declared pretos as a reasonable criterion of fairness generally. Indeed at one point they speculate that the existing policy "may be fostering inequalities in favour of those who declare themselves 'black'" (314)—something that, as we have seen, is regarded in some circles as precisely the purpose of race quotas. In any case, like any simulation, this one must be treated with caution because so much hangs on the assumptions underlying it, and a small change in assumptions could change the entire conclusion. Finally, they separate out applicants according to the type of prevestibular they have attended

---

12. "51.9% dos aprovados da Unicamp é da escola pública," *Correio Popular*, 11 February 2016; "82% dos aprovados em Medicina na Unicamp são da escola pública," *Estado de São Paulo*, 12 February 2016; see also Venturini and Feres Júnior 2018.

and find, sadly, that the grades of applicants who had studied at the non-paying *comunitario* PVCs did not reflect any benefit from them. Of course, as we have seen in the case of EDUCAFRO, this is not always the only purpose of their leaders, but if reliable, it is disappointing.

The UNICAMP experience and this study may tell us that there are simpler ways to achieve the sought-after compensatory effect, or racial parity, among the students who gain admission than through tortuous questions about racial self-assignment and its authenticity. Despite the lack of a clear causal effect of colour on vestibular marks, the data still reinforce the idea that a socioeconomic quota can help level the playing field for blacks. What it cannot do is compensate for poor schooling unless universities provide supplementary teaching to upgrade poorly prepared entrants. The non-professional PVCs are apparently of little help.

It is therefore not surprising that, citing both Brazilian and US researchers (Saperstein 2006; Muniz 2010), the authors rightly warn that "care must be taken when studying performance differentials between self-declared whites and blacks" (Mendes et al. 2016: 321). As they say, the reporting of one's colour carries all sorts of political and psychological motives, conscious and subconscious, that would destabilize an interpretation based solely on colour—and based therefore also on the effects of discrimination and a legacy of exclusion. The ambiguity of results can be seen in a recent paper by Valente, which used a very large database from the end-of-schooling ENEM test in the state of São Paulo to assess the effects of race on students' marks. The purpose was to see how many of these students would have made the grade for admission to USP, and, controlling for the main intermediate variables, she found a clear negative effect of race: "[T]he odds of being accepted are 34.2 per cent less for black students than for white students and 48.2 per cent less for brown students than for white students" and in Medicine specifically, "the odds of admission into Medicine are 36% less for blacks" compared to whites and (astonishingly) "90% less for browns" (Valente 2016: 9).

Although she refers to the hypotheses advanced by Schwartzman and Marteleto (2012) about the fashion (which Bailey and Peria also remarked upon) for negro identification and self-assignment, Valente says that more research is needed to shed light on this apparently paradoxical finding about the negro-pardo gap—especially when the differences are so stark (Valente 2016: 15). The picture is further complicated by her reminder of the surreal arithmetic of university applications. As in *concursos*, it seems that there is hardly any barrier to entering the process, so tens of thousands enter in the almost certain knowledge that they have no chance at all of admission, thus lowering the odds for everyone but hiding, perhaps, the odds that would appear for different groups once the "no hopers" have been eliminated: "[I]n the case of USP, in November of 2012, about 159,000 people registered for the vestibular, and only 10,982 students were selected" (16). In any case, the Fundação Universitária para o Vestibular (University Foundation for the Management of the Vestibular Examination—FUVEST), which administers entrance examinations for USP, has refused to open its database, which would enable researchers to link individual marks to individual features of the candidates (Rubia Valente, personal communication).

These data show that rough justice in an affirmative action scheme of this kind and on this scale can hardly be avoided. But that is not necessarily an argument against the use of race in this quota system: rules governing quota admissions applying nonracial criteria can also have perverse or unintended effects, as in the case of low-income families that invest in private education and find their children excluded from the state-school quota or when family size distorts socioeconomic classification by per capita income.

However justified, university quotas can still not be properly counted as egalitarian because of the multiple other drivers of inequality in the education system: if benefits are restricted to people who qualify on race grounds and who have completed secondary school and attain adequate marks in the ENEM, those who never even got that far for equally structural and historical reasons are out of the picture. An egalitarian agenda of affirmative action at the university level poses severe problems because, as is widely recognized, it would have to start by abandoning the constitutional prohibition on charging fees of any kind for a public university undergraduate course since that so patently favours the wealthier classes; but no Brazilian politician of any persuasion would dare even to mention such an option on pain of mass demonstrations bringing every major city and public university to a halt for days and weeks. Beyond that, if the group to be included in quotas was limited to persons with very low incomes and was not highly differentiated, then an effect on equality overall might be achieved, but this is not the way the system works. In 2011 the national minimum wage was R$545 while even in the highest-income region of the country—the South—household per capita income was on average only R$700 (*Estatística*, IBGE 2012: 168). Since the quotas have tended to be limited to members of families earning less than *two-and-a-half times* the minimum wage *per capita*, it will be obvious that an extremely large number of people qualify potentially—not only the poorest. There would, however, be little point in tightening this condition, since to lower the income ceiling further would also lower the numbers of those with the educational qualifications necessary to attend university. The effects change as one moves farther down in the prestige hierarchy and farther away from the metropolitan centers: in 2010 the chair of admissions at the Universidade Estadual da Paraiba (State University of Paraiba—UEPB) in Campina Grande in the Northeast told me that opening the university to public school students had lowered its standards and discouraged a certain proportion of potential students who now chose private universities. In short, quotas may have gone as far as they can because of the shortage of qualified school graduates. Valente's results would qualify but not invalidate this point. Race quotas can still be defended as a response to the demand for recognition, but we should have no illusions about their ability to reduce inequality in the population.

In another study, Valente, together with Brian Berry, undertakes a statistical exercise to find out how the cotistas fare after getting into university, when the worst performers have been eliminated (Valente and Berry 2017). Whereas Mendes and his colleagues used marks from entrance exams at one institution alone, Valente and Berry use very large MEC data sets from the Exame Nacional de Desempenho de Estudantes (National Student Progress Examination—ENADE), a nationwide test, which has replaced the *provão*, taken by undergraduates at public and private universities in their first and last years of study as a means of assessing the universities' performance rather than that of the students themselves. Valente and Berry set out to test fears that quotas may be opening the way to a flood of underachieving students set up to fail by overgenerous admissions allowances in the way described by Sander and Taylor in the United States. On the basis of test results for slightly over a million students in four annual exercises in the period 2009–12 they found that in public universities "students admitted through affirmative action . . . score 0.70 points less on the total ENADE score than students admitted through traditional methods" (20). However they then applied further models and found that this was largely a consequence of the negative performance of cotistas admitted on the income criterion and of students in the "other," much smaller, affirmative action category covering people with disabilities. The main finding is that students admitted through public high school quotas and a combination of racial and social quotas actually performed slightly better than those admitted through the main, nonquota competition. Although, inside these averages, race did have a negative impact on performance, it was much smaller than that of income. Note that this dataset is unusual (a) in that 75 percent of the sample are in private universities, and (b) in providing data on students gaining admission through a pure income test separately from the proxy public school channel—a category which is rarely documented for public universities. In the private universities, where overall standards are lower but competition for affirmative action places is fierce because they are allocated on the basis of ENEM marks and bring full or partial exemption from fees (ProUni), it seems that all categories of affirmative action beneficiaries did better overall: again, they were held back by low income, but only to a small extent. As the authors say, these results are subject to further review and elaboration as the quotas system is applied across the entire public system and in a more uniform way, but the policy implications are certainly not negative for supporters of racial quotas as a path to inclusion. Furthermore, they would be a response to those who complain that race quotas allow low achievers into university at the expense of others who have better marks in entrance exams: rather these results point to the interpretation that black students are underperforming due to racial disadvantage at the admissions stage, but that after entering as cotistas they begin to perform at a level nearer to their true potential. Once again it must be emphasized that this does not take into account those who, although they have completed their schooling, never reach the gates of university because of their low marks. Despite their gratifying performance, cotistas, are still held back somewhat by race, and, the negative effects of low income continue to be felt and seem harder to overcome.

Further data on post-admission performance are provided by Mendes in another analysis based on individual students' course marks (similar to a grade point average, or GPA) (Mendes 2014). Using UERJ data he found that, although 30 percent of (combined race and income-based) cotistas dropped out, they were more likely to finish their course and graduate than were their colleagues who had entered via the open competition. (For various reasons dropout rates should not be interpreted as denoting academic failure.) That is the good news, but—echoing Bok and Bowen on the United States—those cotista graduates had systematically lower marks than their peers, and this differential was greatest in the more difficult courses. The university's ProIniciar scheme may have helped with its tiny grant of R$300 per month (38–48), as did tuition schemes in the wealthier universities covered by Bok and Bowen, but not enough to bring their marks up to the average.

If race quotas do more for recognition than for equality, one has to conclude that the policies either of race-based or mixed quotas are something of a wager and cannot be easily defended as carefully calibrated social engineering. To require such policies to live up to a high standard of precise effects is excessive: they are policies of reparatory justice and redistribution of state-controlled resources. In any case evaluations can be undertaken in many ways and on the basis of an infinity of different databases, so the evaluation on a nationwide or even regional basis is never going to be definitive, and this uncertainty is compounded by the underlying fluidity of colour classification and self-assignment and the background of a polemical atmosphere in which one side or another will always find arguments and stylized facts to cast doubt on inconvenient findings. At the same time, though, to persist with the schemes if they achieve little or are counterproductive risks bringing the whole idea of affirmative action, and by implication of reparatory measures generally, into disrepute. A comparable scenario was foreseen by the Supreme Court when it concluded its decision by saying that affirmative action policies based on quotas could only be justified so long as the discrimination in question persisted.

Before concluding this discussion, it should once again be recalled that these debates have focused too heavily on elite institutions. The first thing I was told at UNEB in 2008 was that this was a university that had been born already in 1982 with an "affirmative action vocation," focused principally on teacher training, with satellite campuses located in several places outside the state capital, and it was a pioneer in instituting quotas for black applicants, under the leadership of a black woman rector. In 2008, twenty thousand of its forty thousand students were still on in-service programmes specially established to upgrade the qualifications of schoolteachers. In these circumstances race-based quotas may not have been controversial, but they also may not have made much difference when the target population consisted of poorly paid and underqualified schoolteachers, many in the interior of Bahia.

In Brazil's education system, as in most others, there are numerous financial and nonfinancial sources of support for students, though free residence accommodation and meals, even for a minority, must be quite unusual. All sorts of subsidies are provided by universities from their own budgets, as we saw in the case of UERJ. Thus in 2010 the UEPB offered a battery of support for low-income students, including eight hundred places with free board and lodging in a university residence, and helped rural students by operating satellite campuses for a quarter of its students outside the main centre of Campina Grande (population four hundred thousand). The neighbouring Universidade Federal de Campina Grande (Federal University of Campina Grande—UFCG), which also had several campuses but fewer students (though still a sizable fifteen thousand), offered six hundred free places in its residences and served fifteen hundred free meals a day to low-income students, as well as providing twelve hundred means-tested grants (*bolsas*). Bolsas, when available, tend to be small or even symbolic (R$300 per month was the highest figure I heard, equaling three-fifths of the minimum wage at the time), but the free residential and food benefits are valuable for students from low-income families. The more prestigious Universidade Federal de Pernambuco (the Federal University in the neighbouring state of Pernambuco—UFPE) also provided free residence and meals for some students. Widening access took many forms, of which one was allowing extra marks in the vestibular exam to students from underprivileged sectors; another was to build two satellite campuses, with student residences, in the interior of the state. But still that university selected only six thousand from thirty-seven thousand candidates overall in 2010 and was unable to fill the vacancies in engineering due to a lack of qualified candidates. And at the UEPB, only four thousand out of a surprisingly large number of applicants (thirty-two thousand) were admitted. It must always be remembered that so long as students from low-income families have trouble reaching even the minimum qualifying marks the effect of these benefits on equality will be constrained. The race quotas may well increase the diversity of university student bodies, but because they to some extent dilute the socioeconomic barrier, their effect on equality of educational opportunity among socioeconomic groups will be limited.

Another gesture in the direction of affirmative action is the practice of sending untrained current students to teach aspiring ones. This is not unusual—it is used by UFCG, which sends volunteer students to teach on a prevestibular for local public school pupils, and, as we saw, by USP's INCLUSP programme. It can be interpreted as encouraging community contribution and solidarity or as providing these upgrading courses at almost zero cost. We shall see that Frei David uses the method extensively in EDUCAFRO, where teachers are not paid at all save occasional travel money. But the data from UERJ also raised the question of whether, whatever its consciousness-raising merits, such teaching by untrained teachers is academically worthwhile (Mendes 2016).

Sociological Interpretations

In an article originally published in 1996 (Guimarães 1996, 2003) and also in the essays in his book *Racismo e anti-racismo no Brasil* (Guimarães 2005b), in the early days of the quota debates, the sociologist Antonio Sergio Guimarães took many positions that appeared to place him in the camp of the dissidents: he opposed attacks on universalism and individualism, described by him as values that underpin western democracies; he opposed a "proportionalist or collectivist project that has no basis in concrete reality"; and he did not think that opponents of quotas were closet racists hiding behind an individualist facade. He also emphasized the requirement that affirmative action policies be "anchored" in policies of universalization and educational improvement. Without these anchors they would only benefit a minority. He quoted the findings of research at UFRJ conducted by Marcia Contins and Luiz Carlos Sant'Ana as part of Yvonne Maggie's Ford-funded project Movimentos Negros e a Atuaçao do Estado no Rio de Janeiro (Movimento Negro and the State in Rio de Janeiro) in which leaders of the movimento negro expressed serious reservations about the limited reach of quotas: they argued that they just created a black elite and did not resolve the problem of racism and that very few blacks reached positions of power anyway. In addition the respondents remarked on the "ghettoization" of issues of concern to the black population by their being entrusted only to special agencies, exempting other institutions from confronting the problem (Contins and Sant'Ana 1996: 217).

But Guimarães did not think these arguments clinched the anti-quotas case: he also recalled that the core problem in Brazil was that "discrimination is rooted in an assumption of natural privilege for certain groups of people" (2005b: 195). In line with the well-known formulas of Roberto da Matta (da Matta 1986, 1991; Hess and Da Matta 1995), Guimarães wrote that "racial inequalities are naturalized and people are subsumed within their networks of connections, while the rights of individuals are subordinated to property rights," and these are the decisive forces blocking opportunity for blacks. Agreeing with the critics of an illusory meritocracy and universalism, he said this underlying inequality of treatment in social relations made a mockery of the formal equality of treatment, and therefore "we cannot continue to offer formally equal treatment to people who, in practice, are treated as if they belong to an inferior station" (195).[13] So the campaign for quotas would be better

---

13. His meaning was complicated by the use of the word "equal"—and of the Portuguese "igual"—because it signifies both "the same" and "socially equal": "não podemos

conveyed as a call to abandon the hypocritical practice of offering "opportunities on the same terms to everyone, even to those who are treated as if they belong to an inferior station": the state, he believed, also reinforces a hierarchy of unequally distributed social and material capital expressed in a myriad of small interstitial or capillary pressures and interests, and in social institutions, compounded by the everyday habits of social life. Later in the same passage, Guimarães made it clear that he regarded this correction of the everyday subordination of a vast contingent of people of low status as extremely exceptional—unlike others who would assume that once quotas have been established they would be perpetuated as standard practice: "[F]or this, and only this reason, it is necessary at certain times and in some quite specific spheres of society, to accept the treatment of the underprivileged as privileged people" (195).

By "privileged social sphere" Guimarães may have meant the "top," the elite, or the middle class because access of blacks to the professional middle class—the strata that require a university degree as a minimum qualification—is still paltry, and this would fit with other writings of his where he makes it clear that the pressure for quotas comes from a nascent black middle class and that the development of such a class should be nurtured. After the 1988 Constitution went into effect, rights-based claims for blacks focused for the first time on affirmative actions, whereas previously the focus had been on removing discriminatory practices, as he noted in another paper (Guimarães 2003). Young blacks who were advancing in an education system of whose poor quality they were painfully aware were finding that to earn a worthwhile qualification they had to attend private schools and universities, which in addition to being expensive were also offering poor-quality and low-status qualifications that lacked the recognition of those received at state institutions, even if formally they exhibited the same level and subject. Having overcome one or two hurdles, by completing high school and working their way through university, they were then faced with further obstacles, and Guimarães notes that, although broad swathes of the lower middle class—the generously defined "new middle class" much trumpeted by Lula and Dilma and by the economist Marcelo Neri (Neri 2010, 2011)—were affected by this squeeze, it was those who identified as negros who took up the fight even though they were by no means alone in suffering the consequences of a segmented education system.[14]

---

continuar a dispensar um tratamento formalmente igual aos que, de fato, são tratados como pertenecentes a um estamento inferior."

14. According to Ricardo Paes de Barros, at that time a senior official in IPEA and au-

"Am I Black after All?": Changing Identifications and Racial Affiliations

How could the inherent fluidity of colour assignment and its relation with socioeconomic status be combined in interpreting the pressure for a specifically skin colour criterion? Could this interpretation by Guimarães be rephrased in terms of an awakening by people who, feeling deeply frustrated and thwarted (having had their hopes raised in their school years and then finding new obstacles in their path when trying to get in to university, and later, when facing the labour market), ask themselves if their "bad luck" or poor chances are not just a matter of luck or fate but a result of their skin colour? This would not be surprising since they may feel deeply frustrated and thwarted, having had their hopes raised in school for years only to encounter new obstacles first when trying to get in to university and later when facing the labour market. In this case we would be in the presence not of a shift from "class" to "race," nor of some kind of opportunistic manipulation, but rather of an awakening. People who might be on the borderlines of blackness, whose self-image as mestiços or morenos is a way of demarcating themselves as separate from, even perhaps superior to, the negros and the pretos, might begin to look at themselves differently and demarcate themselves more emphatically from the white population while lowering their resistance to drawing closer to the negro. Maybe this is merely a matter of classification, but it might also be a matter of "groupness"—a "sense of belonging to a distinctive, bounded, solidary group" (Brubaker and Cooper 2000: 20). It is becoming commonplace to observe, on the basis of surveys and qualitative research, that "high-status and darker skinned persons are especially likely to choose *negro* today," leading to the view that "usage of *negro* is . . . likely to continue

---

thor of an earlier study of Brazilian income distribution for the World Bank (Barros et al. 2010), after an extensive study of thirty different criteria, the government established three strata of the middle class, based on monthly per capita family income: the lower middle class (R$291–441), the middle middle class (R$441–641), and the upper middle class (R$641–1,019) (announcement dated 24 July 2013). The subject returns at the end of this chapter. In a recent article Celia Lessa Kerstenetzky and others, including the leading authority on social statistics, Nelson do Valle Silva, have provided detailed survey evidence from the IBGE that underlines the enormous range of living standards covered by Neri's category and above all the lack of a stable sustainable basis for a middle-class lifestyle among them. Although it could also be said that Kerstenetzky's criteria (including owning a car and having a household head with a university education) would apply more to an "upper middle class" and err in the other direction, the generosity of Neri's simple income criteria, in conferring middle-class status on people whose lifestyle is not very securely based, is not in question (Kerstenetzky et al. 2015).

growing if levels of educational attainment continue to increase for the general population" (Bailey and Telles 2006)—a "radical chic," but small, demographic. Already in a 1995 survey, Telles explains that people with higher education were almost three times more likely to describe themselves as "negro" than those who had only attended primary school, and those who had attended middle school were twice as likely to do so (2004: 97, and tables 4.5 and 4.6).[15] Bailey, with Telles again, asks whether, because this tendency is particularly visible among the young, it might be a "passing fad" (Bailey and Telles 2006: 94), but it does not seem to have diminished with time. Telles's data are consistent with Guimarães's tracing of the quotas movement to the rise, and perhaps the frustration, of a black middle class. It might be equally justifiable, however, to ask whether this is not about a middle-class *tout court* without racial qualification, some or maybe many of whom are discovering that they may have racial issues to confront, and that they may indeed be victims of structural discrimination. This would explain to them the frustration that comes from poor-quality schooling, for-profit higher education, and blocked opportunities. They may therefore see no inconsistency in retaining an identity as brown or white, even while classifying themselves black in the eyes of the state, as Luisa Schwartzman explained. After all, the state invents quotas for victims of discrimination: a person may hold to their white identity even while reckoning that they are a victim in the meaning of the state, as they understand it.

This hypothesis runs counter to the long-standing finding that Brazilians tend to deny that they themselves are victims of racism even while recognizing that racism exists in the society. In the opening chapters of her book *Dreaming Equality*, Robin Sheriff elaborated the coexistence within Brazilian discourse and social interaction of a binary classification system with a polysemic way of speaking about skin colour: the binary system is alluded to as the subject of irony and evasion, of awkwardness and euphemism, and jokes that can backfire (Sheriff 2001). This is not so surprising: just as many people would rather not be told or reminded that their ancestors were slaves, so they may prefer not to say or be told that they are victims of racial discrimination, which may make them feel weak or humiliated. The rhetoric of victimhood does not suit everyone (though it may suit them in surprising ways). On the opposite side of this field of claims we can then find people who

15. See pages 80–81 of the Portuguese translation by Ana Arruda Callado of Telles 2004; see also Venturini and Feres Júnior 2018.

adopt a black identity but do not at the same time claim to be victims themselves or even concern themselves much with the victimhood of others—they are uncoupling black identity from victimhood. And then there are many who see in their own or others' black identity a vehicle for antiracist militancy. This kind of unpacking, or what some might call "resemanticization," of identity labels has yet to be explored in the Brazilian or other contexts, just as one should question the automatic association of skin colour with income that has long been set aside in the United States.

There are two (not mutually exclusive) global explanations for the upsurge in black identification and pressure for improved access for black and other dark-skinned students to prestige universities. One of these, which maybe owes more to the cultural inclinations of observers than to everyday inquiry, is that blackness has become fashionable and so is associated with youth cultures—leading to Bailey and Telles's hunch that it might decline with age. This may indeed come to pass, though, by the same logic, future cohorts may also follow that same fashion. But the other hypothesis, which is consistent with the messiness of the survey evidence we have tried to dissect from Schwartzman and the UnB survey, is that there may be a genuine pattern of consciousness-raising whereby people begin to question their own self-image as mere victims of bad luck or cease to blame themselves for not studying hard enough. They begin instead to wonder whether they, too, have not been victims of a pattern of discrimination and, so to speak, look at themselves again in the mirror and think, "Maybe I am black after all,"[16] or "maybe that is the real reason why I was turned down at that interview." This could be seen as the inverse of the once-popular idea that intermediate categories between black and white ("mulato," "pardo," "mestiço," "moreno") were an "escape hatch" (Degler 1971) or safety valve and an obstacle to the development of a black protest movement. Here, in contrast, we may be seeing the black movement acting to convince those people that escape is possible but only thanks to activism in the cause of the black population that includes them but somehow denies or relativizes their status as moreno, pardo, or mulato. They may also be people who, while readily admitting that there is racial discrimination or injustice in their country, would never have thought that it was of concern to them

---

16. In this they would be harking back to a friend of the famous sociologist and literary critic Antonio Candido, who, on reading Gilberto Freyre's *Casa-grande e senzala* at the time of its publication in 1933, remarked, "Acho que sou mulato" (I guess I am mulatto) (Lund and McNee 2006: 10; Lehmann 2008: 208).

personally—and now are changing that view. *De te fabula narratur!* Research on these matters is far more developed in the United States, and so it is interesting to note that a recent paper, which also references the articles I have referenced by Luisa Schwartzman and by Francis and Tannuri-Pianto, notes that in the United States "people of interracial and interethnic ancestry often spend years grappling with their identities, incorporating or rejecting labels based on their interactions and the setting in which they are socialized" (Davenport 2016: 60).

But who counts themselves and who is counted by others as occupying one of these intermediate categories? Telles presented data from a 1995 national survey indicating that people who identified themselves as *pardos* but were classified by interviewers as *brancos* had significantly higher incomes (26 percent higher) than those who were classified both by themselves and by interviewers as pardos: he took this as evidence that the economic positions of pardos and negros are more similar than data based only on self-assignment might indicate. But it also moves me to reiterate the point that socioeconomic status is signaled by much more than the colour of one's skin. To begin with, it is necessary to distinguish race from skin colour because, as Antonio Sergio Guimarães has been saying recently (in lectures delivered at Cambridge University in April 2017), race refers to numerous other physical features apart from skin colour, and then we have to remember that socioeconomic status is further signaled by such things as language use, accent, modes of dress, and musical tastes—things the interviewer would observe even while the interviewees, asked what their "race/colour" is (in the standard Brazilian formula that joins *raça* and *cor* in the same census question), interpret the question in terms of skin colour and state that they are "pardo." In the United States the situation is different because in that country colour is so much more closely associated with accent, cultural preferences, and place of residence, even if the pattern is slowly changing.

In any case, who are we, the observers, to challenge those people's self-assignment? If relatively wealthy people count themselves as dark skinned (pardo), it seems somewhat perverse to decree them to be branco (Telles 2004: table 6.3) unless one allows that "branco" means more than skin colour, as in the previous paragraph. If this happened on a large scale (which it does not) it would look like a mission to perpetuate a narrative of white domination in the face of evidence to the contrary. The counterpart observation to be drawn from Telles's table, which is based on earlier research (Telles and Lim 1998: 469), is that already in 1995 the idea that Brazilians tend to "whiten" their image if the opportunity arises was being questioned, since people whose income might be thought to lead them to present a whitened image to the world were not doing so, or were not doing so very much. Another group, which self-classified as pardo but was judged to be preto by interviewers, declared an income 12 percent lower than the "consistently described" pardos. These people might be thought of as "whitening"—that is, presenting themselves as lighter skinned than their income might warrant—thus fitting the "ideologia de branqueamento" (ideology of whitening) so decried by activists, but they were far fewer in proportion than the self-described pardos who were reclassified as whites. Further indication that Brazilians seem to be less drawn to "whitening" than they are assumed to have been in the past is found in another table in the same article, which seems to show that where there was disagreement between interviewees and their interviewers it tended to go in the opposite direction from what the whitening thesis might predict: 20 percent of those who self-classified as pardo were classified by the interviewers as white, and 40 percent of those who self-classified as black were classified by the interviewers as pardo (Telles and Lim 1998: 469). The trend continues in more recent publications: Marteleto made a comparison of race labeling of themselves and their children by parents between 1982 and 2007, using the PNAD survey, and found not only that the overall levels of education had improved dramatically, at least in terms of school years and university courses completed, but also that the proportion of people labeling themselves black had more than doubled among both men and women with secondary and higher education—though the proportion in 2007 was still below 3.5 percent. Previously there prevailed a simple but nonetheless reasonable assumption that since there is a general tendency to have children with people of a similar educational level, so as blacks become better educated they would be likely to choose partners with similar education and therefore lighter skin than their own, and that they would then most likely label their children's colour lighter than their own (Marteleto 2012). In fact this has been advanced as one reason (among others) for the finding of persistent low incomes and education of blacks (Schwartzman 2009a): a version of the whitening thesis but also a statistical artifact. But Marteleto finds that the probability of black fathers or mothers labeling their children black had gone from negative to positive in those twenty-five years. If the numbers were not so small, one could begin to talk of a "darkening thesis," replacing the "ideology of whitening," albeit one that will take a long time to influence more than a select minority.

The story does not end there. Before we can draw out this idea, Telles and his associates arrive to bring us back to earth, taking the notion of an impartial observer one stage further with the use of a colour palette ("pigmentometer") whereby interviewers in their thousand-person 2010 survey assessed a person's colour classification on the basis not only of the darkness or lightness of their skin on a ten-point scale (Silva and Paixão 2014; Telles 2014), but also on classifications of hair (kinky, curled, or straight). Once again an element of whitening reappears: although on self-assignment blacks were slightly better educated than browns, the palette showed a straightforward pattern of years of education rising in tune with lightening skin colour, with the "hair factor" accentuating the pattern (Silva and Paixão 2014: 204–6). The implications of these findings for affirmative action policies based on self-assignment are not evident because the pigmentometer measures incremental differences while quotas are based on a binary segmentation of the population, and in any case the differences between self-assigned blacks and browns are small, but it does point again to the difference between quotas for recognition and quotas for less inequality. As ever, much depends on the purpose of the policy: if it aims to reduce overall inequality, then it should probably keep to socioeconomic allocation of quotas, since quite a few people who sincerely view themselves as black but are not among the poor are potential beneficiaries of race-based quotas. On the other hand, if the purpose is to recognize blacks and further incorporate them so that many more can join the elite, then the race criterion would be suitable. Once again, I emphasize that this second purpose is perfectly reasonable.

These observations converge to an overall picture in which Brazilians have become less resistant to describing themselves as black; or more precisely, middle- and lower-middle-class Brazilians have chosen increasingly to make a positive choice of black identity. They chime with those of Bailey, quoted above. But more broadly, and taken together with the earlier, somewhat speculative, interpretation derived from Antonio Sergio Guimarães, they constitute an invitation to think about racial identity and also about public discourse on the subject in the light of massive social changes that have taken place in Brazil not only since Gilberto Freyre produced his "model" in the early twentieth century but also since the generations of structuralists set new terms of debate in the early postwar period and later in the 1980s (see Telles 2004: chap. 3; Skidmore 1993, 2002). Education has intruded into the lives of every social stratum, millions more young people reach secondary school, and even the numbers in higher education are in the millions. Despite urban residential segregation by income, people of different income and racial groups cannot avoid constant contact in their daily lives, and continued extreme inequality has not prevented the expansion of the urban lower middle class. Individuals encounter and deploy the vocabulary of race in multiple contexts, pejoratively, ironically, and positively, and it is publicly invoked in connection with religion, police violence, and inequality of life chances. Catchphrases will no longer suffice, nor will "theories of Brazil," like those of Sergio Buarque de Holanda or Gilberto Freyre or Roberto da Matta,[17] any more than would a "theory of Europe" or a "theory of the United States."

The unbundling of race mentioned above seems to parallel the wide acceptance of race and its field of associations as the provider of a terminology that sums up resentment against inequality but also as an expression of pride or positive "groupness" (Brubaker and Cooper 2000; Brubaker 2002). Where once observers voiced their frustration with a public discourse that seemed to them to be enamoured of racial democracy and impervious to the reality of racial discrimination, now some of them, like Bailey (2009), are understandably frustrated by its effectiveness as a multipurpose simplifying cipher for all sorts of inequality, as a term of abuse, and also as a vehicle for the demand to be named. But for politicians and activists, the resulting simplifications are a gift from heaven.

Distinction at Bay

We end by asking how this endless academic debate about race affects the life of academia itself. The protagonists, after all, are people with a skin colour who belong to a social class, and the inequalities incessantly documented and denounced in the campaign for recognition and access were also a feature, or at least a subliminal feature, of the debates. Opponents of quotas and classification tended to be more prestigious, or at least to exhibit higher levels of cultural and symbolic capital, than supporters: they had long held chairs in leading universities of Rio and São Paulo and visiting positions at universities in Europe and the United States; many had been associated with well-connected think tanks such as

---

17. I refer to works such as Buarque de Holanda's *Raizes do Brasil* (which yielded the phrase "homen cordial"; or Freyre, whom we have mentioned; or da Matta's "voce sabe com quem está falando?" (Do you realize who you are talking to?) (da Matta 1991; Hess and da Matta 1995).

CEBRAP), which, initially funded by the Ford Foundation, led the way in formulating a strategy for democratic and peaceful transition in the 1970s and early 1980s. Broadly speaking, they were children of the 1960s who had been schooled in the *marxisant* social science of their generation and had been opponents, and in not a few cases victims, of the military regime of 1964–84, when social sciences became a broad-based academic constituency throughout Brazil. They were also from the upper middle classes in a country that in the 1960s barely had a middle class at all, and they were the privileged ones who studied at university before the advent of mass higher education. Like the most prominent among them, Fernando Henrique Cardoso (leading light of CEBRAP), many (though not all) of this generation, which produced numerous brilliant intellectuals, followed a gradual evolution to a more social democratic or liberal position, but this also meant that many remained firm universalists, hostile to populism and corporatism and thus also distrustful of a policy of quotas for any racial group.

Cardoso's administration can be seen as marking the high point of the predominance of that generation, which despite their politics benefited from the military government's expansion of public higher education and held many leading positions in subsequent governments of varying stripes between 1984 and 2002. The PSDB, which attracted so many of them, especially in its São Paulo power base, drawing them away from early sympathies for the trade-union-based PT, gradually shifted toward the centre or even the centre-right in opposition to the PT, insofar as left and right have any meaning in the Brazilian parliamentary context. During the Cardoso government the rivalry between the PT and the PSDB became bitter, starting from the personal hostility between their leaders and trickling down to the Congress, the intelligentsia, academic life, and the rank and file. If one word were offered to provide the cynosure of this rift it would be "neoliberalism" and especially the (relatively limited) deregulation and privatization undertaken during Cardoso's government. But when Lula came to power and implemented economic policies almost identical to those of his predecessor, while also constructing a coalition with the same allies on the right, minus of course the PSDB itself, including even the landed interest of the "ruralistas," the rift became less ideological and more tribal.

This is the background to the polarization of opinion on these issues of affirmative action and classification among the intelligentsia, which can become quite bitter even in private conversation. Note that the camps are not pitting "whites" against "blacks," nor does anyone deny the reality of racial exclusion. Yet the bitterness ran deep: for example, as we parted after a long interview, a leading figure in the movimento negro described anthropologists as the *cafiches* (pimps) of the Indians, blacks, and others and said that those who deny the existence of race should return their diplomas and doctorates, which are all about race: had they not made their careers out of the blacks and were they not now denying that they exist?

These remarks reveal a certain racial tension, which is not entirely unique: sometimes, in the nooks and crannies, there are hints. We can see such a hint in a 2003 publication from the usually highly technical INEP. (Once again we see militancy penetrating the bureaucracy, though in the case of INEP it was a unique instance.) Introduced by the editor as a collection by "autores militantes" (several of whom are highly respected academics), it was designed to commemorate National Black Consciousness Day by publishing a series of papers about access to higher education. Yet what seems to me to be a carefully crafted paragraph by Valter Silvério reveals a racial dimension to the tension in academic disputes: Silvério says that certain authors and texts only accord to the movimento negro a very "timid" place in their interpretations, and that this leads one to formulate hypotheses (by which he means suspicions) about "racism in the academic field," and about the superficial acquaintance even among authors expert in the subject with the organization of contemporary social movements. And then he goes on to comment on those writers' own criticisms, levied against black intellectuals, of "mistakes" or "errors" (scare quotes in the original) derived from their American counterparts—mistakes and errors that are then contrasted sarcastically with the "well-founded, depoliticized and accurate contribution" of other, Brazilian, "non-black interpreters" (Silvério 2003: 71). The assumption has to be that the bibliographic references that follow are all to white Brazilian academics (which indeed they are).[18] The language is coded, and the essay is hardly published in a place that is going to command much publicity, but it does give a rare insight into a sense of re-

---

18. "Um conjunto de hipóteses de como opera o racismo no campo acadêmico, . . . o pouco conhecimento que vários autores, alguns inclusive que lidam com o tema, têm do movimento e das novas formas de organização dos movimentos sociais contemporâneos. Um problema adicional tem sido . . . uma certa acusação da existência de 'equívocos' ou 'erros' interpretativos e analíticos, por parte de intelectuais negros e/ou do movimento negro que imitam e/ou copiam o seu congênere norte-americano, contrabalançada pela rica, bem fundamentada, despolitizada e acertada contribuição de outros intérpretes não-negros" (Silvério 2003: 71). The authors and texts cited were Fry 2000; Grin 2001; Maggie 2001; Schwarcz 1999; and Sansone 1998.

sentiment against the racially tinged "hauteur" of the white academic elite, Silvério's outlook is further illustrated by his remark to me in our interview that the black people's agenda had been "captured" by people who had no record of commitment to the cause. For him, the campaign had taken the cause onto the national stage, but black people were not adequately included in decision-making forums. This, he remarked resignedly, is the way Brazil is (uma coisa do Brasil).

The gulf between the camps was not only ideological: it was also social and probably generational—something we saw at work in the edited anti-quotas volume *Divisões Perigosas*. The social gap can be gauged from an enumeration of the signatories of manifestoes sent to the Brazilian Congress and the Supreme Court by groups of intellectuals in 2006 and 2007 concerning legislative proposals and judicial decisions that eventually were concretized in 2012.[19] The mere fact of the writing and publication of these manifestoes, signed exclusively by academics with their institutional and departmental affiliations, is an illustration of the political standing of universities and the academic profession in Brazilian public life. For they were concerned not only with a matter specific to their professional lives but also with the broad issue of race equality and the Estatuto de Igualdade Racial (Racial Equality Statute), which was being actively considered at the same time after lying dormant for a long time in the Senate. They also continued to be recalled for years in conversations and publications on the subject.

The June 2006 manifesto in support of a proposed "quotas law" had 421 signatories (excluding students) of whom only 79 (18.8 percent) were from the following five universities, chosen because they are the foremost institutions in what is widely recognized as the "golden triangle" of Rio, São Paulo, and Brasilia: USP, UNICAMP, UnB, UFRJ, and UERJ. In contrast, there were two dissenting manifestoes, a short one sent to the National Congress to protest the draft Estatuto da Igualdade Racial and a longer one sent to the Supreme Court, which was in the process of deciding on the constitutionality of admissions quotas. Both of these were signed by 113 people, though they were not exactly the same ones, among whom 40.7 and 42.5 percent were from those five institutions. All three lists of signatories were heavily dominated by social sciences and the humanities. It is a very rough index, but the contrasting percentages do surely tell us that the supporters of quotas were more likely to be located

19. The two manifestoes appeared, among many other places, in the *Folha de São Paulo*, July 6, 2006. They can be read at the following site: http://www1.folha.uol.com.br/folha/educacao/ult305u18773.shtml

nearer to the social and economic periphery.[20] The authors of the pro-quota manifesto, published just a month later, have no doubts as to their opponents' position in the social hierarchy: they describe the "113"—a number that remained fixed in the collective memory—as belonging to "elite institutions," and as "members of the elite of a multiethnic and multiracial society with a recent history of slavery and systematic genocide." Of course, the signatories are not a sample of opinion, but the comparison does show that anti-quotas activism was concentrated in these institutions. In the end, despite their undoubted cultural and social capital, the dissenters did not win the battle: but they could be said to have "held the line" on two central issues of concern to them, namely racial classification and the efficacy in terms of social justice or collective benefit of race-based quotas. In the end, as we know, the quotas law did not openly espouse binary race classification (though by combining pretos and pardos in one category, together with the indigenous, for the purposes of quota qualification, it did do so in practice) and did not adopt a purely racial criterion for quota place allocation either, combining it with socioeconomic criteria based on students' household income and their type of schooling.

Conclusion

I have analyzed the idea of affirmative action as practiced in Brazil in the light of a limited range of contemporary liberal democratic ideas, above all those associated with Rawls, but in the end one cannot expect practical politics to live up to the demanding purism of Rawls's fairness tests, and I fell back on Sen's capabilities approach, which is less finely calibrated. I would argue that to clarify underlying purposes and also differences of opinion it is necessary to consider the difference between the pursuit of racial equality, of reparation, of consciousness-raising in the name of self-recognition, and of social justice or reduced overall social inequality. On the basis of this discussion it seems to me that the real issue at stake has been access of blacks to the elite and that this argument is reinforced by the crude data in Ricardo Henriques's IPEA paper showing that most of the racial (black-white) inequality in Brazil is due to the absence of blacks in the top 5 percent of income earners, and by the careful survey results of Biderman and Guimarães and of Stanley Bailey and his colleagues, both of

---

20. São Paulo's USP was in 2012 on the verge of joining the top two hundred world universities compiled by the London-based *Times Higher*, but it remained there in 2014. UNICAMP ranked between 301st and 350th but was 28th in the rankings of universities established in the last fifty years.

which show a similar pattern using more elaborate and reliable statistical methods (Biderman and Guimarães 2004; Bailey et al. 2013). An early paper by Telles (1994) based on a very large data set from seventy-four metropolitan areas in Brazil in 1980 also showed that in the upper reaches of Brazilian society race trumps class and that, although industrialization had reduced racial inequalities among blue-collar workers, it had left them unaffected or even more unequal at the managerial and professional levels, even when controlling for education. The pattern may have changed since 1980, because of the development of the middle and above all lower middle class and, perhaps more important for the present purposes, the slow and in the long run perhaps limited replacement of the "ideology of whitening" with an "ideology of darkening." Thus, the recent interpretation by Guimarães of a "racial formation" constituted by negros and morenos as a defensive homogeneous community could appear in a different light as an inclusive category reaching out and indeed upwards in the social hierarchy (Guimarães 2017: 10). The evidence that upwardly mobile blacks are less interested than in the past in adopting a lighter-coloured or eventually white choice of colour assignment would support an argument for the declining relevance of race and the growing importance of socioeconomic status (or class) as a device for resource allocation in pursuit of reduced overall inequality.

However, this might still not crack open the elite for blacks since racial exclusion is so powerful at that level: therefore if the underlying purpose of the movimento negro is, as I have posited, to gain enhanced recognition and access to the elite for blacks, then there would be no reason to cast doubt on the use of the race criterion in allocating university places that expands one necessary step to the "top," especially in a society where the concentration of power and resources in the top five percent is far greater than almost anywhere else.

The other hypothesis is that the political elite, seeing this upsurge in black consciousness, has reacted in the interests of social cohesion (perhaps even self-preservation) and, unlike the academic dissidents, has cast ideological purity aside and tossed out some crumbs from the table (for these affirmative actions are very cheap) or, stated in less cynical terms, fearing the danger of racial conflict as in other countries, has opened up opportunities for a black middle class. But if this is the case they should beware, for there is no guarantee that a substantial increase in the number of blacks graduating from university will translate into success in the labour market, especially in the country's current parlous economic condition, or even if it does achieve that next step, that it will lead to reduced tension in race relations. Indeed, the contrary may happen, as some might say has happened in the United States following civil rights and the establishment of a degree of affirmative action. The much-derided "subtlety" of Brazilian discrimination is owed precisely to the socioeconomic inequality that accompanies racial exclusion, but if a substantial black middle class develops then that disguise will not be so readily available. The study of the black middle class in the New York area by Michèle Lamont and others should act as a warning. This is part of a multinational study of the United States, Brazil, and Israel, and the following conclusions about New York are striking in the light of the fifty years that have passed since passage of the Civil Rights Act and all that went with it.

> We found that African-American respondents mention more incidents of stigmatization and discrimination than the other interviewed groups considered in this book. What we defined as stigmatization or "assault on worth" is more frequently mentioned than discrimination. . . . Contrary to our expectations, given the growing inequality among blacks, narratives about stigmatizing and discriminatory incidents are largely similar for the African-American middle class and working class, except that middle class blacks are twice as likely to say they have been underestimated or stereotyped as poor, low status, or uneducated blacks. (Lamont et al. 2016: 59)

This reflects the sharp edge of social relations among people of different colours and the sensitivities that have arisen with the development of a black middle class, admittedly in a society where de facto vertical and horizontal segregation persists. Even informal segregation is unlikely to develop in Brazil, but the passage shows how the injuries of race, hidden for generations behind the subtlety of discrimination that so infuriates black leaders, could give way to more tension, not less. Indeed, a recent study using a 2008 survey points tentatively to a pattern similar to that detected by Lamont, whereby although only a minority claimed to have suffered discrimination in their daily life, the people who described themselves as preto and could be counted as middle class by virtue of their education and income were the most likely to do so (Daflon et al. 2017). Meanwhile, we shift in the next chapter to another kind of subtlety—that is, the soft lines of conflict engineered by a heritage of corporatism that has enabled the movimento negro to achieve success even while it has failed to put down roots among a potential mass following.

FIVE

The Movimento Negro between State, Civil Society, and Market

Real Social Movements?

In Latin America of the 1980s and 1990s, left-wing ideologies of transformation were built around a strong enthusiasm for civil society and "new social movements" and exhibited a quasi-religious reverence for the innocent and unspoiled voice of the truly disinherited, which I called *basismo* (Lehmann 1990). The movements were found in urban areas promoting self-managed projects to alleviate poverty, for example, by establishing educational initiatives and kindergartens, and also to raise consciousness, often in Christian Base Communities (CEBs) which some theologians saw as seedbeds of a grassroots-led transformation (Boff 1985; Mariz 1993; Burdick 1994). In rural areas they were devoted to the defense of human rights against violence perpetrated by landlords and sometimes their backers in the state, and to the demand for land reform (Martins 1980; Martins 1986). My "quasi-religious" description alludes to the enthusiasm of the protagonists but also to the involvement of priests, nuns, and other religious, a network of think tanks and documentation centres operating under the protection (though not necessarily the control) of the Catholic Church (Doimo 1995) and to the influence of liberation theology on their language and methods. This moment was also marked by the appeal of post-Marxist political philosophy and the methods of teaching and learning inspired by the educator Paulo Freire.[1]

---

1. For a small sample of a vast literature, including some early disenchantments, see Banck 1980; Lehmann 1990; Oxhorn 1994; Holston 1996; Assies 1999; and Eckstein 2001.

However, Alain Touraine, grand theorist of social movements and the Latin American scene, sounded a note of dissent. In a wide-ranging panorama of modern Latin America entitled *La Parole et le Sang* (Speech and Blood),[2] and in appearances at seminars and conferences around the region, he argued that subordination to the state is an inescapable and defining feature of Latin American social movements, although he did not mean that they are totally absorbed by it, as would be the case in totalitarian regimes (Touraine 1988: 162). This contradicted the hopes of the basistas. Nonetheless, in the end, Touraine admitted that, although the "new" social movements were not of the kind that would redirect the course of society because they were not affecting the core reproduction of the system, they nonetheless could qualify (curiously) as "historical movements" rather than "social movements," effective in demanding respect for persons and their human rights, citizenship, and a place in the nation for family, community, and ethnic group (253–57) but lacking a grand "historical project." In thus describing them he was using a set of concepts that he had long deployed in the analysis of social movements, notably the defining feature that they must call into question those core mechanisms of reproduction of society and propose broad-based projects of cultural transformation (mutation culturelle), as well as displaying the three principles that for him defined a social movement: the principle of identity, denoting a "historical subject" in whose name the movement mobilized, the principle of opposition denoting the social groups against which the movement was engaged; and a historical project (Touraine 1965, 1977, 1985). The ideologues of basismo, many of them exponents of liberation theology, like the Boff brothers in Brazil (Boff 1985; Levine 1992; Lehmann 1996), but also secular theorists of grassroots mobilization, like Touraine's former pupil Manuel Castells (Castells 1983), were of a different opinion: they hoped that these movements would escape the twin dangers of subordination to a populist, Marxist, or quasi-Marxist, authoritarian leadership, or to corporatist connivance in the management of capitalism, by remaining faithful to the grass roots—the same political sensibility sustained by some national and international NGOs (Oxhorn 1994, 1995; Bebbington and Lehmann 1997; Assies 1999). In developing a mobilization that was as direct an expression as possible of the voice of the voiceless and eschewed the

---

2. The book has not been translated into English or Spanish though its ideas have been widely published in papers and articles written by Touraine.

construction of movement hierarchies, they seemed to be driven by expressive more than instrumental motives.

Yet, even before the transition to elected civilian rule in Brazil in the 1980s, the anthropologist Ruth Cardoso had written a famous, or notorious, paper that questioned the basista orthodoxy of urban social movement theorists, pointing out that the movements tended to turn into pressure groups focused on extracting resources from the state and thus open to clientelistic temptations, even during the military regime, while others, like Willem Assies, pointed to the role of "external actors" (Cardoso 1983, 1992; Assies 1999). Later, in the early 1990s, Michael Hanchard commented on a similar pattern in the movimento negro, writing of the "dependence of many Afro-Brazilian organizations on non-community funding sources, particular those of grant institutions outside of Brazil" (1994: 129). More recently, alluding to their lack of a mass base or structured organizations, Tianna Paschel remarked wryly of black movements in both Colombia and Brazil that they "were not exactly poster children of an effective movement" (2016: 221). This question of social movements and their relationship with the state, international aid agencies, and NGOs would not go away. In the concluding chapter I will develop further a concept of social movements that is organizationally less demanding but insists, rather, that to "deserve the name," a social movement has to encompass a wide range of interests and ideas, and even ideologies, and of overlapping and laterally connected organizations and sensibilities.

The Landless Workers' Movement and Quilombolas

Both the sceptics and the followers of Touraine may find support for their views in the example of one of the most famous and successful achievements of grassroots basismo, the Movimento dos Trabalhadores Rurais Sem-Terra (Landless Workers' Movement—MST), which had a very high profile in the period of democratic transition and has suffered the assassination of many local leaders in a struggle for land involving both political pressure for land reform and peaceful land occupations. The MST's high profile continued through the Cardoso presidency, but it has now faded from view, although it has hardly disappeared. At a certain point it managed 161 cooperatives (*assentamentos*), 140 agribusinesses, and a university, as well as organizing many other educational activities for its followers in the cooperatives (Burdick 2004: 99–138;

Carter 2010). At the same time its leaders conducted noisy campaigns against Cardoso's and Lula's neoliberalism while campaigning on ecological issues like transgenic seeds. Yet despite this extensive empire of productive and educational activities, and a social base incomparably larger than the movimento negro, during the governments of its erstwhile ally, Lula, the MST lost influence, and by 2013 land expropriation and redistribution came to a halt while the government alliance with agribusiness (the *ruralista* lobby) consolidated. Its intellectual support group has also lost enthusiasm as the space it once occupied in cause-oriented research and academic advocacy has been largely taken over by race, indigenous survival, and the environment. Below the radar of high politics, especially at the local level, the MST has remained a force to be reckoned with, keeping close to the state apparatus—the hand that feeds it and its followers. Its cooperatives remain dependent on state banks for their survival (Gómez Bruera 2015: 585),[3] and its leaders are constantly interacting with the land reform agency INCRA: there are sympathizers inside INCRA, which sometimes hires an MST official as a political appointee. In one account a regional INCRA office provides the stage for an annual ritual in which MST leaders bring their followers to demonstrate at INCRA offices, occupy them, and even kidnap officials while they negotiate various budgetary and resource demands (Wolford 2016). Members of INCRA's staff, for their part, regularly pursue their own ideological agendas and contest governments both on land reform policy and on their own wage demands. Wolford's comment could serve also to describe the relationship between the movimento negro and the Brazilian state: "The idea that there are two arenas, state and civil society, that are distinct even if overlapping, is problematic . . . given the extent to which state actors in Brazil engage in protest and the extent to which social movement actors engage in self-governance" (81). The movimento negro itself may not kidnap university officials, but its presence is palpable among academics, and we have seen that administrators sometimes absorb its ideas (Schwartzman and Silva 2012).

The MST does to some extent fit with Touraine's requirements: it has a vast mass base, its leaders have nursed a grand project to change the

---

3. See the interview of the MST leader João Pedro Stedile with the Brazilian Press Association (ABI), 3 January 2014, on the ABI website, http://www.abi.org.br/joao-pedro-stedile-avanco-do-capital-no-campo-impede-a-reforma-agraria/. It also had to face politically motivated accusations of financial mismanagement (found to be without foundation by a congressional inquiry—CPI—in 2011). A factual summary can be found at http://www.conversaafiada.com.br/politica/2011/02/22/cpi-do-mst-derrota-katia-cerra-e-globo/

basis of Brazil's economy and society, and their target is a powerful agro-industrial business, which, as producer of a significant proportion of the country's exports, does resemble a core mechanism of reproduction. Yet the infinitely smaller quilombo advocacy network, which, as explained in chapter 1, has harnessed the ethnic theme to traditional claims for land redistribution, or perhaps vice versa, has in recent years made more headway in the sphere of official and public recognition, illustrating the central place of relations with the state for social movements or proto-social movements.

Quilombo advocacy has been led by intellectual activism in the image of the quotas movement and has also managed to achieve much in the superstructure, carving out niches in the state—both in INCRA and SEPPIR—even though its achievements on the ground, in terms of land redistribution, have been infinitely smaller than those of the MST. Its trajectory is the opposite of that of the MST, which spent two decades building up its rank and file before gaining traction in forcing the pace of land reform in the 1990s. *Quilombola* advocacy is not a social movement but rather a network in which anthropologists have taken the forefront—not only in promoting the cause in the Constituent Assembly, the Congress, and the executive branch but also in persuading people on the ground that they are entitled to land as *quilombolas* (members, in a loose sense, of a quilombo), be it as descendants of fugitive slaves or simply as communities with a history of settlement in an area (see Véran and Boyer for one point of view, and O'Dwyer and Wagner de Almeida for the advocates: O'Dwyer 2002; Véran 2003, 2013; Almeida 1989). Small wonder that the person responsible for quilombolas in SEPPIR in 2008 told me that sometimes "the community itself does not recognize itself as a quilombo" and that the important task was to "ensure that they get the chance to recognize themselves." The quilombo advocates first moved ahead in the superstructure, with constitutional and legal provisions and a presidential decree in 2003. These measures gradually widened the criteria for formal recognition of quilombos as a particular legal form of community and also for eventual access to land. The threat of quilombo claims to the landed interest is minuscule compared to the ambitions of the MST, and maybe for that reason PT governments, despite the party's historical links to the MST, have been inclined to encourage this small and identity-driven pressure group led mostly by intellectuals, with only a limited social base of grassroots activists and academic experts (Capinan 2009; Boyer 2011, 2014, 2016; Ribas Guerrero 2012; Lehmann 2017). The comparison can also be made with the Lula and

Dilma governments' abandonment of the Amazonian Indian and environmental causes: since the new Constitution was passed Brazil's indigenous population, mostly in the Amazonian basin, has grown in political visibility, and its leaders have shown increasing confidence and competence in the political sphere nationally and internationally. The demarcation of Indian lands in the wake of the Constitution also advanced significantly, rendering them inalienable and out of bounds to agribusiness and deforestation while the state also tried to limit deforestation on environmental grounds. The PT governments gradually deserted both the indigenous and environmental causes, leaving populations vulnerable to repeated and sometimes atrocious violence and allowing deforestation to continue legally and illegally. Yet amid all this the quilombo cause has sustained its low-key advance through the corridors of power. Both have enjoyed substantial support from the Ford Foundation, a subject to which we now turn.

NGOs and the Ford Foundation

Apart from the state, an additional major influence on Latin American social movements has been the international NGO network. These relationships have become so strong that since at least the 1990s, it has been possible to speak convincingly of an established regime in which international NGOs develop relationships with governments and multilateral partners in a wide range of fields as fully fledged partners in the international development community (Fox and Brown 1998; Keck and Sikkink 1998; Brysk 2000). The relationships between international NGOs and domestic nongovernmental partners, sometimes thought of as grassroots organizations, tend to be close and, often, long term, so once they have committed themselves they may follow local leaders even in directions they had not foreseen. Conversely, organization leaders must assess their own objectives or ideals against those of prospective sponsors and possibly modify them accordingly (Thayer 2017).[4]

We can illustrate this model by comparing the relationships of the MST and the quilombolas with the Ford Foundation. The MST has a mass base and a high international profile and has received support from other sources, so it seems to have made limited efforts to raise

---

4. Thayer quotes a 2003 survey by the Brazilian Association of NGOs (ABONG—Associação Brasileira de Organizações Não-Governamentais) to the effect that 58 percent of the respondents received more than 60 percent of their income from international NGOs (Thayer 2017: 175).

funds from Ford. In contrast, Ford's inclination toward race and gender issues and identity-driven movements, at least as far as Brazil and Spanish America are concerned, has enabled quilombo campaigners to overcome the disadvantages inherent in their narrow base, their small number of active supporters among the intelligentsia, and their patchy presence on the ground. The official history of the foundation's first forty years in Brazil makes no mention of any contributions to the MST (Brooke and Wytoshinky 2002): recalling his contacts with the MST ten years after he left the foundation, the former head of the Rio office, Nigel Brooke, told me that he had "serious misgivings as to their democratic credentials" and that "they got infiltrated by radical environmentalists who also believe in direct action." In addition he described the MST's agrarian reform objectives as "anachronistic," and he had found little evidence of "successful *assentamentos* from the point of view of production and the improvement of living standards for the rural poor."

Whereas the MST has, at least in Brasilia, become a voice in the wilderness, the very small quilombola movement, in addition to rarely documented local initiatives that are independent of NGO support,[5] has gained a sympathetic hearing among decision-makers due in no small part to Ford's support for advocacy through the Brazilian Anthropological Association (ABA). The foundation granted US$300,000 to the ABA in the period 1993–2002 to conduct applied research in support of quilombo and indigenous land rights together with the Núcleo de Estudos Etnico-Raciais (Ethnic and Racial Research Center—NUER) at the Universidade Federal de Santa Catarina (Federal University of Santa Catarina—UFSC), which also between 1994 and 2002 received $600,000 in grants for teacher training, preparation of teaching materials, and legal assistance related to the same issues.[6] Ford also sponsored important meetings that led to the recognition of anthropologists as experts by the judiciary and the Ministério Público in land demarcations (Boyer 2014; Lehmann 2017).[7]

---

5. As an example, along the Trombetas River in Amazonia the journalist Sue Branford has documented an active and broad-based campaign that has met with some success. See her report for the Latin America Bureau, http://lab.org.uk/rio-trombetas-the-last-quilombo

6. This information is drawn from the Ford Foundation Archive, held at the Rockefeller Foundation Archive at Sleepy Hollow, New York, and also from abundant grant information published on the foundation's website fordfound.org

7. "Carta de Ponta das Canas," a document that emerged from a workshop on "laudos antropológicos" (anthropological expert opinions) organized by the ABA and NUER in Florianópolis between 15 and 18 November 2000.

This support for quilombolas, like the foundation's support for the movimento negro and the quotas cause, has been built on long-standing and carefully nurtured relations with the Brazilian social science community. The foundation played a prominent role in the institutionalization of the social sciences in Brazil in the form of the Associação Nacional de Pós-Graduação e Pesquisa em Ciências Sociais (Brazilian Social Science Association—ANPOCS) and the ABA, and contributed indispensably to the survival of research, and sometimes of scholars themselves, during the military government. During the late 1990s the foundation worldwide gave massive support to the preparation of the Durban Conference and later to follow-up activities, and this also had repercussions in Brazil, where it funded NGO participation in the drafting of the government's position paper and the travel of the large number of NGO participants to the conference itself. In Brazil, as elsewhere, the foundation has moved away from the investments in predominantly academic activity for which it first gained a reputation, and since the 1990s has leveraged its academic networks in support of causes "on the ground," notably land issues, litigation, and legal precedent-setting in the racial sphere—this last modeled on its funding of landmark civil rights cases in the United States. Eventually it began to replace the heading "research" with "applied research" in classifying its grants. Thus we see a strong, though not exclusive, commitment to race and activism and a unique foundation culture (which has yet to be described in depth) built up independent of any Ford family involvement.[8] The commitment was also supported by strength in stock markets, which has helped Ford to achieve its place, in some estimates, as the second-largest foundation in the United States in terms of capitalization ($12 billion, second only to Gates's $44 billion).[9]

---

8. In 1976 the remaining members of the Ford family severed their connection with the foundation, which was founded in 1936 by Edsel Ford, son of the first Henry Ford. There were technical as well as political reasons for this, according to Brad Smith, vice-president of the foundation in 1995–2005: the foundation was in the embarrassing position of relying entirely on the 95 percent of the share capital of the Ford Motor Company that had been donated by Ford family members, but like any responsible charitable concern it had to diversify its holdings. The other reason was contained in two letters written at the time by the Ford family member on the foundation's Board of Trustees in which he called on the foundation to do more to strengthen the economic system rather than insistently criticizing it. "Henry Ford II was the last Ford family member to sit on the foundation board. He resigned in 1976, detailing his "frustration" and "plain irritation" in a letter to then chairman Alexander Heard. Ford alleged that too many foundation staffers failed to appreciate that the largesse they could distribute was "the fruits of our economic system," proving that "the foundation is a creature of capitalism." Detroit News, 3 June 2015.

9. Given the complications of tax, offshore locations, and regulation, this estimate of

The emphasis on legal and activist projects is evidenced in four grants to GELEDES, totaling $680,000 in the 1990s, and a further grant of $200,000 to set up GELEDES' "SOS-Racismo" service offering legal support to victims of specific acts of discrimination. The legal priority was vindicated when GELEDES and the Centro de Estudos das Relações de Trabalho e Desigualdade (Centre for Labour and Inequality Studies—CEERT) achieved a precedent-setting legal recognition by placing marriages celebrated by an Afro-Brazilian *pãe* or *mãe de santo* on the same footing as those celebrated by Catholic and other priests and pastors, but Denise Dora, human rights officer in Ford's Brazil office in the early 2000s, told me that the idea of promoting precedent-setting legal cases was based on the mistaken idea that precedent works in the Brazilian legal system as it does in the United States, a difference I have already pointed out.

The Rio office of the foundation continued to emphasize the importance of race-awareness in education and legal education under the leadership of the sociologist Edward Telles, its human rights officer in Brazil from 1997 to 2000, and Denise Dora, who told me that during a ten-year period she funded several masters programmes in human rights, including the one at USP's Law Faculty. The significance of this last was twofold: first, at her insistence, affirmative action places were created for students on those programmes, something unheard of at USP at that time; and, second, the dean of the Law Faculty at the time was Ricardo Lewandowski, who later was appointed to the Supreme Court and acted as its rapporteur in the 2012 quotas case. In tune with the foundation's approach, this grant combined the foundation's commitment to affirmative action with the maintenance of close long-term relations with their grantees.

Telles has written that "Ford began to fund research specifically about affirmative action policy" around 1998 (during his tenure), with full grants awarded on "ways to reduce racial inequality" (2003: 40, 41). In 2001 the foundation launched a competition entitled "Colour in Higher Education," inviting project proposals, of which 40 were successful. The cheapest, according to another source, was for R$60,000 (c. US$50,000 at the time), so this was a major investment. For the period 2006–14 one can access a spreadsheet on the foundation's website that contains de-

---

relative size should be taken only as an order of magnitude. The data do not seem to cover non-US foundations and there are no doubt many that have all sorts of arrangements. See the website of the Foundation Center, a resource institution established in New York by major foundations for the benefit of philanthropists and grant applicants, http://data. foundationcenter.org/#/foundations/all/nationwide/top:assets/list/2014 tailed information on grants worldwide. In Brazil this consists of 583 grants totaling $120 million, or $12 million per year. It does not include grants from Pathways, a stand-alone foundation programme intended to bolster access to universities by disadvantaged groups worldwide and which funded PPCor. GELEDES received almost annual grants, which together amounted to $1.7 million, and $1.55 million went to the Centre for Labour and Inequality Studies (Centro de Estudos das Relações de Trabalho e Desigualdade—CEERT), also based in São Paulo. Grants to both these organizations specifically mentioned litigation, including the creation of legal precedents for the punishment of racial discrimination. Several grants reflect support for identity-driven organizations such as ACMUN in the southern city of Porto Alegre, which received $700,000, and ABPN, whose single grant of $100,000 was small compared to the major contribution to the development of a memorial for the patriarch of the movimento negro, Abdias do Nascimento, covering the preparation of an archive for his papers and a prize in his name ($600,000 in all).

The foundation's priorities in Brazil can be confirmed by classifying the grants by beneficiary.[10] In table 1, I have therefore used its column entitled "Benefiting Population" to see how far the indigenous and Afro-Brazilian populations (as Ford describes them) were prioritized. The results show that the foundation's Brazil office has directed half its grants and half its grant money to the cause of indigenous and black Brazilians, including quilombolas.

I identified 31 grantee organizations associated with indigenous causes and the defense or promotion of black and quilombola rights and human rights (including the borderline case of the Central Unica das Favelas). I describe these as "research and activism related to black, indigenous, and quilombola identity, rights, and land." Between them, in the period 2006–15, they held 275 grants, and the size of the grants was almost standard—apparently because officers have discretion to allocate grant monies up to a certain size. The organizations received a total of $36.2 million, and an average of $1.17 million over the period. If we exclude the Federation of Agencies for Social and Educational Assistance

10. The foundation does itself classify more than half its grants as coming under "initiatives," but these are excessively broad categories and in any case 246 grants are listed as "noninitiative." The initiatives are Advancing Media Rights and Access (90 grants), Advancing Racial Justice and Minority Rights (54), Climate Change Responses That Strengthen Rural Communities (24), Expanding Community Rights over Natural Resources (81), Just Films (2), Higher Education for Social Justice (10), Promoting Transparent, Effective, and Accountable Government (3), and Strengthening Human Rights Worldwide (72). https://www.fordfoundation.org/work/our-grants/grants-database/

(Federação de Órgãos para Assistência Social e Educacional—FASE), an NGO identified more as a project manager than the bearer of a particular cause, and the Human Rights Fund, which received a major capital injection, the average is $903,000 and the total is $26.2 million. Contrary to what clientelistic assumptions might lead one to expect, there does not seem to be an inordinate concentration in a small number of "favourites": the top 11 received $21 million, and an average of $1.9 million, while the remaining 17 received an average of $431,000. Denise Dora said that the office received between 500 and 600 proposals a year, of which half were in the field of human rights, and of these only 20 were successful, and, although these figures reflect the desire to nurture some organizations to maturity and effectiveness, they do not give the impression of a closed shop.

Ford has involved many people in its processes—in committees; in consultations; and not least when the military was in power, in its very strong commitment to human rights, people threatened by repression who were helped in different ways. The late Fulvia Rosemberg, director of the Brazilian operation of the International Fellowship Program (IFP,) founded by Ford as a separate institution to enable people from disadvantaged groups to undertake graduate studies, told me that it was part of her project to involve many people in the process of selection, recommendation, and teaching so that they would be drawn toward its aim of advancing the causes of blacks and indigenous people. The foundation also appointed the rector of UERJ, Nilsea Freire, as head of its Rio office

TABLE 1. Number and Size of Grants Benefiting Minority Populations from the Ford Foundation's Rio de Janeiro Office, 2006–15

Benefiting Population	Number of Grants	Value (US$millions)	Average Grant Size (US$)
Indigenous	118	29.4	250,000
Afro-Brazilian	103	21.1	204,800
Indigenous and Afro-Brazilian	37	8.3	224,300
Quilombola only	17	3.2	188,200
Total	275	62.0	225,500
As percentage of total grants from the Rio office	47.3	51.7	

Source: Ford Foundation grants database, https://www.fordfoundation.org/work/our-grants/grants-database/

Note: The categories are mutually exclusive: quite a few grants have two benefiting populations, hence the dual category "Indigenous and Afro-Brazilian." The classification here uses the foundation's own categorization of benefiting populations.

after she had overseen the introduction of affirmative action at the university. In this way we can see that Ford has developed dense relationships in Brazilian academia during the fifty years since it established an office in Rio, not just because there are beneficiaries of its grant giving but also because it has involved so many Brazilian academics in its activities.

Civil Society in Brazil: A Critique

These figures, combined with mentions of Ford support in previous chapters, are provided here in support of an argument that civil society does not mean the same in Latin American studies as it does in political theory and that the connotation of independence vis-à-vis the state and of grassroots protagonism underplays the reliance of social movements both on the state and on external support from international NGOs. Latin Americanists and Latin American social scientists themselves use the term civil society to refer to concrete collective agents, either social movements in general or NGOs, whereas in political theory the term has a long history, going back to the Enlightenment and earlier, as an assemblage of rights and obligations that demarcate civil society from the state while governing their relations. The Latin Americanist literature on the subject in English can be said to have first emerged in the 1980s with the publication of writings by political scientists, notably Alfred Stepan and Margaret Keck, mostly about Brazil (Stepan 1985, 1988; Keck 1986, 1992; Keck and Sikkink 1998), followed by Philip Oxhorn, James Holston, Jonathan Fox, and many others (Fox 1994; Oxhorn 1994, 1995, 2011; Holston 1995). Among Latin American scholars there is little discussion involving the concept in terms of political theory but much writing on social movements that are taken to be coterminous with civil society. The one exception is Leonardo Avritzer, who questions the assimilation of social movements to civil society by distinguishing two aspects of civil society—on one hand markets and on the other "an autonomous locus of producing social solidarity" on the grounds that markets cannot satisfy the demands of solidarity (Avritzer 2017: 46). Like others he starts from the autonomy shown by social movements vis-à-vis the state in periods of democratic transition and also like others he recognizes the approximation that then occurred between the two, but he then argues that sceptics ignore a "substantial core of religious associations" that retain a degree of autonomy. In this he is right, though by religious associations he refers to those falling within the scope of Catholicism. It should be noted, however, that this autonomy may be related to the sort of activity those associations are involved in—that is to say, activities that do not require much in the way of material resources, especially since religious personnel often provide basic management and sometimes also leadership. Once the organizations get into projects they look outside to the state and to international NGOs. The other reservation is that, like others writing on the subject, Avritzer does not include the most massive phenomenon of all, namely the evangelical churches, which disrupt his and all the other schemata. The omission is understandable, for the evangelical churches use a radically different language, and evoke radically different emotional responses, from those usually associated with social movements and solidarity—but can their exclusion from a discussion of civil society be justified? We will return to the question below.

Guillermo O'Donnell, in his writing about Latin America, eschewed this usage and instead offered a strong critique of pared-down concepts of rights and an expansive liberal idea of citizenship, but, although they have clear implications in his development of the concept of the subject as agent, he does not apply the notion of civil society or social movements in the way it is used by Latin Americanists. If he had done, he might have found that his concept of the subject as agent clashed with the basista notion of *el pueblo* or particular ethnic or even racial groups as agents. As a sort of counterpoint, O'Donnell's development of the concept of corporatism decades earlier, and later of delegative democracy, built up a picture of a state that is in a position to suffocate or co-opt social movements rather than encouraging their autonomy (O'Donnell 1977, 1978, 1999, 2010).

A raft of recently published articles on Brazil offers instructive findings on both the use and misuse of civil society and especially of the relationships between the PT in government and social movements, also known as civil society organizations (CSOs). At a macrolevel David Samuels and César Zucco claim that PT penetration in society and by implication its establishment of local offices—which proliferated after Lula's arrival in power in 2003—depend heavily on what they call civil society. Using a large database they find that the "effects of establishing party presence do . . . vary with civil society density—but only for the PT," not for other parties. Other parties, we can infer, build on ties of clientelism and loyalty to individual politicians, while "the PT is unable to cultivate affective partisan attachments" where civil society is weak (Samuels and Zucco 2015: 771). This procedure of using simplified statistics from the IBGE to construct an indicator of civil society presence is repeated in another recent article chronicling the PT's highly successful penetration of the Northeast of the country where it had but a sketchy presence before 2002 (van Dyck and Montero 2015).

The Samuels and Zucco paper does not define civil society and offers no examples of how this mechanism of recruitment works, and it is not within its scope to ask whether the organizations covered by the term may not themselves be proactively cultivating their relations with the PT, especially in the period after it gained the presidency and thus access to resources in 2003. They take it for granted that involvement with a political party seeking to build up its base is compatible with the notion of a civil society organization. Although there is nothing wrong with such involvement by local interest groups, I do question the appropriateness of the term civil society in referring to them and above all the assumption that they are independent of the party and the state. For a more analytically aware account of these relationships, we need case studies, such as that by Abigail Friendly of housing-related pressure groups and neighbourhood associations in the Rio de Janeiro town of Niteroi in the 1990s (population around half a million). The study—in which the PT is much less prominent than other more "traditional" parties—does not take refuge in euphemisms: after describing numerous disputes over party alliances among the organizations she says that in general "civil society came to depend on resources and institutional favours" and that the "usual pattern" is for parties with representation in municipal government (in the form of elected councilors) to appoint leaders to positions in the bureaucracy. In the words of a "municipal technocrat," "all the community leaders have in one form or another become employees or assumed other positions in the municipality or with councillors" (Friendly 2016: 231–32).

The PT has a special relationship with transformation-oriented CSOs since they share an ethos driven by grassroots mobilization and hostility toward the pervasive clientelism of Brazilian political culture, which were dominant themes in the PT's origins amid the mobilizations of the democratic transition. But after reaching government the PT seems to have converted this affinity into an institutionalized pattern of recruitment and the relationship "became more reward-based" (Gómez Bruera 2015: 575).

The party itself has become more hierarchical, reducing the role of its grassroots units (unidades de base) in decision-making and internal elections, and increasing its reliance on business for contributions to its finances—culminating in the spectacular corruption scandals known as *mensalão* and *lava-jato*.[11] After the election of Lula it made abundant use of the patronage available to the executive, especially by rewarding its associates and supporters in trade unions, whose peak organization, the Central Unica dos Trabalhadores (National Trade Union Central—CUT), is described by (the admittedly unsympathetic) Ribeiro as an "ancillary organization of the PT" (2014: 102). Ribeiro estimates that approximately twenty-one thousand positions are open for appointment by the president and ministers in the federal government alone, and that by 2010 "at least 3000 federally appointed positions were occupied by party members" (219). Although this is standard practice, the innovation was the distribution among different PT factions and "thematic groups," which presumably refers, among others, to people who had played prominent roles in social movements. Similarly (the equally unsympathetic) Gómez Bruera also quotes a study by D'Araujo (2009) claiming that 45 percent of all the top-level federal positions (Direções de Assessoramento Superior) were held by trade unionist members (Gómez Bruera 2015: 579). D'Araujo's data, based on a sample of 519 holders of senior positions, show that the federal civil service has a very high rate of trade union membership anyhow, and since so many of the people in these positions are recruited from the civil service into these political appointments, it is hardly surprising that a high proportion are trade union members—the figure was 78 percent in 1998 (67). If they were officeholders, that would be more significant, but her data do not give those details.[12]

Gómez Bruera also writes, quoting Ribeiro, that between 1997 and 2007 almost two-thirds of "middle level elites" in the PT have maintained "some kind of participation" in a CSO—a category that importantly includes trade unions and a large number of housing-related pressure groups and movements (2015: 571). He cites a survey among federal depu-

---

11. The *mensalão* scandal involved raising money from kickbacks on contracts with the Post Office and other agencies, and using it to make monthly payments to politicians from small parties so that they would vote through Lula's legislation. It brought down Lula's closest adviser, José Dirceu, as well as his Minister of Finance Antonio Palocci, among others. The *lava-jato* (car wash) was a network of operations involving kickbacks on Petrobras contracts: it provided the pretext for the assault on Dilma Roussef's presidency and the beginning of a campaign leading to her impeachment—though she was not accused of involvement. It led to the imprisonment of dozens of business people and some politicians and eventually the conviction of Lula himself in 2017. As of 2018 lava-jato cases continue in the courts.

12. D'Araujo tries to show that these political appointments grew substantially during Lula's tenure, but her table shows only a very gradual increase of 18 percent from 2003 to 2012 (2009: 26).

ties for the 1997–2002 period in which 62 percent acknowledged that they owed their election to connections with a social movement and dedicated about half their time to their electoral bases, which are mainly CSOs. At local level he alludes to the distribution of jobs by PT mayors to people from CSOs, notably in São Paulo and doubtless in response to unrelenting demonstrations and pestering: in São Paulo Luisa Erundina (1989–93) had to dole out jobs to housing activists to get them literally off her door-step, and Marta Suplicy (2000–2004) did the same—more apparently to neutralize them than to implement the measures they demanded. (Non-PT mayors presumably also respond in similar ways, but social protests on behalf of underprivileged groups touch a particularly sensitive chord in the PT.) Both these former mayors of São Paulo have since left the PT.

A recent detailed and analytically sophisticated study by Lucy Earle thickens out this portrayal of the logic of social movements on the basis, again, of São Paulo's housing crisis. In Earle's account, although there is much variation in the extent to which the housing movements are pre-pared to trust the authorities, in the end even those which pride them-selves on an autonomist posture and a rhetoric of fierce confrontation engage with them. Some leading figures work as paid advisors to politi-cians, or are appointed to senior positions, mainly at the level of the city's municipal government, while continuing their more or less full time movement activity. Earle does not describe this as co-option nor does she imply that leaders have been "bought off": on the contrary, as the title of her book says, she sees it as a "transgressive citizenship" of permanent mobilization whose effectiveness is enhanced by the patchy rule of law and a political class able to bend real estate and land markets to their will. The strategy is particularly favoured by São Paulo, where movements find a broad activist base, nurtured in the dissident discourse of the city's intelligentsia (Earle 2017: 214–18).

The literature quoted tends to impute initiative to the PT and other politicians, but from our point of view it surely reflects an underlying standard strategy whereby social movements mobilize in order to extract resources from the city or state and to find "slots" for their leaders and activists in the state bureaucracy. One reason is that, with the exception of the trade unions, they have no independent sources of funding, which is where international NGOs and funding agencies come in. But even the trade unions, who do possess substantial resources, depend on the state for the discounting of dues direct from wage packets "known as the union tax" (imposto sindical).[13]

---

13. This provision, dating back to the 1930s, whereby workers have to donate one day's

The interdependence of state and civil society is illustrated by the celebrated participatory budgeting that was pioneered by the PT in Porto Alegre in the 1980s and later reproduced across the country, especially after Lula's election. The original experiment can be interpreted either from the viewpoint of the grassroots, according to which there was a structured opportunity for citizens to participate so long as they were affiliated to a CSO, and a system for proposals to be processed "up" to the Mayor's office (Avritzer 2009), or from the point of view of PT decision-makers in a city which was a party fiefdom, according to which the whole process was orchestrated, though not manipulated, from the Mayor's office—a conclusion I drew from Abers (2000). By the time Lula's and Dilma's governments had come and gone, a certain consensus was emerging among the champions of social movements and civil society that, whereas religious associations showed a stable level of popular participation, when it came to public policies "varies according to the willingness of the state to establish or to derail forms of collaboration with CSOs" (Avritzer 2017: 58). In the same volume Baiocchi and Teixeira, having listed the numerous instances of participation and dialogue established by Lula's government, involving "tens of millions" of Brazilians in "some form or another" debating government policies, go on to lament that this is largely a sham and that the government had sacrificed its participatory commitments to "congressional compromise" (Baiocchi and Teixeira: 289–90).

My purpose is not to discredit these grassroots organizations, or CSOs, or the trade unions, or the movimento negro itself, nor to cast doubt on their motivations or those of their leaders, nor do I make anything approaching a claim that the state is monopolizing political space. Both Baiocchi and Teixeira and Avritzer seem to have concluded that the relationship between social movements and the state tends to oscillate according to the dispositions of governments (not of the movements themselves), never reaching extremes either of co-optation or total autonomy. I also recognize that today's corporatism is less elaborate and less institutionalized structurally than that which was established in the 1930s in Brazil and Mexico and a little later in Argentina. My purpose is to draw attention to an established way of doing politics, especially of bringing political pressure on the part both of groups that suffer different sorts of exclusion

pay per year to their union, was threatened by reforms proposed in 2017 and as of October it looked as if it would be abolished. However, a law cannot be implemented without the corresponding 'regulation' and this had still not been provided by the Ministry of Labour. Its removal had already been proposed and then stopped at the time of the Constituent Assembly in the 1980s.

(in work, in housing, in race relations, in education) and of powerful interests, which is different from the politics assumed to exist under ready-made liberal assumptions. It is less institutionalized than it was during the high tide of dirigiste development strategies because that system was destabilized by debt crises, by "structural adjustment," and by globalization, which then forced or encouraged governments to privatize and deregulate. But this supposed triumph of neoliberalism has been far from complete in Brazil (or in Mexico or Argentina), as the persistence of acute crises over the pensions of government employees, over labour market regulation, over the management of state enterprises, and over subsidies to big business illustrate.

For this reason liberal assumptions about civil society as a sphere independent of the state, at least the more simplistic ones, have some application in Latin America, but it is limited, especially in the political sphere. The one sphere where regulation has all but collapsed is that of religion (Mariano 2011; Lehmann 2013b, 2016d). The hegemony of Catholicism was not enforced by the state in the strict sense of the word in the twentieth century, but it still benefited from crucial passive and informal state support, and today an autonomous evangelical movement has advanced to the point where, in Brazil and Chile for example, evangelicals constitute more than 20 percent of the population.

In his pathbreaking work on evangelical Christianity in Latin America, David Martin was optimistic that the "tongues of fire" of his title would free Latin American society from its heritage of corporatism and Catholic conformism, carve a space for secularization and liberal individualism, release a cascade of entrepreneurial energy, and unlock the shackles of patronage and clientelism, which he also associated with Catholic hegemony (1990). But we now observe a dual trajectory whereby classic Pentecostal churches have indeed carved out a very large and multifarious sphere of autonomous action largely independent of the state, with hundreds of thousands of mostly small churches, while a parallel neo-Pentecostal sphere has also developed with a much higher mediatic and political profile, represented famously by Brazil's Universal Church of the Kingdom of God. Both types are funded by the contributions of followers, but the neo-Pentecostals have drawn closer to the state if only to protect their media interests and precious tax exemptions. Today the evangelical caucus (*bancada*) in the Brazilian Congress, representing both broad currents, is equivalent in size to the proportion of its followers in the population as a whole (80–90 out of 513 deputies) and the Universal Church has a political party of its own, which sometimes succeeds in placing its representatives in Ministerial positions. We will have to wait and see whether this is an indication of a future convergence along corporatist lines. For the moment, it remains a striking fact that the evangelical churches are the one significant movement that enjoys substantial autonomy from the state, yet they are also largely ignored by the theorists of civil society.

In this section I have drawn attention to the special meaning of civil society in the Brazilian context and contrasted it with standard European usages, and I have adduced examples to show that social movements are usually intertwined with the state, concluding by drawing attention to the relative autonomy of evangelical churches. I have avoided the question why the churches have an autonomy that the movements do not have, but I have introduced them briefly to highlight the need to broaden the conventional approach, which tends to blank them out of the picture even though they clearly are part of civil society and they are more autonomous vis-à-vis the state than social movements as conventionally defined.

Independence and Self-Help in the Movimento Negro

If one is looking for something approaching a conventional view of civil society in the field of black advancement, one can find it among various initiatives that have remained independent of the institutional fields that have so far been at the centre of my interpretation. They do not figure among the universities adopting quotas, their leaders do not write in the op-ed pages of the *Folha de São Paulo,* and they scarcely figure in the literature produced by SECAD or in the many sociological and statistical studies around affirmative action. But they are not insignificant, and the leader of one of them has been the most rhetorically uncompromising advocate of affirmative action in the media. In covering this quite different dimension, I shall rely mostly on interviews to describe three ventures that represent different approaches or sectors in the cause of black advancement—one more *basista* or *comunitario,* the others more market oriented, providing education targeted at "aspirational" black students. Frei David's EDUCAFRO contains a mixture of these two traits, while the Faculdade Zumbi dos Palmares in São Paulo and the Steve Biko Institute in Salvador represent more the latter in that they are relatively apolitical and charge fees.

Frei David and EDUCAFRO

This *comunitario* venture is based entirely on voluntary work by student teachers and charges a nominal fee. Frei David, a Franciscan friar, himself emerged from the ranks of Catholic activism inspired by liberation theology, although his exclusive emphasis on the empowerment of "meu povo negro" (my black people) sets him apart from the more universalist orientation of that school of thought.[14] In March 2013 Renato Emerson dos Santos, who had been an important figure in the early stages of Frei David's pioneering initiative in Rio de Janeiro, used the phrase "formato CEB" to describe the style of the "comunitario" PVCs, and their educational self-management: they are very much in the line of "new social movements" with their ethos of voluntarism and their origins in Catholic basismo (Lehmann 1996; Brandão 2007). Emerson's phrase was a reference to the "format" of the CEBs, emphasizing autonomy from the state and grassroots inspiration—although it has frequently been observed that they were dependent for their continuity on the guidance of priests and bishops (Hewitt 1991). Their programmes also include an element of consciousness-raising and political debate: an account of the Rocinha PVC, a breakaway from Frei David's first prevestibular organization in the enormous Rio favela of Rocinha, describes the tension between consciousness-raising and conventional learning in the early 2000s (da Silva 2008).[15] But their work seems detached from that of campaigners inside the public universities. Indeed, there are signs of a social distancing in the movimento negro: while the people who have been at the centre of this quotas narrative have operated in the higher education sphere, mostly in prestige universities, as well as in the federal bureaucracy, the PVCs—apart from those linked to the universities themselves, which were sponsored by SECAD or the local NEAB—have operated in a separate sphere, especially in urban low-income neighbourhoods, and have not been heavily involved in policy elaboration. Frei David himself, as an advocate of quotas in all sorts of spheres (the civil service for ex-

---

14. The expression "povo negro" came into common currency with the Church's 1988 Campanha da Fraternidade. This is an annual "Campaign of Fraternity," which the Church organizes with a different theme each year. In 1988, the centenary of the abolition of slavery, the theme was "I heard the cry of my people," evoking the Exodus of the Israelite slaves from Egypt and referring particularly to the condition of Brazil's black population. See Exodus 3:7.

15. Although Rocinha is usually described as a favela, it has long outgrown that description on account of its population size and developing infrastructure. It is officially recognized as a neighbourhood.

ample), is something of a loner, operating independently of the bureaucratic and academic insiders we have observed and focused principally on his own EDUCAFRO operation. His talent for public relations and media exposure was illustrated when he chained himself to the railings at USP. At the 2012 Rio Fashion Week a group of men and women students paraded topless with "EDUCAFRO" emblazoned on their bodies to highlight the absence of black models in the shows. (I doubt whether Frei David was involved in planning this particular stunt.) In 2013, as reported on the GELEDES website, EDUCAFRO signed an agreement with the Fashion Week, with the involvement of CEPPIR (Coordenadoria Especial de Políticas de Promoção da Igualdade Racial—the city's equivalent of the federal SEPPIR), under which Fashion Week would include a minimum of 10 percent black models. A similar agreement was reached with the São Paulo Fashion Week—though in neither case do we know if there has been implementation.

In an interview in April 2010, Frei David highlighted several themes in his life. One was his attachment to the Church, a second was his sense of himself as a controversial figure promoting the cause of "meu povo negro," and a third was the insistence on placing black self-recognition (asumir) at the heart of black social advancement—overcoming the complex of "negros de jabuticaba"— black on the outside and white on the inside like the jabuticaba fruit. At the same time he emphasized self-reliance, entrepreneurship, and risk-taking, and so the fourth theme was the "racial democratization of higher education." He also expressed a deep distrust of the non-PT Left (the Partido Comunista do Brasil [Communist Party of Brazil—PCdoB]; and the Partido Socialismo e Liberdade [Socialism and Freedom Party—PSol]), whose supporters have tried to co-opt or seize control of the organizations he has founded. This combination of themes does not easily fit into an ideological mould. David's resistance to state monopoly is one source of his conflict with political forces for which progressive politics is synonymous with state involvement and which therefore oppose his deals with the Catholic and other private universities from which his graduates obtain financial support. Others saw his unwillingness to accept funds or even pay teachers more than their travel costs as a way to keep power to himself.

Frei David speaks of himself as a public figure, sometimes in the third person, for example, as "David guerreiro"—David the warrior—and recounts the events of his life as formative experiences that prefigure his emergence as a leading campaigner for black advancement and quotas. His trajectory started with his vocation as a Franciscan friar and priest, motivated principally by the role a priest could play as a social activist: in the lower-class area where he lived as a child and teenager from a middle-class family that had fallen on hard times, there were no public services like police or emergency medical attention—only a lone Spanish Jesuit riding through the mud on his motor scooter. David gained admission to university to study engineering, but eventually his "subconscious" told him that this was the cowardly choice, and in 1976 he entered a Franciscan seminary.

By this time he had already experienced a first humiliation, when he applied to join Itamaraty the Diplomatic Service and, as mentioned in the previous chapter, was told that a person of his background did not have a chance. He did not see this as a racial slur at the time, but an experience three months after he arrived at the seminary brought him face to face with a black identity that had not before occurred to him.[16] The occasion was a sketch ("gozação") mounted by the German- and Italian-descended seminarians of his year: a table was placed in the centre of the refectory decorated to represent a slave ship, and the black members of the group (eight or nine out of thirty-seven) were told to go to it, but David did not go, and when the organizer said "someone is missing" he found himself picked up and transported bodily to the "slave ship." David lost control and walked out, ready to abandon the seminary: he had been insulted by being called a negro. His master, a friar of German origin, persuaded him to stay, but the manner in which he did so challenged David in such a way as to change his life. Did he not say he wanted to change the world as a priest, and now was he going to give up at the first hurdle? The master told him he was suffering from a disease known as the "ideology of whitening" and asked to see photos of David's parents. First the novice showed him one of his mother, but only with further prompting did he show one of his darker-skinned father. The master's words were "Congratulations! Your father is *negro*." There, in David's words decades later, was the "proof of the crime."

David was in a "state of shock"; he even had suicidal thoughts, but

---

16. He describes this in his contribution to a volume of short autobiographical essays by seventeen public and especially cultural figures edited by Haroldo Costa, first published in 1982 and republished with fourteen additional contributions in 2009 (Costa 2009). He was still speaking of it in very similar words thirty years later in 2010. The emblematic character of the aspiration to the Diplomatic Service and of the service's racially exclusive recruitment until quite recently appear in another article in the same book by a Roman law professor, Jose Pompilio da Hora (44), who recounts how twice he was firmly and explicitly told by prominent Itamaraty figures that as a negro he could never enter. This was despite—or perhaps because of—the fact that he was tutor to the daughter of one of them.

under the guidance of the master he plunged into his new identity. Having looked in vain in the library for books on black history he found some in the nearby town and devoured them. From that time he decided he would serve his "povo negro" to enable them to appreciate their "beauty" and to speed up their "amadurecimento," their coming of age. He became obsessed: he would count black people at any place and on any occasion. And when it came to the end of his novitiate, and he had to commit himself definitively to the order and take a vow of obedience, even though the vow is supposed to be unconditional, he said he would only do so if he could devote himself to their cause.

So Frei David spent the early 1980s in the parish of São João de Meriti in the lower-class areas of Rio's Baixada Fluminense region (thirteen municipalities, innumerable low- and middle-income neighborhoods, population four million), where the bishop was the prominent advocate of liberation theology and bitter opponent of the military government Dom Mauro Morelli (dos Santos 2007). São João de Meriti became well known in Church circles as David initiated discussion groups on the race question among parishioners and with fellow religious. This brought the criticism that he was "fomenting racism in Brazil," but "Frei David guerreiro" was, in his words, growing and maturing day by day. At this time the bishop supported race relations work, but within the framework of human rights,[17] while David—though he did not say this to me—was to some extent striking out on his own with a distinctive "black" theme. Eventually he tired of endless debates about whether to involve the church in these struggles and decided that rather than found yet another black activist group that would be no different from the others, he would take the struggle into the Church hierarchy itself. According to others, he also was in touch with Pentecostal and Protestant churches.

Inevitably, David ran into conflicts with Cardinal Eugenio Salles, archbishop of Rio de Janeiro: a meeting he organized in 1987 of black Franciscans (Encontro de Franciscanos Negros) was promptly forbidden by the cardinal, and Frei David's comment was, "[T]he communists won't let me speak, the Church won't let me speak." By "communists" he referred to his subsequent conflicts in the PVNC and EDUCAFRO.

Seeking advice from the widely admired intellectual and human rights advocate Betinho about how to deal with the cardinal's ban,[18] Frei

17. This information was provided by Professor Edlaine Gomes, who was involved in human rights work with the diocese at that time.

18. Herbert José de Souza, "Betinho" (1935–97) was the founder of the Instituto Brasileiro de Análise Social y Económica (Brazilian Institute for Social and Economic

David alerted the media, which reveled in the scandal of the forbidden meeting ("Cardinal Bans Blacks from Meeting Together" read the head-lines), which as a result attracted male and female religious from far and wide. Betinho told him that "for a few hours or days you can be a prophet," As a result of the ban, forty people withdrew their registration, but then sixty joined in, and the meeting opened with another of David's hallmarks—a "missa Afro"—a celebration of the Mass with African themes and symbols designed in accordance with the "theology of incul-turation," which was current among some Catholic theologians, though not to be confused with the theology of liberation (Shorter 1988; de Theije and Mariz 2008).

In the Baixada he had the support of his bishop and worked with the "Pastoral Negro," a unit of lay and religious working for the defense and advancement of the black population.[19] David toured the area with a slide show entitled "A historia que não foi contada" (The Untold Story), which brought the history of blacks to an uninitiated audience, told, in the consecrated phrase from liberation theology, "from the point of view of the oppressed." According to Frei David audiences would leave the show feeling angry. Then in a follow-up session he would make a further presentation entitled "A vida renasce da luta" (Life Is Reborn through Struggle). As so often in his career, his purpose was to provoke a debate, and he says this one spread like wildfire through the suburbs of the Baixada. His message was uncompromising: discrimination against blacks was more than just bad behaviour or everyday racism—it was the result of a deliberate project to exclude the black population, embodied in "seven laws" decreed during the country's five-hundred-year history, a theme he was still reiterating in 2010.

In the 1990s Frei David's activism turned toward university admis-sions. At the first National Black Students' Seminar (SENUN), which took place in Rio in 1993, the small number of blacks at universities, es-pecially the prestigious ones, was a subject for discussion, and partici-

Analysis IBASE) and a leading public figure and advocate for HIV sufferers—among whom him and his brother, who contracted and eventually died from the disease as a result of contaminated blood transfusions to treat their hemophilia.

19. In the wake of Vatican II the Church in Latin America has established numerous pastoral agencies devoted to specific social issues, for example, Indians, rural workers and small farmers, and urban youth (Conselho Indigenista Missionário, Comissão Pastoral da Terra, Pastoral do Negro, and Pastoral do Menor for young people), which in Brazil oper-ate under the auspices of the National Bishops' Conference and incorporate laypeople as well as religious. Some of their people have been persecuted and even killed in land con-flicts in Amazonia.

pants were inspired by the experience of the Steve Biko Institute in Salvador to establish prevestibular courses for blacks and people of low income on the basis of independent funding and volunteer teachers (dos Santos 2007). Frei David then founded a pioneering PVN, (Prevestibular para Negros, i.e., for Black Students), taught by volunteer teachers and students, which was able to take advantage of opportunities that came through the Church, notably in the form of scholarships for his graduates to study at the prestigious and very expensive PUC in Rio. The venture expanded rapidly to seventy-seven "núcleos" in 1999, but then split and in 2001 was reduced to thirty-two as a result of internal conflicts. A group of teachers said they could not work in an organization that had "negros" in its name because that detracted from what in their view was the class-based nature of the problem: this conflict went on for two years until a compromise was reached to rename it "Prevestibular para Negros e Carentes" (PVNC—i.e., for blacks and people in need). Frei David's personalistic leadership style and his resistance to the creation of institutional mechanisms of governance were also a source of tension (dos Santos 2011), and he admitted readily to me that he was forever "envolvido em conflitos" (getting into fights)—while adding that he relished these conflicts because they offered opportunities for consciousness-raising. In any case, he saw them as attempts by parties of the Left (notably the PCdoB) to gain control.[20] These, in Renato Emerson dos Santos's detailed account, were not the only forces in contention: there was a "spontaneist" group, a free-thinking leftist group, and so on, and there were also those who did not identify with Frei David's closeness to the Church. Some described his supporters pejoratively as the "campo negro-eclesial." "Closeness" does not mean he was under instructions from any hierarchical figure but rather that his identity as a priest and friar lay at the heart of his life, and this is confirmed by his remark to me describing his project as "radicalmente da Igreja" (a project deeply rooted in the Church). This is a statement about his identity: unlike those who identify with liberation theology, he rarely if ever evokes theology, or even Christian morality, in his public advocacy—but his personal identity is tightly bound up with his role as a priest, with the Church, and with the Franciscan Order.

Another source of conflict within the Rio PVNC was Frei David's entrepreneurial talent, as exemplified in the scholarships at Rio's PUC,

20. Despite its name, the PCdoB is not really a left-wing party anymore, although its grassroots members seem still to have been firm Marxists at the time of this dispute.

which were awarded to students personally recommended by him. Despite this advantage to the students, the university's private (albeit non-profit-making) status gave rise to (or was the pretext for) a fierce dispute with people who would not countenance scholarships granted to a non-state institution, whatever the benefit for the students. These arguments went to and fro in the Rio PVC in the years 1994–97 between Frei David, volunteer teachers, and some students, punctuated by assemblies in which it seems whoever came along could vote. Renato Emerson dos Santos spoke of seven to eight hundred people taking part. At one point the assembly forbade David from taking the public universities to court, which was part of his campaign to have the vestibular exam fee declared discriminatory against candidates from low-income families: his opponents argued that this was against public universities and thus brought discredit to the principle of public education. Frei David's case was that a flat fee for all students discriminated against those who were worse off. His characteristic response was to undertake the lawsuit anyway, but since such a suit could only be brought by an institution, he had to persuade a judge that he himself was an institution—and he succeeded both in this and in the suit itself. These conflicts continued until eventually he parted company with the Rio PVNC and, on the advice of the "good bishops" who supported him and those in the Church who shared his commitment, went off to study for a masters degree in liturgical theology in São Paulo, in which he developed a theological basis for the Missa-Afro: a mass in African style.[21] Thus he found a symbolic way to bring black identity into church ritual.

After finishing his degree, Frei David set up a new PVNC, EDUCAFRO, in São Paulo in which he vowed that political parties would have no part. It seems, however, that when he fell ill in 2006 and had to leave EDUCAFRO in the hands of the less experienced Frei Valney, there was almost a coup by supporters of the PSol—the leftist breakaway from the PT. The ideological motive, once again, was disagreement with David's unwillingness to mix the black struggle with the struggle against capitalism and all other inequalities.[22]

21. One reason for the bishops' encouragement was that they were worried that Rome would eventually be alerted by the "confusion" of Missa-Afro, Missa-Indio, and Missa Nordestina (to suit the culture of people from the Northeast of Brazil) and were looking for a theological justification for these multicultural versions of the rite.

22. A letter of resignation from several of the people who had worked at the EDUCAFRO headquarters during his absence, published in January 2009, refers repeatedly to David's centralizing and authoritarian leadership, and also to these ideological issues. The letter was dated 24 January 2009 and reported online on 20 October 2012 by Círculo Pal-

At that point the Franciscan Order had withdrawn financial support for fear of legal-financial risks under new philanthropy laws, and David claimed he had to ask his family for funding. Nevertheless, EDUCAFRO continues to occupy premises in São Paulo on the lower floors of the church of São Francisco and next door to the historic building of USP's Law Faculty on the Largo São Francisco.

In 2008 I was told that thirteen thousand students were studying in EDUCAFRO "núcleos," that they were mostly women and mostly under twenty-five, and that many had children. Most of the teachers, said in 2013 to number a thousand, were also women. By 2010 there were 124 "núcleos" in the São Paulo metropolitan area where school graduates were being prepared for the vestibular. He was also developing relationships with private universities and partnerships with private companies—arranging internships with the major bank Banco Itaú for example—and was talking of operating microcredit schemes through the núcleos, although at the time these were just outlines of an idea. He had also started to offer English courses. These aspirations reflect his ambition to show that a venture can be funded through the "little man's own efforts." He tried to apply this in quite practical ways so that, although tuition at EDUCAFRO is free of charge, some kind of tax is levied on former students who hold EDUCAFRO scholarships at universities and someone is employed to keep in touch with them. They are asked to contribute financially or by teaching, working in the administration, or fund-raising. In an introductory meeting for interested students in 2013 it was explained that a person who helped by bringing in thirty students by leafleting or running a raffle, opening a local nucleus, or working six hours a week for EDUCAFRO would qualify for a grant paying full fees at a university—and private universities valued EDUCAFRO graduates because "they study, don't mess around, get good results, are punctual, and have low rates of absenteeism." In 2017 EDUCAFRO had five regional bases in the interior of São Paulo, Minas Gerais and Brasilia.

At EDUCAFRO consciousness-raising (under the title "cidadanía"— "citizenship") is an indispensable part of all courses. I accompanied an induction class in which the leader spoke of the racist nature of Brazilian society, of the students' own racism, and of the pervasiveness of negative stereotypes of women, disabled people, and "nordestinos" ("northeasterners" from the region of Brazil whence millions of migrants have come

marino, a self-described tendency within the movimento negro, but the website is no longer available.

to the big cities of the south). An example quoted was of an overweight black woman, automatically described as an "orixá"—a candomblé priestess. A fifteen-minute film was shown spelling out the history of laws against black people in Brazil (Frei David's "seven laws"). The speaker told me that these are "sort of political" events at which it is made clear to prospective students that EDUCAFRO is not just a place to study—it is also part of a movement. They were offering courses preparatory to going to study medicine and other subjects in Cuba, but students were warned about the political system there. Rather the political message was about their own lives: people who benefit from EDUCAFRO by gaining admission to a university and getting a grant should also "give something back," helping others by teaching or otherwise supporting the institution—and indeed I met two graduates who were then studying at the Faculdade Zumbi dos Palmares and were volunteering at EDU-CAFRO. Frei David joined the meeting at a certain point and said, "[I]f you came just to get into university, you need not come back, but if you came to help the cause of black advancement, then stay."

The emphasis on blackness and the background presence of the Church were illustrated by an event for EDUCAFRO students staged at the auditorium of the Memorial de América Latina in São Paulo—a cultural centre and library designed in his distinctive curvy modernist style by Oscar Niemeyer in the 1990s. Apart from the encouragement to engage in education and advocate affirmative actions, the event opened with a brief allusion to Axé—the word used in candomblé for life force—and continued with a performance of African-style dancing and singing led by a member of a Franciscan women's congregation, including a song in praise of Zumbi and the living quilombo.

The rhetoric of black empowerment that permeates Frei David's discourse is combined with an aspirational ethos reminiscent of that transmitted in evangelical churches—and indeed many EDUCAFRO students, like students generally, are evangelicals. Taken together these multiple orientations and attachments make him a movement leader, for a movement grows on the basis of links and attachments between people of otherwise quite varied convictions. As a man of God, an organizer, a warrior, and a teacher with a taste for controversy, prepared to promote the advancement of black people in whatever ways are available, Frei David's willingness to act without too much attention to ideological niceties is well suited to promoting a broad-based cause.

Although I did not visit an EDUCAFRO núcleo, I was able to read a masters thesis written by Renato dos Santos Gomes, the leader of a PVNC núcleo linked to EDUCAFRO, on the subject of the núcleo itself. The thesis was sent to me thanks to Amy Jaffa, a British student who worked with Renato (Gomes 2015). The thesis and Amy Jaffa's description provide an eloquent condensation of the social and political ethos of the organization, as well as indications of its contribution to local community life—something not usually mentioned because discussions tend to focus narrowly on educational opportunities. Located in Vila Operária in the suburban municipality of Nova Iguaçu (population eight hundred thousand), this núcleo started out in 1997 and offers weekend classes given by volunteer teachers who receive little more than their travel expenses. Students pay a nominal amount as a gesture of commitment but are expected to contribute by working as teachers after graduating. Subjects taught are Portuguese, science, mathematics, geography, history, Afro-Brazilian culture, and the all-important citizenship course. Originally they taught in premises lent by a local school, but this arrangement was ended and the operation came to depend very heavily on Renato and his wife and on the venue provided by his mother in her nursery school. The aftermath of the loss of those premises was itself instructive as a sign of the atmosphere of activism mixed in with neighbourly bonhomie that surrounds the initiative: for two days classes were given under an almond tree in a small square until a solution was found (Gomes 2015: 39). The PVNC attracted the attention of local politicians who brought improved street lighting and paving to the area and also encouraged the creation of preparatory courses for aspiring naval cadets or people looking to qualify for technical schools. It organized musical and sporting events and a Parents' Association to discuss attendance and absenteeism issues. Success in university admission was marked with social gatherings celebrating the realization of their hopes and the chance of social mobility, to the accompaniment of food (*feijoada*) and displays of *capoeira*. Its students also published a newsletter called *Azânia*—in homage to South African nationalism. But the "Pré," as it is known locally (an abbreviation of "prevestibular"), was very poor and had to "beg and borrow" notebooks, chairs, and desks from universities—equipment that also served the nursery used by the PVNC on the weekend. Separately from the PVNC, Renato ran a scheme offering "education and mentoring for young people getting out of drug trafficking." According to Amy Jaffa, "Renato would regularly go and speak to drug traffickers and try and convince them to come to his project."

These "halo effects," reminiscent of the self-managed projects associated with CEBs and the "formato CEB," are rarely mentioned in the educational or *engagé* literature on PVCs or indeed affirmative action in general. In contrast, the description of the courses and management in Renato Gomes's thesis fits well with the "official" movimento negro story and with that of Renato Emerson dos Santos, whom the thesis quotes (dos Santos 2011). The educational philosophy of the "Pré" and EDU-CAFRO, expressed in its core course on culture and citizenship, is grounded in a valorization of the knowledge and lifeways of the popular classes and in the project of forming political actors (militantes políticos) who know how to state their case, paying serious attention only to "grounded" and applicable ideas. There was, in Amy Jaffa's words, "a strong political element to the course." The valorization of the people's knowledge brought a certain distrust of official or erudite culture. Renato's thesis describes how teachers were asked to avoid "paternalism," which might undermine students' already low self-esteem, and there was some (gentle) criticism of the dated taste in music chosen by teachers for social events, notably that of the Musica Popular Brasileira (MPB) school associated with internationally famous Brazilian artists and composers of the 1970s and 1980s such as Tom Jobim, Chico Buarque, Caetano Velloso, Paulinho da Viola, and María Bethania—not surprising coming from students more accustomed to rap, hip-hop, and funk.

As in Emerson dos Santos's account of the Rocinha Comunitario PVC (dos Santos 2011: chap. 5), decisions were taken in entirely open assemblies, seminars, and forums, and the disputes about the acceptability of external funding, private or public, were also present, setting the "Christian wing" against others. There was even an attempted "coup" by a left-wing faction. But in the final analysis the operation was heavily dependent on three support mechanisms familiar to observers of Brazilian social movements. One is the commitment of family members, in this case Renato, his wife, and his mother; another is the patronage of the Catholic Church, as mediated by Frei David, via scholarships for its graduates who gained entrance to the prestigious PUC of Rio de Janeiro (37); while the third consists of occasional donations from politicians.

The financial precariousness of this venture is illustrated in Amy Jaffa's account of the project's relationship with a potential international supporter:

> I did introduce an international education charity to Renato's project, in the hope that he could get some more stable funding. The CEO came and visited and told Renato that she was going to help him. She spoke of building libraries and computer suites and provid-

ing the project with regular financial support, but I am not sure how much of this materialised. I translated correspondence between them for about a year afterwards but nothing had really taken off by then.

A More Entrepreneurial Model: Faculdade Zumbi Dos Palmares

An even more hybrid version of of black empowerment and the entrepreneurial spirit is the Faculdade Zumbi dos Palmares, a higher education institution established in 2002 in São Paulo by an entrepreneur and former police officer linked to the Partido do Movimento Democrático do Brasil (Brazilian Democratic Movement Party—PMDB), built on a private enterprise model but with major support from the city's former mayor, Gilberto Kassab (2006–12), who in effect donated to it the sizable and well-located premises of a bankrupt Rowing Club (Clube de Regatas Tietê).[23] The Faculdade Zumbi is committed to admitting 50 percent black students, and to some extent the content of the teaching is designed to attract students drawn to the more politically progressive branches of the subjects taught. Thus the law course highlights themes such as social inclusion, diversity, minority rights, and affirmative action. I attended a first- and a second-year class and could see the prominence of racism in Brazil as the point of departure.

Zumbi has a well-designed and lively website containing much information translated into English, which combines an affirmation of black identity and opportunity, and an emphasis on partnerships with business, offering employment opportunities while students pursue their studies and attaching a positive value to entrepreneurship.[24] Fees in 2010 were modest—R$300 per month (c. US$140 at that time), and classes are taught in the evening. As a "faculdade" it does not have the status of a university, but it is recognized as a higher education institution and its diplomas count as professional qualifications. Not everyone involved in the quotas campaign, though, approves of the Faculdade Zumbi because it charges fees and perhaps also because of the political background to its creation, which owed much to the founder's connections to the PSDB, to Paulo Renato de Souza, and later to Mayor Kassab, who, though at

---

23. The club had fallen on hard times as the elite migrated away from the area, and it owed millions in taxes, so its premises now belonged to the municipality, which made it available on very generous terms. Kassab has more recently been a minister in the Temer government. When I visited SECAD in 2008 I was told that there was a "project" to support the Faculdade Zumbi, but I do not know if anything came of that.

24. See the Zumbi website, http://www.zumbidospalmares.edu.br

that time technically attached to a "right-wing" party, the Democratas (universally known as DEM), was close to José Serra, a leading PSDB figure, at various times Mayor and Governor of São Paulo, Minister of Health and of Foreign Affairs and twice Presidential candidate. Paulo Renato told me he had helped the Faculdade Zumbi write its project and that the venture had received funding from the powerful educational entrepreneur João Carlos di Genio, whom we have already encountered. People involved ideologically in the movimento negro, with their conviction that the excluded should put pressure on the state so as to claim what is rightfully theirs, may also not entirely sympathize with the self-help ethos propounded by Faculdade Zumbi and, in a more populist register, EDUCAFRO. In 2010 the Faculdade Zumbi had almost two thousand students (all taking evening classes) of whom 80 percent were black and 60 percent were women, and was offering courses in subjects like law, business, teacher training (*pedagogia*), and transport technology (a 2.5-year course in partnership with the city's transport system). In an interview in April 2010 the Faculdade's academic director said that access to paid internships was one of its main attractions, which I was told had benefited six hundred of its two thousand students. Echoing what I had already heard at GELEDES, the director said they had found a more positive response among US-based multinationals than among Brazilian companies. The Faculdade also qualified for ProUni funding and provided fee reductions of up to 100 percent with funding from the French supermarket group Carrefour. To be sure, the fees are so low that this is not an expensive proposition for sponsors.

Fashioning a Black Middle Class: The Instituto Cultural Steve Biko

The Instituto Cultural Steve Biko (ISB—Steve Biko Institute often known simply as "Biko") in Salvador is the most structured of the nonprofit prevestibular courses I have visited or read about. In 2014 it was still occupying premises lent by a religious institution in the city's historic colonial centre, and was planning to move into new, more modern premises in a central location ceded by the municipality (in a deal similar to the Zumbi case) for a twenty-year period and due to be refurbished with the help of the Coca-Cola Corporation—which, I was told, also supports the Faculdade Zumbi. Once again a major municipality has said it would make a substantial capital contribution to a nonprofit, modestly fee-paying, educational body catering to a black clientele with a self-help ethos—but as of 2017 the ISB was still at the same address.

The ISB was founded in 1992 as a cooperative by economics students at the UFBA and named after the founder of the black consciousness movement in South Africa, murdered by the authorities while in detention in 1977. Since then it has offered after-school classes for secondary school students from Salvador and its suburbs to enable them to prepare for the vestibular.

The idea of black pride, or pride in blackness, remains a prominent theme in the institute's public presence, but it handles the subject with care: in a CD entitled *Bikud@s*,[25] produced to mark its twentieth anniversary, the opening sequence speaks of "consciência negra" as an attitude of mind (atitude mental) and not a question of skin colour. The commentary and testimonies focus on the achievements of Biko's graduates who went on to study medicine or to become professionals. In contrast to the discourse heard from Frei David, the accent is on future prospects rather than the exclusion and poverty of the black population, although these are mentioned. Two of the interviewees on this highly professional CD cannot hold back their tears as they describe their appreciation for the institute and how it boosted their prospects. The word "boost" is important here because of the emphasis on self-confidence: "It is the mind of the oppressed that is the most effective weapon of the oppressor." The CD is strongly marked by the black consciousness idea: for example, one speaker describes herself as "working for the black community based on black knowledge and concepts" and says, "We need a black university, and all our struggle has to lead up to that." Another black consciousness theme—that of a people unaware of their own history—also appeared in 2009 when I interviewed the institute's accountant, himself an ISB graduate who went on to study economics at UFBA. To illustrate the poor quality of school education, he described students who come to study having learned in school that "the US and Europe always set the standard for everything, especially in education and culture, and often they think Africa is just a country, not realizing it is a continent with many countries."

A second person I interviewed, in 2014, a graduate of the Salvador

---

25. The title is a play on the Biko name and the word "bicudos," meaning "pointed" or perhaps "pointy," derived from "bico"—a beak.

PUC, remarked on moderate resistance on the part of Brazilian corporate sponsors to being identified with race-based interpretations of exclusion and his feeling that the institute is better known abroad than in Brazil—witness an exchange programme with Morehouse College in Atlanta and the Coca-Cola sponsorship—but it has received support from the electricity company CHESF and from the local Secretariat for Racial Equality (SEPROMI), which supported the above-mentioned video among other things. The institute's only regular source of income (as distinct from lumpy project support) are the fees paid by students. There is a desire to convert it into a higher education institution—a "faculdade" like the Faculdade Zumbi—but this remains a long-term project: it was planned for 2012, but the date mentioned during my 2014 interview was 2018.

Like EDUCAFRO the institute ensures that each course includes citizenship and black consciousness, human rights, and the "recovery of history." The theme of black awareness is further reflected in the institute's exchange agreements with historical black colleges in the United States, like Morehouse, and in the foregrounding of images, expressions, and symbols associated in popular culture with blackness. Thus a programme aiming to get young blacks into science subjects is called OGUN-TECH, after Ogun, a supernatural figure in the candomblé pantheon. Another programme, called the Projeto Mentes e Portas Abertas (Open Minds and Open Doors—POMPA), evoking the idea of "pomp," or pride and theatrical stylishness, works with university students and aims to insert people into strategic positions so they can contribute to policy-making. The institute is also represented in performances at the Salvador carnival.

The emphasis at Biko is on getting black students not just into university but also into prestige professions, so priority is given to preparation for entrance into public universities in Bahia—UFBA and the state university, UNEB. The OGUNTECH programme, which ran for four years but was not running in 2014 due to a lack of external funding, was designed to help secondary school students improve their science education so they could gain entrance into science courses at university. My 2014 informant estimated that some five thousand students have passed through the institute and of these "about" a thousand went on to a public university—which means fifty per year. But numbers fluctuate due to short-term and unstable funding: when the institute received support from SECAD in the early 2000s, its student numbers swelled to over three hundred, only then to fall back to seventy.

Although it was a forerunner of the idea of the PVC, the Steve Biko Institute has not been reproduced: it has a more solid administrative structure than many others, does not rely on volunteer teachers, charges fees, and has its own line on black consciousness. Emerson Renato dos Santos spoke of it a little dismissively as a "black middle class project." Of course, Biko staff and students took part in demonstrations in favor of quotas, but the black consciousness brand does set them apart from the some in the movimento negro and also discourages the identification of the movimento with any particular ideological commitment.[26]

The Limits of Educational Intervention

Does all this activity actually improve the life chances of the students? Apart from the disappointing finding by Mendes et al. (2016) that students from PVCs did not perform well in the UERJ vestibular exam, we have no systematic evaluation, but it is salutary to return to Amy Jaffa's report because it reminds us that while these proliferating organizations can create enthusiasm and commitment at the grass roots, and while they also raise awareness of discrimination and racial exclusion, the road to visible improvement in their students' life chances after school and university, in the labour market and in access to the elite, is long and grueling and requires concerted and sustained state intervention.

Jaffa followed some students through to their next stage when she attended a social work course at Rio's PUC and reports that it was "made up entirely of *bolsistas* [scholarship holders] from Rio's favelas and many of them had been able to pass the vestibular exam and get a place at PUC by attending a PVC." But the post-education story is less encouraging: her former colleagues tell sobering stories about the brick wall that faces graduates from stigmatized groups when they enter the labour market.

> I was told in February 2017 that only three people from the group of some 35 in my cohort at the PUC have been able to get a job (and only one has a paid job as a qualified social worker). There was also a wider feeling with people I spoke to that the use of any resources designed for "carentes e negros" would be detrimental to them—friends

---

26. This may be related to the name of the institute, Biko having been a controversial figure in South Africa in the anti-apartheid movement, contested by people following a more orthodox Marxist line of thought, because of his ideas about black consciousness. There is a long history of differences between Biko's ideas and the African National Congress party's steadfast structuralism and universalism, which resisted racial specificity.

of mine would not use the subsidies they are allowed to enter *concur-sos* etc. because they said anyone who can be identified with such things would immediately be discounted. Some of this stigma may also exist in signing up to a course advertised as designed specifically for "carentes e negros."

This is not peculiar to Brazil and serves as a reminder that improving access to education is far from the "end of the story": we have already mentioned extensive research in France showing that discrimination is much more severe in the search for work than in education or indeed in the workplace itself once people have found a job (Brinbaum et al. 2012; Beauchemin et al. 2016), and we saw earlier that beneficiaries of affirmative action in prestigious US universities have an unusually high rate of failure when they are hired by prestigious law firms. The authors who produced that finding laid the blame at the feet of the affirmative action system that had placed them under excessive pressure and did not think to ask whether discrimination or stigma at work itself had anything to do with it (Sander and Taylor 2012). The 1992 Brazilian data analyzed by Biderman and Guimarães (2004) showed that race discrimination in the labour market was severe mostly in the upper reaches and affected men above all, while sex discrimination affected women.

Conclusion

It might seem, at first glance, that the examples in the last section should nuance my emphasis on corporatism and the involvement with the state. But I do not think it would do more than offer precisely that—a "nuance." The reason is that all three face structural limitations because they are outside the charmed circle, or maybe iron gates, of state-protected higher education. Frei David's venture sends a few of its graduates to the competitive Catholic universities, but for the most part they go to for-profit private sector universities, which are widely assumed to offer a second-best option. The institutionalization of EDUCAFRO seemed a little precarious, and the article by Mendes and his colleagues cast some doubt on the quality of what can be offered with untrained volunteer teachers (Mendes 2016). The extent of control or coordination by Frei David's tiny and mostly volunteer central staff on the very large number of núcleos is unknown: I did not visit any of them, and although I did meet people from them at the head office they did not seem very eager for me to visit. Renato Gomes's thesis describes his venture as totally independent, something like a franchise-holder of Frei David's Rio de Janeiro organization. The PVC phenomenon may be or may have been widespread and quite deeply rooted, especially if Antonio Sergio Guimaraes and Renato Emerson dos Santos were right to estimate its numbers at around eight hundred, but it remains unresearched, unevaluated, and undocumented. A small number of PVCs were run by universities themselves and so presumably had a more solid institutional basis, and some of those benefited from SECAD's initiatives while they lasted, but if they were sustainable on any significant scale they would have formed some sort of national association, which they have not. There is also some doubt about their survival now that the MEC has established the end-of-schooling ENEM exam as an alternative path to university admission in place of at least the first stage of the vestibular—the more competitive institutions have a second and even a third stage; but EDUCAFRO seems to continue as active as ever.

With its premises, political backing, a substantial student clientele, and its reputation for arranging internships, the Faculdade Zumbi seems to have a firmer institutional basis. But it is only a faculdade and would need a major capital injection to aspire to full university status. Its debt to political sponsorship obviously resonates with the corporatism thesis, although there is little institutional permanence built into such arrangements.

The Steve Biko Institute shows signs of permanence, but it is reliant on private sector donations to survive through fluctuations in its student numbers, and it does not seem to have generated the widespread appeal or the sort of imitators that might be hoped for given the large numbers of school graduates who aspire to attend university. The acquisition of new premises, if indeed it comes to fruition, may herald future growth.

In the early parts of this chapter I cast some doubt on whether the movimento negro is "really" a social movement, on account of the lack of a historical project for society as a whole and the dependence of its many manifestations on the state and international NGOs. I have documented the variety of manifestations of the movimento that show the wide range of projects, as well as debates and think tanks, gathered under the very broad motto of black advancement, without a centralized leadership—for the strength of movements lies in loose ties among groups, communities, projects, and idea factories rather than centralized leadership. The ties may sometimes be intangible affinities, but they are nonetheless real in their effects. If a centre of gravity must be found, then for this movement it must be in academia, for it is through academic institutions that sections of the movement have achieved a degree of power, it is there that its ideas are debated and transmitted, and the movement's base consists principally of people aspiring to attend academic institutions. The PVCs, the Faculdade Zumbi, and EDUCAFRO are something like a periphery to that central focus. They look "up" to the university—not to political power or business success. Other movements may be weakened by a lack of diversity in their networks. The quilombo movement would not exist at all but for the involvement of anthropologists. The MST has lost influence after breaking with the state at the national (though not the local) level and becoming distanced from the intelligentsia. Environmentalism relies heavily on international support, and it remains to be seen whether the indigenous leadership that has grown up can develop links beyond the anthropological profession.

The movimento negro's dependence on external support may be disappointing for a true believing *basista* who looks to social movements as the authentic expression of grassroots culture and claims. But it is now quite normal for local struggles to transcend national and cultural frontiers, and for their movements to form part of worldwide movements. In Latin America especially, struggles for the recognition of ethnic identity and racial equality, like struggles for the protection of human rights, are permeated by the invocation of international legal instruments, like the International Labour Organization's Convention no. 169, by the involvement of multilateral institutions, and by the support of international foundations and NGOs. In these circumstances, social mobilizations must be interpreted with regard to their international as well as their national dimension. Even then, however, the almost irresistible draw of the state remains, and it is to this that we return in the final chapter.

SIX

The Campaign and Theories of Social Movements

The "movimento negro" is difficult to fit into the theory and definition of social movements, not least because it is singularly short of formal organization. One of the standard, though somewhat dated, theoretical approaches to social movements, the "resource mobilization" school, assumes that movements are composed of formal organizations, even if many informal networks are useful and even necessary for them to achieve their goals (McCarthy and Zald 1977). The assumption that movements have defined goals narrows the scope and excludes the very diversity of visions that enables them to mobilize large contingents and wide-ranging interests. Likewise formality does not allow for the allusive or lateral associations of thought and community that together go to make collective identities. The assumption of formality also restricts its relevance to many situations in countries where the civic culture or material resources available to many sectors of society, do not lend themselves easily to formal organization. Although the notion of a "social movement industry" is also contained in McCarthy and Zald's model (1210), pointing to the interconnections whereby organizations contribute constituencies and resources to each other in pursuit of shared or overlapping ideals and goals, I would emphasize more the unenunciated connections behind rhetoric and strategies. The *variety* of ideas, identities, and affiliations present among activists and followers enables a movement to reach out to and draw resources from different interests and ideals: in the Brazilian context the social movement industry in the field of racial equality brings together support from people connected to feminism; to organizations defending human rights, employment rights, the environment, and health; and to a residual legacy from the CEBs—in addition to the pervasive academic presence in the humanities and social sciences. It has shown some capacity to create the linkages a movement requires between people of different classes, different ideological leanings, and different professions and subcultures. There has been only limited research on activity in support of black advancement within powerful groups such as the OAB (Ordem dos Advogados do Brasil—Brazilian Bar Association) and the trade union movement (principally the CUT), but the OAB has national and state-level commissions tasked with fighting racism and promoting racial equality, and within the CUT there is a coordinating group, or "coletivo," devoted to the fight against racism. The MST seems to have shown little interest in the subject, nor has it supported the quilombolas. Militant activity in support of the black cause is woven into the fabric of certain sectors of academic life and the quasi-academic network of NGOs, but the resulting activism has quite a narrow social base and hardly goes to make up a mass movement. In the language of resource mobilization theory these organizations or networks are almost entirely populated with conscience-driven or cause-oriented constituents and followers: the potential beneficiaries of their actions are elsewhere. Resource mobilization theory, reflecting the US context in which it was first developed, speaks of issues separating, for example, intellectuals and worker members in trade unions, or blacks and whites in the civil rights movement (McCarthy and Zald 1977: 1232), but at least they are or were in the same organizations: in these Brazilian cases the conscience-driven constituents and the beneficiaries inhabit quite different worlds, and one is forced to ask whether the absence of a mobilized beneficiary constituency is the stark manifestation of class distance. We see this in the lack of interest among quota campaigners in private universities, which receive the thousands of low-income and black beneficiaries of ProUni. Nevertheless, the softer requirement of an allusive appeal across different spheres of social and political life, and of the spread of a sensibility that is certainly hard to pinpoint, does surely appear in Brazil, as the cause of black advancement springs up and continues to grow in many different contexts. After President Roussef's impeachment we must wait and see whether it continues to grow now that the state is evidently less receptive.

Resource mobilization theory bears the imprint of its time and place, when civil rights, black empowerment, and the antiwar movement were riding high in the United States. By the 2000s evidence was emerging in the United States to document the twin trends of declining levels of participation in civic life and the growing dominance of professional organizers in volunteer and pressure groups (Putnam 2000; Skocpol 2003). In Latin America also, there were once episodes of massive collective popular mobilization: Argentina was the scene of both massive demonstrations in the street and also dramatic confrontations of organized political apparatuses and unions in the postwar period and again in the early 1970s; in Chile the combination of large-scale street presence and a background of urban and rural unions and party organization underlay the crisis that culminated in the 1973 coup; in Brazil trade unions and also the Peasant Leagues figured prominently in the conflicts that led to the 1964 coup, and the São Paulo trade unions played an important mobilizing role in the transition to democracy in the late 1970s and 1980s (Lehmann 1978; Valenzuela 1978; O'Donnell 1988, 1999 [1993]; Stepan 1988; Garretón 1989). But times have changed. Only in Chile have we seen sustained mass mobilization, in the student movement (Fleet and Guzmán-Concha 2017), which translated into university reforms in the 2014–17 period. If the scale of protest marchers in the street, rather than organization, was a deciding factor, the Brazilian government would have fallen already in 2013 when millions went down into the street to march against corruption, the World Cup, poor public services, transport price hikes, and so on. Perhaps because they were mobilized through social media, they lacked an organizational backbone, and trade unions, ensconced in their hybrid "system," were absent (Tavares de Almeida 1996, 1997). The protests lasted over a month but led to little save some delayed hikes in urban transport prices. But not all was lost: discretely, in response to demands to fight corruption, President Dilma successfully proposed a law allowing plea-bargaining, which became a key (some say abused) instrument enabling judges to convict businessmen and some politicians in the scandals of 2015–17.

In the absence of large-scale organizational strength, social movements in Brazil today rely on NGO and state support and, perhaps as a result, their practical activity tends to focus on self-managed projects. When nationwide events do occur, like the national CONAPIR conference on racial equality, they are organized and underwritten by SEPPIR. In Brazil one of the few articulated popular movement organizations— that is, an organization with a structure capable of reproducing itself, and with cadres and resources of its own—has been the MST (Branford and Rocha 2002; Carter 2010), yet its *assentamentos* are heavily dependent financially on government support through bank credit. Basismo, too, at its height, expressed in the CEBs, which were present at the birth

of the MST in Rio Grande do Sul in the 1970s, relied on Church personnel for leadership and on international NGOs for resources and had little to fall back on when Pope John Paul turned on the priests and religious who constituted its support network.

A Constituency

The quotas campaign itself is not a grassroots movement in the manner
of basismo, since its strength and social base are concentrated among
intellectuals and potential university students rather than the socially excluded and voiceless. It has not developed an infrastructure of local organizations with regular meetings and activities. So does it qualify as a
social movement rather than a pressure group? Does it herald a turning
point in the mechanisms of reproduction of society?

To answer this question we may return to the Touraine model—which
dates back even further than resource mobilization theory—built on a
tripod of "identity, opposition and a project of cultural transformation"
(Touraine 1988: 256). Clearly the campaign we are discussing, as part of
the movimento negro, does have a principle of identity in the black population of Brazil and has devoted much time and energy to the expansion of that constituency by convincing people—with some success—to
"asumir" their blackness, while also persuading Brazilian society as a
whole to recognize them, more than bearers of a cultural heritage, above
all as full citizens. Its practical project has achieved a remarkable public
relations success by distilling the many demands that can arise from a
history of oppression and a contemporary reality of exclusion into a single word—Quotas! This word condenses the aim of bringing about reparation for the injustices of the distant and recent past, to get black people
into the elite, and to darken the face of Brazilian higher education. Its
appeal can therefore be very wide indeed, and the same can be said of its
constituency, consisting according to some of almost half the country's
population. The clamour for higher education spreads ever more widely.
Members of the country's growing lower middle class—popularly known
by the marketing category "Classe C"—have begun to aspire to a university education, and they need it if they or their children are to make
headway in the better-paid and more secure sectors of the labour market. In addition, the very ambiguity about "who qualifies" as a black person and the generous official quota criteria of "pretos, pardos, e indígenas" broaden the constituency of the movimento negro still further, and
to this may be added people who have never thought of themselves as

black or pardo but come to do so not for opportunistic reasons but because they genuinely begin to interpret their disadvantage in racial terms. In addition, apart from elite exclusion, other dimensions of black disadvantage or worse are becoming more and more prominent in the public sphere and can strengthen identification with the black cause, notably the disproportionate number of black victims of police violence in a country with a horrifying record of police killings perpetrated against poor people (Waiselfisz 2012; French 2014).

The numbers involved in the quotas campaign strictly understood are small in relation to the theoretical constituency of potential university entrants, which could be the entire population of eighteen- to twenty-four-year-olds, but most of those do not reach the minimum standard of education needed to gain admission to a public university. A 2012 research paper from UNICAMP, based on the 2009 PNAD survey, found that in the poorest quintile 77 percent of children did not get beyond "ensino fundamental" (in principle for ages seven to fourteen) and only 3 percent reached higher education. Among the wealthiest quintile the corresponding proportions were 15 and 60 percent (Andrade 2012).[1] The pressure for access to higher education can only increase.

The movimento negro can claim that it has achieved a great deal and not only for black students: low-income students were swept up in the legislation driven by race-based claims without so to speak "lifting a finger," and the movement has pressed for *bolsas de permanencia* (bursaries),[2] which are not allocated on a race basis, it has benefited students in federal institutions coming from low-income families. This is important in light of the need for students in the most competitive courses to study full time, and of the (probably exaggerated) 30 percent dropout rate found in Mendes's study of UERJ (2014).[3] The success of affirmative action and its beneficiaries calls for supplementary supervision, mentoring, and tu-

---

1. Thirty-three percent of the population aged eighteen to twenty-four had completed *ensino medio* (high school) and a further 19 percent were in higher education, leaving 21 percent who did not even complete *ensino fundamental* and a further 27 percent who completed "ensino fundamental" but then either left school or continued but did not complete "ensino medio"—in principle for those aged fifteen to seventeen.

2. I have used the very English term "bursaries" because these are grants paid on the basis of need rather than academic achievement. To qualify students must show that they are attending their classes. Blacks do not get any racial preference, but indigenous and quilombola students get twice that sum to allow for extra expenses since they generally live in rural areas far from university campuses. See the websites of the MEC (Information as of May 2017), http://permanencia.mec.gov.br and http://portal.mec.gov.br/pnaes

3. I say "probably exaggerated" because, as the author points out, the dropout rate may be due to reasons other than failure or renunciation of higher education.

toring, since by definition these students arrive at university with lower marks than their peers. This applies especially, as Valente showed, to students from low-income backgrounds who have come via the socioeconomic quota. But affirmative action is not accompanied by additional budgetary allocations to universities, although the extra administrative cost is not negligible, many having created administrative units ("pro-Reitorias") to manage affirmative actions. On the other hand financial support for non–racially classified low-income students in public universities has risen substantially. In 2017 the "bolsas permanência" are worth R$400 (c. US$120) monthly and are paid to students from families with an income equal to or less than 1.5 minimum wages per capita at federal universities (cotistas and noncotistas). Since 2010 the federal government has administered a hardship fund, the Plano Nacional de Assistência Estudiantil (National Plan for Student Financial Support—PNAES), to help students with living expenses and budgeted at R$650 million in 2013 (c. US$300 million at the time). We have also seen that students have access to research internships. These sums are far in excess of the estimated R$100 million cost in 2016 of the ProUni programme, which pays fees for qualifying students in private institutions, but on the other hand far less than the loan fund for students in private higher education institutions (FIES), which was budgeted to receive $R1.2 billion in 2017.[4] Nonetheless, significant quantitative and qualitative changes in the public universities arising from the quotas will unfold over the coming years, despite severe budgetary pressures.

The growth potential for the movimento negro, for its part, looks very positive, to the point where it could shake off its minority victim status and become a voice for a much wider constituency. The number of young blacks applying and being admitted to public and private universities is likely to continue increasing. It is to be hoped also that their large numbers, due to the broad-brush criteria for quota admission and the large number of quota places available, will help to avoid the problems of self-confidence and isolation that seem to have affected both the well-being and the grades of some students admitted through affirmative action in the United States. To them we may add the effect of growing

---

4. Note that these items are not strictly comparable because, while the payments to students are in cash, FIES is a loan fund that in theory will one day see its loans repaid, and the cost of ProUni is in terms of tax and social security payments foregone. I cannot find the PNAES budget for 2017. For other data, see the statement from MEC at http://portal.mec.gov.br/projeto-escola-que-protege/40-perguntas-frequentes-911936531/prouni-1484253965/5821-sp-117675771

black consciousness and self-recognition on the size of the potential constituency of the movimento negro. As we have noted, the ideologues of the black movement seek to expand the numbers of their constituency, and so very large numbers of people could be persuaded to renounce their sense of nonblackness and join in supporting the cause—a cause that by the same token would broaden its appeal and become increasingly representative of the population as a whole. If there were eventually to be a convergence of the cause of black advancement and the cause of young people as a whole, it would be a remarkable inversion of the premonitions of a narrowing identity politics amid growing racial tension. Instead of deepening divisions, the call of black identity would transcend them, and the concept of difference underlying fears of neutralization or mestiço co-optation would dissipate. "Black" could then become the whole of Brazil.

For the moment, however, we may point to a striking contrast between the narrow constituency of the Brazilian quotas campaign as it has developed so far and the movement in Chile for free higher education. The Chilean student movement, which has been a mass movement, though led by students from prestige public universities, placed the abolition of fee-paying education at all levels at the top of its demands (Fleet 2011). Chilean public universities, unlike their Brazilian counterparts, are also fee paying, so their students had a direct interest in this issue, but they also fought for the reform of private universities, which are a thriving business in Chile as well, despite legal prohibitions on profit-making in education. So their aims were broader-based, and their movement achieved a major success when the Congress and the Bachelet government decreed a gradual abolition of all fees in higher education over a five-year period starting in 2016. In contrast to Brazil, Chilean academics seem to have played little role in the movement. Just as in Brazil, however, public universities are not receiving extra funding to manage quotas, so Chilean public universities are not receiving sufficient extra funds to compensate for the lost income from fees. They are now also far more dependent on the political conjuncture, and as of early 2018 even quite high prestige private institutions were dismissing staff and closing departments.

An Adversary?

The quotas movement cannot be said to possess or to have constructed the clear adversary that the Touraine model—built as it is on the experience of European working-class and social democratic movements—

requires. The universities themselves can hardly be thought of as an enemy—rather they and the field of policy, law, and regulation in which they operate, are arenas in which the struggle is pursued. Whatever might be said about patterns of exclusion and racial prejudice, few would claim that blacks are engaged in a struggle against a white supremacist elite inspired by a doctrine of racial supremacy bent on keeping them out of higher education and blocking their social advancement. Strategies to weaken the opposition to quotas have been conducted in this field and its associated professional associations, and rarely have they identified an enemy "bloc"—their enemy has rather been an idea or a climate of denial and indifference. Frei David's separate campaign stands out for its confrontational stance, but he, too, cooperates extensively with the private sector, whose dubious standards and profit-making vocation he does not publicly criticize.

The quotas campaign thus far could be described as a campaign against exclusion from quite specific institutions and against a system of racial exclusion from the elite of society. The demand for quotas would have been much more conflictive if the university system had been stagnant, since it would have brought a visible replacement of lighter-skinned middle-income students by darker-skinned lower-income students: Mendes did detect some of this, but if the system had been stagnant the competition would have been much more severe. Instead, new public universities were being created and student numbers were increasing. Despite the criticism of higher education institutions, especially those in São Paulo (USP and UNICAMP), for their resistance and what some brand their underlying racist culture, the movimento did not challenge their continued leading role presumably because its members respect their brand names and their role as prime channels to the elite. (The same can be said of campaigns in Britain to widen, socially and racially, admissions to Oxford and Cambridge.) The tension between rising demand and stagnant university budgets, which is likely to continue for many years, may, however, bring new conflicts over affirmative action.

There is therefore little alternative to an institutional engagement that has both short- and long-term fruits: in the short term the "browning" of the university, or at least of its student population; and in the long run the browning of the elite and perhaps one day even of the professoriate.

Reorienting the Cultural Reproduction of Inequality

Does the movement also impinge on the core mechanisms of reproduction of society, as Touraine requires? For campaigners universities are institutions for the reproduction of racial inequality: their role in the reproduction of inequality in general is a secondary issue, at least on the face of it. This is not a criticism of the campaigners, who are from the black movement, and that is their cause. The relative "whiteness" of universities is part of the reproduction of the system, not a consequence of a doctrine of racial supremacy or even of conscious racial attitudes, but it is part of the institution's "persona"—that is, when a rare black person appears in class in a law school he or she will feel different, as also would a person who bears the marks of poverty or speaks in a different accent—although the sense of difference would be softened in a sociology class or an education school, compared to medicine or engineering. But the quotas, with the darker faces they are bringing to lecture halls, are changing this, as we learn from Cicaló (2012b). Apart from study and learning or academic qualification, the social experience of university can enable people from different backgrounds to learn a new language, a new accent, and new habits—and if it encourages them to retain and even display the apanage of their racial or class or regional identities, and to appropriate *each others'* habits of speech and dress, or their use of leisure time, the effect is to transform the signification of those identities by conferring a positive charge upon them. The effect of an influx of black professors would be even greater.

It is precisely the place of the university as a highly selective stage on the path to elite status that attracts the quotas movement. Had this selectivity and elitism themselves been under attack, the country would have seen a movement, more like that which has taken place in Chile, to change the structures of higher education themselves. The lack of resistance among the political and economic elite may also indicate a confidence that these institutions will not "massify"—that they will remain as relatively narrow funnels—and so a change in their "colour" will not bring a change in that function: the opposition to quotas, after all, has come from within the academic world and from the leading newspapers, whereas the Supreme Court and the Congress waved the idea through with little opposition. If this reasoning is correct then the elite is less concerned with the colour of its membership than with keeping itself small. Alternatively, we may see the development of expensive private and selective nonprofit universities: they would have to be nonprofit (like Mexico's Instituto Tecnológico de Monterrey, for example) if they were to fulfill the role of elite reproduction: there is a widespread awareness in Brazil and elsewhere that for-profit education does not produce quality education. In the short run, however, the current dual structure of Brazilian higher education, with its vast low-quality for-profit private sector, will remain—but the face of the student population in prestige institutions darkens.

The Epidemiology of Ideas

A social movement can be distinguished from pressure or interest groups by the ability of an idea to "catch on" among otherwise unconnected groups and individuals, as in McCarthy and Zald's "social movement industry"—a "substructure" of participants or activists who bind together strands from different social movement organizations (1977: 1210). But I would go further: the role of these multipurpose activists who bridge different organizations is of course important, but beyond the quasi professionals and cadres a movement can plug into disparate themes and motifs, creating, if it succeeds, a broad spread of thin affiliation to complement the core of thick commitment to any particular theme. If this does not happen then the movement can resemble an interest group or, if over-focused, a sect rather than a movement. We can observe thin or loose affiliation in contemporary "alternative" or dissident subcultures at the intersection of antiglobal, environmentalist, feminist, indigenist, and cognate causes, whose followers share incidental features that vary from place to place and group to group: some may share an inclination toward alternative lifestyles, others may like to go to demonstrations, some may be statist, and others libertarian, but their connections multiply through lateral features and social as well as ideological connections, for reasons neither conscious nor willed. This is why I speak of the epidemiological features of social movements by analogy with Dan Sperber's concept of the epidemiology of representations (1996). An idea may spread through the efforts of people consciously to promote it—like religious missionaries and political campaigners—but it may also more stealthily incorporate itself into the "web of intuitive beliefs" that enables a population to communicate (96). The term intersectionality translates this "web" into a more explicit or visible strategy. By developing a halo of nonconfrontational progressive politics and broadening its constituency to include people who had not thought of themselves as black, the movimento negro has been highly successful in propagating the idea of quotas, as evidenced by the absence of controversy when they spread beyond education into the federal public service and also into the São Paulo municipality.[5]

---

5. In a decree issued in 2013.

This approach also finds support in two of the most quoted ever articles in sociology, by Mark Granovetter, on the "strength of weak ties" (Granovetter 1973, 1983), a model reflected many years later in Putnam's *Bowling Alone* where he writes of "bridging" and "bonding" forms of social capital. Granovetter started with a simple proposition that was concerned with the success of individuals and community groups in achieving desired outcomes of interest to them, and he adduces theoretical argument and empirical evidence to show the advantages brought to them by weak ties enabling people and community leaders to both learn from and communicate with people who could be quite remote from their immediate circle. Community here refers to diversified groupings—but intense local bonding without bridging ties between cliques or groupings within the community actually weakens leaders' abilities to achieve anything and individuals' ability to achieve their goals in the labour market and elsewhere: "the more local bridges (per person?) in a community and the greater their degree, the more cohesive the community and the more capable of acting in concert" (Granovetter 1973: 1376). The important resulting claim counteracts the widely held intuition that solidarity and internal cohesion are essential to successful claims-making on behalf of societal groupings: "social systems lacking in weak ties will be fragmented and incoherent. New ideas will spread slowly, scientific endeavors will be handicapped, and subgroups separated by race, ethnicity, geography, or other characteristics will have difficulty reaching a modus vivendi" (Granovetter 1983: 202). I would add that this implies also that even organized claims-making on behalf of a racial or religious group is open to the same proviso: it has to reflect diversity within the group and resist an over-homogenized concept of its own social base. The affinity of this model with my explanation of social movement success is evident, as also is its affinity with Putnam's lament over the decline of associative life in the United States: even while "joining" remained vigorous he points out that the joining is disproportionately concentrated in evangelical churches whose members prioritize care of each other ("bonding social capital") over looking beyond their immediate grouping ("bridging" again), while leadership in civil society organizations has become ever more professionalized and their membership, however large, ever more passive (Putnam 2000).

A successful social movement embodies ideas that spread beyond their point of origin and beyond organizations formally engaged with it; a range of organizations, parties, bureaucracies, interest groups, and professional associations are drawn to an idea and, importantly, its ap-

peal extends across class boundaries, so that many organizations that
share some goals or whose followers frequent overlapping social worlds
are inclined to support it even if it is not principally their concern, while
others who might have doubts feel free to keep quiet. This serves to
broaden alliances and legitimate the idea, projecting it beyond a narrow
base of enthusiasts, and bringing together people with diverse interests
and ideological allegiances. If one thinks of movements as subcultures
living under the sign of ideals, symbols, and emblems that can be shared
across such frontiers, and are thus capable of bringing pressure to
change from many directions, then there is space for tightly or loosely
organized interest groups and institutions within them. To some extent
this has been the achievement of the movimento negro, combining a
small number of key players loosely linked by networks rather than leadership structures to a much larger constituency of interested people, and
a wide appeal grounded in an idea of citizenship. Despite its lack of a
mass base, it achieved public recognition of the racial exclusion that (to
simplify a little), until President Cardoso spoke out very late in the twentieth century, was the dirty secret of Brazilian society.

Not everyone, of course, agrees: for Michael Hanchard this multifariousness is not an advantage, His pioneering (English-language) study
conducted in the early 1990s offers many good reasons for his frustration
with the movement as it was then, grounded, among other things, in an
implicit view that the civil rights movement and its Black Power offshoot
in the United States are the models for racial dissent and achieving
change. Hanchard wrote of political blackness in Brazil as a point of encounter for various ideological currents coming from the United States,
Africa, and local Brazilian ideological sources, implying that this mix
distracted from a focus on race (1994: 90). He was critical of the cultural
themes so central to Brazilian black consciousness and black resistance,
noting that samba and candomblé do not work as drivers of black mobilization because they are emblems of Brazilian national identity and not
of black empowerment, and blaming "culturalism" for leading the movement "away from strategies of contemporary political change . . . . towards symbolic protest and a fetishization of Afro-Brazilian culture"
(99). He also regretted that "Black Soul," which had been "an expression of resistance," as well as "a form of commodified leisure," was "ap-
propriated for mass consumption" (99), and he criticized "the absence
of Afro-Brazilian versions of boycotting, sit-ins, civil disobedience and
armed struggle" (!) (138). Hanchard's view is to be contrasted with that
of Benedita da Silva, whom he quoted. For long Benedita—an unusual

figure as a black woman, an evangelical and a politician of the Left—was a lone black voice in Brazilian institutional politics and, in contrast to Hanchard's call for a more focused campaign, distinguished a social movement, which in her view could not have a common ideology because of the diversity within it, from a political party—by which she meant her own party, the PT. So she recognized a common cause in the movimento negro but did not see the need for it to have a common ideology (97).

The movement for black awareness, rights, and empowerment in the United States may have brought about far more legal and institutional change in that society than the movimento negro has achieved in Brazil, but the multifariousness that Hanchard regrets does have the potential of infusing the question of racial exclusion and black rights into many spheres of public life. The spread of ideas, jargon or habits of speech, symbols, and even lifestyle features like modes of dress, hairstyles, badges, and t-shirt slogans plus the incremental spread of discussion groups and action groups not to speak of the multiplier effects of social media, are further "epidemiological" features. In the academy a history of absence of black faces means that as they begin to appear in more than token numbers a quasi-political atmosphere is created, though not necessarily a conflictive one. And with their appearance come interest groups, study groups, ginger groups, and also targeted financial support allocated with an element of affirmative action. With these sources of support undergraduates get their first taste of research, as well as a sense of shared black identity coupled with a sense of entitlement and the confidence that comes with it. An important contrast with the United States is that they exist in sufficient numbers not to "stand out," not to feel so easily singled out or "under observation," as representatives of a group—as seems to happen in prestige universities there.

This pattern of coming together is more in evidence among social science and humanities students than others, and this ties in with the politicized character of social science activity in Brazil, similar to what one observes of race and gender in North America and Europe.[6] We also saw in the SECAD-sponsored studies that there has been an expectation—not always met—that beneficiaries of affirmative action would find in the teaching staff a ready response to their race-related interests and con-

---

6. By "politicized" I refer to the superimposition of normative positions on institutional boundaries, on publication outlets, and, sometimes, on decisions about appointments, though in Brazil, as I have said, affirmative action in academic appointments is still not on the agenda or even among the movimento negro's demands.

cerns. Elected student representatives sit on the top policy-making councils of public universities and get involved in academic politics:[7] as staff and teaching programmes develop an aura of favouring one or another point of view or cause, some students are drawn to particular positions, schools of thought, or political ideologies. From time to time, sections of the student body irrupt in the midst of academic proceedings, as when students more or less laid siege to the UFBA University Council in Salvador during its debate on affirmative action in 2004, and in an inaugural lecture at the Faculty of Philosophy and Letters at USP in February 2016, which was interrupted by a protest over the small number of black students at the university.[8] But generally, with the exception of UFBA, the role of students in pressing for quotas had been limited until conflicts concerning this and many other issues became severe at USP in 2014–16.

The cause may command widespread support, but it is not a support limited to a particular demographic or race-based identity and thus is very rarely affected by inward-looking sectarianism. Stan Bailey's surveys in 2001, 2010, and 2012 showed widespread support for quotas with some very moderate decline among the more educated and, interestingly, among blacks and pardos (Bailey 2014: 12, 16), and in any case far higher support for affirmative action than in the United States. In Brazil there is no ghettoization of research and study on issues of concern to the black population. Academic bodies concerned with race issues in Brazil identify with the cause of black advancement and with the demand for quotas, but they have a more racially diverse staff than equivalent institutions in other countries. The NEABs and research groups, like João Feres's GEMAA and the centres for African and Oriental or Afro-Asian studies at UFBA and UERJ and LAESER at UFRJ, do not exhibit a black homogeneity among their staffs or students. Valter Silvério, for example, said that half the students who worked on projects in his NEAB were white, and he also said that during the time he worked at SECAD (2004–7) it had twenty-four professors, of whom only two were black; as we have seen, he spoke somewhat regretfully of the "capture" of the "black people's agenda" by people who did not have a record of commitment to the

---

7. As an example, student representatives constitute twelve of the fifty-nine members of the UFBA University Council.

8. The information on UFBA comes from an interview I conducted with Jocelio Teles dos Santos in 2010. The USP incident involved a lecture by José de Souza Martins. Martins himself wrote to many friends and colleagues on the subject. See the comment at http://outraspalavras.net/alceucastilho/2016/02/29/ativistas-calam-jose-de-souza-martins-na-usp-mas-eles-conhecem-sua-historia/

subject, and of black underrepresentation in decision-making forums, but he did not hint that they should be monopolized by blacks. It would be astonishing if these units did not have more than the average numbers of black students or staff, but there does not appear to be a determined push to raise their number for its own sake. While the representation of black voices is a matter of concern and of reparation for their past exclusion, any notion that they should be privileged voices in matters of race encounters resistance among black and white interlocutors alike. Indeed, a black professor at the Universidade Federal do Estado do Rio de Janeiro (Federal University of the State of Rio de Janeiro—UNIRIO) complained indignantly to me about a move in the ABPN, the black researchers' association, to restrict discussion or legitimacy to subjects relevant to blacks. She had responded by saying it was an association of black researchers not black studies only. White researchers have recounted troubling occasions when their legitimacy as analysts of race issues was questioned because of their colour—but these are extremely isolated cases, and the professor from UNIRIO was not alone in her reservations. In a 2008 interview, Nilma Lino Gomes, whom we encountered in chapter 2, and who has held a series of prominent appointments, spoke of the pressure on black academics to carve out a niche for themselves (consolidar um lugar) and remarked that some people used the word "contaminated" in describing blacks producing knowledge about themselves. According to my notes she said this "laughing, without bitterness," remarking that Brazilian blacks, like members of sexuality-based movements of gays and others, are criticized for "producing our own subjects." Despite her prominence in institutions and interest groups promoting black access, Nilma also said that the low representation of blacks in academic subjects outside the social sciences and humanities was "a very sensitive topic" because people have genuine doubts as to whether they wish to be seen as scientists or activists, reflecting the different culture prevailing in those subjects.

The issue has not been entirely buried. In 2017 the ABPN suffered a disagreeable rebuff when it applied to the Santa Catarina State Research Fund (Fapesc) for the very small sum of R$15,000 (US$4,800) to support a meeting in the state's capital Florianopolis. The reply was negative, in part because the amount to be spent on food was considered excessive but most insensitively because Fapesc believed that the meeting should be more inclusive ("abrangente") and bring in "other academic segments," a point it clarified by noting that "the meeting's programme involved exclusively (or almost exclusively) representatives of a single race."[9] There followed a denial by ABPN that the meeting was to be attended only by people of one race, accusations of institutional racism in the agency, and an ironic observation that the agency had not voiced the same criticism when meetings were proposed with exclusively white participation.

The formation of professional associations—notably ABPN–and the holding of frequent seminars and conferences on black advancement and its obstacles, constitute efforts to create professional-institutional spaces for black academics and intellectuals, which are surely a reasonable way of enabling black people to gain representation in academic institutions. But the pattern observed in the United States, where universities have created separate fully-fledged departments of ethnic studies, black studies, Afro-American studies or for that matter women's and gender studies, with predominant representation among their staff members of the groups concerned, is not observed in Brazil.

The comparison lends itself to a double-edged hypothesis: on one hand many US universities have invested significantly and long term in these subjects and in the staff and students they are likely to attract, but on the other hand they incur the criticism that they are enclaves created as gestures that (in academia's obsession with an infinity of status markers) do not receive the same respect that more traditional discipline-based or "mainstream" departments do. In contrast the units devoted to Afro-Brazilian subjects in Brazil are rarely fully fledged, permanently funded, independent academic departments, and those that do exist (such as GEMAA at UERJ's IESP, UFBA's CEAO, and the NEABs) depend on external funding and the contributions of tenured professors from other departments. But they are not enclaves.

The notion that there should be a prescribed place for black academics in studying or teaching subjects affecting the black population has to do with what Sansone already in 2002 called "race without ethnicity" (2002). For Sansone, one reason for misinterpretations of Brazil by people accustomed to race relations in the United States and countries of the former British Empire is that while differences of skin colour are a source of recognition they are not superimposed on a range of other differences, religious, cultural, socioeconomic, residential, or linguistic, on ways of speaking, on choices of first names, and so on. Some priests and priestesses of candomblé may proclaim their Yoruba authenticity, but they count innumerable white-skinned people (who might also claim African

9. "da forma como está formatado, sobretudo, a programação envolve exclusivamente (ou quase) representantes de uma só raça," *Diario Catarinense*, 7 July 2017.

descent, if that were relevant) among their peers and followers. Likewise the assumption about Afro-descendant identity is far from universally shared: Stanley Bailey's surveys, it will be recalled, found many people who while readily recognizing themselves as black had no interest in or knowledge of Africa (Bailey 2008). This is a point well-articulated by Moraes Silva in distinguishing weak symbolic boundaries from strong social (or structural, socioeconomic) boundaries (Moraes Silva 2016: 80).

In other words, this is a field plagued, or mined, with false dichotomies, of which the—admittedly tentative—description of the quotas controversies as a "culture war" in Brazilian academia (Bailey and Peria 2010) are an example: the record shows that the cultural aspect of these conflicts, though present, is tangential to the main themes of citizenship, racial equality, class status and class origin among the protagonists, as well as the competition for power and influence among intellectual interest groups. In fact, although Bailey and Perla use the phrase "culture wars," they readily point to common ground and "struggles to construct new forms of political identity and to define them in terms of political engagement" (602). Maybe "culture skirmishes" would be more apt.

It is, however, true that limited culture wars have recently erupted in Brazil and that, surprisingly, they do mirror those raging in the United States and Europe, fueled by evangelical pastor-politicians on campaigns against gay marriage and similar subjects,[10] and by occasional, but persistent, acts of aggression on the part of people from the Universal Church of the Kingdom of God against *terreiros* and *pães* and *mães de santo*. From time to time one of these pastors makes an inflammatory statement about blacks, but such confrontations, like others over personal morality or even the Satanism of the possession cults, are far removed from those concerning quotas: those who disagree about affirmative action have shared conceptions of human rights, citizenship, and the private character of religious affiliation, which are not shared by the pastors in ques-

---

10. In February 2013 the appointment of Deputy and Pastor Marco Feliciano to the chair of the Congressional Committee on Human Rights provoked an outcry on account of his tweets against gay sex and provocative remarks about black people. His appointment remained, however, since it was part of a set of interparty deals allocating such positions. In May 2014 the Ministério Público supported a group of people, headed by Ivanir dos Santos, in a petition to the courts to force YouTube to withdraw sixteen videos containing virulent attacks on African-originating religions (religiões de matriz africana) for practicing "witchcraft and Satanism" (bruxaria e satanismo); they obtained a temporary suspension order while the court decided its final position on 13 June 2014. In the course of this process there was another outcry, this time against a judge who took the view that these religions could not be counted as such because they do not have sacred scriptures. The judge later changed this phrase but not his ruling, which was overturned by a temporary suspension order. *O Globo*, 13 June 2014.

tion or by some politicians of the extreme right. But any complacency may be misplaced: Bailey and Perla published in 2010; in 2018 the country is embroiled in multiple crises, and a politician who has repeatedly denigrated blacks and indigenous people, as well as gays, Jair Bolsonaro, is climbing in the polls.

The quotas campaign has advanced by means of the gradual creation and conquest of spaces, within academia and government and in the NGO world. Without ever bringing about a confrontational parliamentary debate, it has found platforms for the promotion of its cause in the federal government. Without a supportive press outlet, and on the defensive on television, which pays it limited attention (and when it does subjects its spokespeople to fierce polemical exchanges), the campaign has had to rely on its academic cottage industry of projects, centres, institutes, seminars, and conferences, through which it develops its own ideological or intellectual apparatus. This effervescent space of intellectual activity fulfills a core feature of Touraine's model of a social movement because it acts as a seedbed of ideas and projects—what he calls more ambitiously a project of historical transformation. At the same time it also reflects the way the campaign has been absorbed by overlapping networks, by "sociality" rather than confrontation. In this perspective, it has followed the course contemplated by Benedita da Silva rather than that apparently preferred by Michael Hanchard, and it has achieved some success. To be sure, there are those who disagree and would prefer the monistic strategy of a totalizing race-based movement, but in Brazil this runs against the grain of a society where the centrifugal tyranny of small differences is countered by the centripetal attraction of small resemblances.

At the same time it is also a society in which insurgent movements are drawn to the state, or sometimes are directly run by it. This does not in itself mean they have no independence, for it is extremely common throughout the world for governments to fund or have agreements with NGOs, and it cannot be assumed a priori that the NGOs are simply co-opted.[11] But in the case of black advancement in Brazil, the absence of a sustainable material base separate from state funding does leave a field more open to top-down management than would otherwise be the case. There have, for example, been three CONAPIR conferences held in Brasilia since 2005, and a fourth was scheduled to take place in November 2017 (though as mentioned earlier, it has been postponed to "the

---

11. The extent to which priorities and agendas are negotiated was extensively discussed in the development literature in the 1990s (Carroll 1992; Hulme and Edwards 1996; Bebbington 1997; Bebbington and Lehmann 1997; Fox and Brown 1998).

second half of 2018"). The first one attracted a thousand delegates and two thousand other participants, but more importantly some ninety thousand took part in the preparatory phases at municipal and state levels involving consultations with indigenous and quilombo populations, with representatives of the "religiões de matriz africana" (African-originating religions), and of *ciganos* (gypsies) (IPEA 2005: 137). The whole operation was orchestrated by SEPPIR, yet it had few repercussions: my interviewees, who did mention the first Zumbi March in 1995 and the process of consultation in the lead-up to Durban, made no mention of this conference or its successors despite SEPPIR's claim that they had emerged from such extensive grassroots participation. The risks of closeness to the state are again illustrated by the second Zumbi March in 2005, which was complicated by differences over relations with political parties and trade unions, ending up with two separate marches on different days and separate lists of demands presented to president Lula (IPEA 2006: 159). Finally celebrations for the annual Dia Nacional da Consciência Negra also seem to be funded by SEPPIR—in 2011 to the tune of R$1.37 million (c. US$600,000 at the time).[12]

Tianna Paschel's remark that the movimento negro is hardly a "poster-child" for an effective movement, is right if by effective is meant a movement like Touraine's "mouvement historique," a movement that can—without violence—bring millions onto the streets, bring change to a regime of cultural reproduction, and transform institutions. Above all, if by effectiveness is meant a high degree of independence vis-à-vis the state, then she is also right. But if by effective is meant that it can claim substantial achievements, then it has been effective especially in the quotas campaign, and it does deserve the name.

Conclusion

In these last two chapters I have brought together the themes of corporatism, civil society, and social movements. The argument is sensitive because it can be interpreted as a way to diminish the movimento negro and its achievements, and also as questioning the radicalism of its leading figures. But in deciphering the sometimes confrontational rhetoric of Brazilian politics and racial protest, analysis also has to remember that very often it is a prelude to, and occasionally provides a smoke screen for, absorption and accommodation. I gave examples of this when discussing the literature on civil society and challenging assumptions about the au-

---

12. See the list of SEPPIR tenders in (IPEA 2013: 455).

tonomy of social movements that thrived under the banners of *basismo* in the years of the transition. I also drew attention to the evolution of the PT itself, which even sustained a leftist or leftish rhetoric after Lula, in his June 2002 *Carta aos Brasileiros*, renounced the party's earlier commitments to wholesale structural and nationalist transformation of the economy. Once in power, Lula sidelined sacred cows such as restrictions on foreign capital, repudiation of the foreign debt, land reform, and income redistribution, in favour of bolsa família and above-inflation increases in the real minimum wage, funded by the commodities boom. Although a degree of income redistribution was achieved thanks to increasing formal sector employment and rises in the minimum wage, it was vulnerable to reversal when the boom ended. At the same time the party was using time-honored methods to consolidate its position in the state by appointing thousands of people to discretionary posts in the bureaucracy and by co-opting local organizations; the cause of black advancement, in its many guises, also benefited from these opportunities. In addition I have documented the dependence of the quotas campaign on the Ford Foundation and placed this in the context of the lack of autonomy of social movements generally and their reliance on funding from the state and international NGOs. This is how the Brazilian state historically and recently has dealt with nascent collective social actors to prevent the development of sharp confrontations. To be sure, this implies that the full range of demands are not met, and sometimes that movements are completely betrayed by their leaders or by the state, but in the case of race in particular, the dangers of confrontation along racial lines, and thus the merits of policies that would avoid it, have to be taken into account, and on the other side I have heard only the word "compromise," not "betrayal." In any case, the leaders did not command substantial resources or followings that would have given substance to the word "betrayal" had there been any cases.

This therefore is an attempt, in discussing the definition of social movement, to place the quotas campaign in the context of the structure and culture of the Brazilian state and of theories of social movements, which, admittedly, are rather demanding and Eurocentric or "US-centric." Touraine's model is very useful, but he does not claim that it is the only way to achieve social change.

Several aspects of my interpretation still remain hypothetical: the political scientists whose interpretation of the PT's growth I have criticized on the grounds that they have not looked at the mechanisms of the relationship between the party and civil society groups could well respond that I have not done the required detailed research either, relying on localized case studies. Also, returning to my general interpretation of the movimento negro and the quotas campaign, the claim that the real objective of the quotas campaign was to get blacks into the upper reaches of the country's decision-making elite is based on deductions from observed strategies and from statistics and surveys of inequality, which show that there is a spike in the racial component of inequality in the top 10 percent of income earners (Biderman and Guimarães 2004; Henriques 2001). This hypothesis needs to be explored more directly, though it may not be easy, because people questioned might well resist such an interpretation, preferring not to be seen as proto-elitists. Likewise my interpretation of the instability of racial self-assignment also requires detailed inquiry. When I imagine people saying to themselves that maybe their bad luck is in reality a matter of discrimination I am doing precisely that: imagining. But how to conduct such an inquiry? The design and conduct of interviews aiming to uncover such changes is challenging. Prolonged immersion in the student or teenager milieu would be a better approach, something that so far only André Cicaló has achieved. The fourth theme requiring further work is my hypothesis about the motivations of the political elite in accepting the case for quotas and adopting, in Congress, an unusually radical proposal: for a political class otherwise noted for its venality and conservative instincts to set aside, at a stroke, half of all places in prestige institutions for disadvantaged people who previously had largely been unable to gain access is, to say the least, surprising. Maybe they just regarded it as a matter of little importance, to be dismissed as "coisa de negro," as someone said to me when describing congressional indifference to race issues? That would be a very embittered interpretation. My interpretation of why they did this, and why they did it unanimously, needs to be put to the test in interviews with the deputies and senators. Brazil's supposed "preconceito de não ter preconceito"— the "prejudice" expressed in avoidance of the slightest expression of prejudice—like the frequently mentioned subtlety of everyday discrimination, may have been criticized, especially by those looking to raise consciousness among black people of their own oppression, but the affirmative actions in university admissions, and later in recruitment by the federal government, did get adopted. In a country already suffering under the weight of accumulated and intractable problems of inequality and a distorted political economy, and in a world beset by dark forces of racism and nationalism unleashed in the Middle East, Eastern and Western Europe, and the United States, that "prejudice against prejudice" may be a cause less for regret than for celebration.

Appendix A

Selected Indicators on the Growth of the Brazilian Higher Education System (2003–2014)

	2003	2011	2014
Undergraduate students registered in federal, state, and municipal public higher education institutions (millions)	0.83	1.6	1.82
Undergraduate students registered in private higher education institutions (millions) (Table 5.1; excluding distance learning)	1.54	4.15	4.66
Number of public higher education institutions (Table 1.1)	192	284	298
Number of private higher education institutions (Table 1.1)	905	2,081	2,070
Number of undergraduates registered in federal universities (millions) (excluding distance learning) (Table 5.1)	0.442	0.927	1.08
Number of beneficiaries of ProUni scholarships (cumulative)	95,608 (2005)	1,096,348 (2012)	

Source: Last row: MEC, *Sinopse das Ações do Ministério da Educação*, December 2012. Otherwise: INEP, *Sinopses Estatísticas da Educação Superior* (Statistical Sinopses of Higher Education) for the corresponding years. They follow a standardized format and the relevant Tables are indicated. See http://portal.inep.gov.br/web/guest/sinopses-estatisticas-da-educacao-superior

Note: The *Sinopse* is a 125-page glossy pamphlet produced for publicity more than for scientific use, so the figures here are given for illustrative purposes. The text has some further figures. The decipherment and interpretation of the abundant statistics published by INEP, the MEC's highly respected statistical institute, requires specialist familiarity with its definitions and procedures. An example of the difficulties involved is the problem of how to discover and represent part-time students, especially in the private sector or how to reflect the different numbers of years students take to complete the same course of study and obtain their degrees. Thus the data presented here are intended only to indicate orders of magnitude.

Appendix B

Interviews Carried Out between 2008 and 2014

Rio de Janeiro

Denise Dora (Ford Foundation; first interview)
Renato Emerson dos Santos (PPCor, UERJ)
Nelson do Valle Silva (IUPERJ)
Ivanir dos Santos (CEAP)
Angela Paiva (PUC, Rio de Janeiro)
Elielma Ayres Machado (UERJ)
CRIOLA
Zeze da Motta (Secretary for Racial Equality for the state of Rio de Janeiro, prominent film, theatre and TV star)
Renato Ferreira (PPCor)
Peter Fry (anthropologist, former Ford Foundation officer and Brazil representative)
Jean-François Veran (anthropologist, UFRJ)
Sueli Carneiro (founder of GELEDES)
Paulo Sergio Pinheiro (UN human rights rapporteur, former head of the Human Rights Secretariat in Brazil; telephone interview)
João Feres Jr. (Instituto de Estudos Politicos UERJ; expert on quotas)
Bernardo Sorj (sociologist UFRJ)

São Paulo

Denise Dora (former Ford Foundation; second interview)
Faculdade Zumbi dos Palmares (academic coordinator)

Fulvia Rosemberg (Ford Foundation International Fellowship
  Programme)
GELEDES—Instituto da Mulher Negra (coordinator of Labour and
  Income Management Programme, lawyer in charge of SOS
  Racismo)
EDUCAFRO (Interim Coordinator Frei Valnei; coordinator for alumni)
Edilene Machado (IFP fellow)
Elisabete Pinto (Office for the Health of the Black Population in the
  São Paulo Municipality, later UFBA Psychology)
Frci David Raimundo dos Santos (founder and leader of EDUCAFRO)
Fernando Henrique Cardoso (former President of the Republic)
Manuela Carneiro da Cunha and Mauro Almeida (anthropologists and
  prime movers of indigenous rights in the 1987 Constitutional
  Assembly)
Quirino Augusto Carmello Camargo (USP, PASUSP; telephone
  interview)
Valter Silvério (sociologist UFSCar)

Belo Horizonte

Nigel Brooke (educational researcher at UFMG and former Ford
  Foundation officer and representative in Brazil)
Nilma Lino Gomes (professor of education at UFMG, later rector of
  UNILAB and head of SEPPIR)
Ana Gomes (coordinator of university training course for indigenous
  teachers at UFMG)
Deborah Lima (anthropologist at UFMG and expert consultant in
  quilombo cases)

Brasilia

Giovanni Harvey (SEPPIR)
Aleixandre Reis (SEPPIR)
Ivair dos Santos (professor de pensamento negro at UnB and leading
  adviser to SEPPIR)
Arsenio Schmidt (head of SECAD)
Leonor Araujo (Conexões de Saberes programme, SECAD)
Paulo Renato de Souza (Federal Deputy for São Paulo and former
  Minister of Education)
José Jorge de Carvalho (anthropologist at UnB and leading figure in
  promotion of affirmative action there and in Brazil as a whole)

Jussara Gruber (educator and expert in indigenous education)

Itamaraty (Ministry of Foreign Affairs) (Ana Cabral; Sylvio Albuquerque e Silva; Director of Affirmative Action Programme)

Givania Silva (INCRA, coordinator of Department of Quilombola Land)

Salvador

SEPRO (adviser to head of the secretariat)

Wilson Mattos (adviser to the *pro-reitor* [Pro-Rector] in charge of research and postgraduate education, UNEB)

Jocelio Teles dos Santos (anthropologist, CEAO)

Instituto Steve Biko (interviews with administrative staff)

Campina Grande

Ivan Barroso Santos (in charge of admissions and social inclusion UEPB)

Eliana Maia (Pro-Reitora UEPB in charge of undergraduate teaching)

UFCG (Vice-Rector)

Mercia Batista and Jose Gabriel Correa (sociologists, UFCG)

Lemuel Guerra (sociologist, UFCG)

Recife

IFPE (Vice-Rector and three heads of departments)

UFPE (Director de Controle Academico—director of student records)

Moises Santana (social scientist, UFRPE and UFAl)

Fabio George (procuradoria da republica—public prosecutor's office, Pernambuco)

Los Angeles

Edward Telles (sociologist, former Ford Foundation officer in Brazil)

New York

Brad Smith (President, The Foundation Center, former Ford Foundation Representative in Brazil)

Glossary

alfabetização: literacy training, teaching people to read and write.

apostila: course book essential for the preparation of competitive examinations for civil service positions (*concursos*).

assentamento: literally, settlement, a cooperative of beneficiaries of land reform.

assistencialismo: doling out favors, usually on a clientelistic basis, by politicians or bureaucrats, to damp down a conflict or assuage demands from the populace on a short-term basis.

asumir: to recognize oneself as having a particular identity, notably as a black.

bancada evangélica: Evangelical Congressional Caucus.

basismo: a disposition to favour grassroots political action and distrust government support as mere *assistencialismo*.

blocos de carnival: carnival floats and their accompanying dancers.

Bolsa Família: the programme of conditional cash transfers to female household heads in very low income groups.

bolsas de iniciação científica: research internships for undergraduate students receiving a small stipend.

bolsas de permanência: subsidies, bursaries, or grants that enable low-income students to cover the cost of their studies.

candomblé: generic term referring to possession cults in the Afro-Brazilian tradition.

capoeira: a style of dance that can be performed by a single person which, when performed by two people, comes to resemble martial arts with elaborately choreographed moves. In both popular and erudite imaginaries it is associated with Afro-Brazilian culture.

cidadanía: citizenship.

comunitário: community based (as in PVC *comunitário*—community-based PVC).

concurso: competitive examination for an established permanent position in the public service. Note that to be selected does not guarantee an appointment, which has to await the availability of budgetary allocations.

cota/cotistas: quota and students benefiting from quota places in affirmative action programmes.

cursinho: private schools offering courses to prepare for the vestibular exam.

edital (*pl.* editais): a call for tenders or an announcement of a public examination (*concurso*) by a state agency.

ensino fundamental: first cycle of schooling, in principle for children aged seven to fourteen.

ensino medio: second cycle of schooling (high school), in principle for students aged fifteen to seventeen.

feijoada: a hotpot of black beans, jerked (sun-dried) beef, and pork, cooked for several hours and consumed at family gatherings and celebrations.

integrismo: a political movement of the 1930s which reproduced the ideas of European fascism.

laudo: expert opinions, in this context produced by anthropologists to certify the authenticity of *quilombola* or indigenous land claims.

Mestiçagem: racial mixture or, slightly anachronistically, miscegenation (cf. Portuguese *mestiço*; French *métissage*).

moreno: brown-skinned.

movimento negro: Brazilian black movement.

núcleo: local branch or gathering.

pães and mães de santo: candomblé priests and priestesses.

pardo: brown-skinned.

petista: supporter of the PT party.

portaría: administrative decree emitted by a ministry.

preto: literally "black," denoting the deepest black skin colour, a term mostly used in official statistics and classifications that do not use the term *negro*.

prevestibular: non-fee or low-fee courses that prepare students for the vestibular exam: a popular *cursinho*.

pro-reitor: appointed head of a major department in university of administration.

provão: literally "the big test." Officially known as the Exame Nacional de Curso, this test is taken by higher education students, but its purpose is to evaluate the courses they take and their institutions.

quilombo/quilombola: settlements originally founded by escaped slaves and the people who live in them.

reitor: rector of a university.

terreiros: sites belonging to *pães* and *mães de santo* where candomblé ceremonies are carried out.

vestibular: university entrance examination set by the universities themselves.

vice-reitor: vice-rector. Usually elected by the same voting college that elects the rector.

Bibliography

Abel, Sarah (2018). "Of African Descent? Blackness and the Concept of Origins in Cultural Perspective." *Genealogy* 2 (1).

Abers, Rebecca (2000). *Inventing Local Democracy: Grassroots Politics in Brazil.* London: Lynne Rienner.

Agier, Michel (2000). *Anthopologie du Carnaval: la ville, la fête, et l'Afrique à Bahia.* Marseilles: Parenthèses.

Alberto, Paulina (2011). *Terms of Inclusion: Black Intellectuals in Twentieth-Century Brazil.* Chapel Hill: University of North Carolina Press.

Almeida, Alfredo Wagner Berna de (1989). "Terras de Preto, Terras De Santo, e Terras de Índio: Uso Comum e Conflito." *Cadernos do NAEA: Núcleo de Altos Estudos Amazônicos da Universidade Federal do Pará* 10:163–96.

Almeida, Nina Paiva (2008). *Diversidade na Universidade: O BID e as Políticas Educacionais de Inclusão Étnico-Racial no Brasil.* Masters thesis, Universidade Federal do Rio de Janeiro, Museu Nacional.

Almeida Filho, Naomar, Maerbal Bittencourt Marinho, Manoel José de Carvalho, and Jocelio Teles dos Santos (2005). *Ações afirmativas na universidade pública: O caso da UFBA.* Salvador: Centro de Estudos Afro-Orientais da UFBA.

Altglas, Véronique (2005). *Le Nouvel Hindouisme Occidental.* Paris, CNRS Editions.

Altglas, Véronique (2014). *From Yoga to Kabbalah: Religious Exoticism and the Logics of Bricolage.* New York: Oxford University Press.

Alvarez, Sonia, Jeffrey Rubin, Millie Thayer, Gianpaolo Baiocchi, and Agustín Laó-Montes, eds. (2017). *Beyond Civil Society: Activism, Participation, and Protest in Latin America.* Durham: Duke University Press.

Alves Cordeiro, Maria José de Jesus (2007). "Tres Anos de Efetiva Presença de Negros nas Salas de Aula da UEMS: Primeiras análises." In A. A. Brandão, ed. (2007).

Andrade, Cibele Yahn (2012). "Acesso ao Ensino Superior no Brasil: Equidade e Desigualdade Social." *Ensino Superior* 6. https://www.revistaensinosuperior.gr.unicamp.br/artigos/acesso-ao-ensino-superior-no-brasil-equidade-e-desigualdade-social

Andrés, Aparecida (2008). *O Programa Universidade Para Todos.* Brasilia: Cámara de Deputados, Consultoria Legislativa.

Andrews, George Reid (1991). *Blacks and Whites in São Paulo, Brazil, 1888–1988.* Madison: University of Wisconsin Press.

Appiah, Kwame A. (2005). *The Ethics of Identity*. Princeton: Princeton University Press.

Assies, Willem (1993). "Urban Social Movements and Democracy in Brazil." *European Review of Latin American and Caribbean Studies* 55:39–58.

Assies, Willem (1999). "Theory, Practice, and 'External Actors' in the Making of New Social Movements in Brazil." *Bulletin of Latin American Research* 18 (2): 1211–26.

Avritzer, Leonardo (2009). *Participatory Institutions in Democratic Brazil*. Baltimore: Johns Hopkins University Press.

Avritzer, Leonardo (2017). "Civil Society in Brazil: From State Autonomy to Political Interdependency." In S. Alvarez et al., eds. 45–62 (2017).

Bacha, Edmar L., and Lance Taylor (1978). "Brazilian Income Distribution in the 1960s: 'Facts,' Model Results, and the Controversy." *Journal of Development Studies* 14 (3): 271–97.

Bailey, S. R. (2008). "Unmixing for Race-Making in Brazil." *American Journal of Sociology* 114 (3): 577–614.

Bailey, Stanley (2009). *Legacies of Race: Identities, Attitudes, and Politics in Brazil*. Stanford, CA: Stanford University Press.

Bailey, Stanley, et al. (2013). "'Race' and the Analysis of Racial Equality in Brazil." *Social Science Research* 42:106–19.

Bailey, Stanley, Fabricio Fialho, and Michelle Perla (2016). "Support for Race-Targeted Affirmative Action in Brazil." *Ethnicities*. https://doi.org/10.1177/1468796814567787

Bailey, Stanley R., and Michelle Peria (2010). "Racial Quotas and the Culture War in Brazilian Academia." *Sociology Compass* 4 (8): 592–604.

Bailey, Stanley R., and Edward E. Telles (2006). "Multiracial versus Collective Black Categories: Examining Census Classification Debates in Brazil." *Ethnicities* 6 (1): 74–101.

Baiocchi, Gianpaolo, and Ana Claudia Teixeira (2017). "Brazil: Back to the Streets?" In S. Alvarez et al., eds., 45–62 (2017).

Banck, Geert (1986). "Cultural Dilemmas Behind Strategy: Brazilian Neighbourhood Movements and Catholic Discourse." *European Journal of Development Research* 2 (1): 65–88.

Barbosa, Lucia Maria de Assunção, Petronilha Gonçalves e Silva, and Valter Silverio, eds. (2002). *De preto a afro-descendente: trajetos de pesquisa sobre o negro, cultura negra e relações étnico-raciais no Brasil*. São Carlos: Editora da Universidade Federal de São Carlos.

Barros, Ricardo, et al. (2010). "Markets, the State, and the Dynamics of Inequality in Brazil." In *Declining Inequality in Latin America: A Decade of Progress?*, edited by L. F. Lopez-Calvo and N. Lustig. Washington, DC: Brookings Institution.

Barth, Fredrik (1969). *Ethnic Groups and Boundaries: The Social Organization of Culture Difference*. Boston: Little, Brown.

Batista, Gilda Alves (2007). "Relações raciais e educação: Uma análise do programa políticas da cor na educação brasileira (PPCOR)." Masters thesis, Education, Catholic University, Rio de Janeiro.

Beauchemin, Cris, et al., eds. (2016). *Trajectoires et Origines: Enquête sur la diversité des Populations en France*. Paris: Institut National d'Etudes Démographiques (INED).

Bebbington, Anthony (1997). "New States, New NGOs? Crises and Transitions among Rural Development Organizations in the Andean Region." *World Development* 25 (11): 1755–65.

Bebbington, Anthony, and David Lehmann (1997). "NGOs, the State, and the Development Process: Dilemmas of Institutionalization." In *The Changing Role of the State in Latin America*, edited by M. Vellinga. Boulder: Westview.

Becho, Renato (2017). "Binding Precedents as a Way to Reduce Tax Lawsuits in Brazil." Paper delivered at the conference of the Association of Brazilianists in Europe (ABRE), Leiden.

Benedito, Vera Lúcia (2007). "País de Cidadãos: Ações afirmativas desafiando paradigmas na Universidade Estadual de Mato Grosso do Sul." In Braga and da Silveira, eds., 113–57 (2007).

Benhabib, Seyla (2002). *The Claims of Culture: Equality and Diversity in the Global Era.* Princeton: Princeton University Press.

Bethell, Leslie (2010). "Brazil and 'Latin America.'" *Journal of Latin American Studies* 42 (3): 457–85.

Biderman, Ciro, and Nadya Araujo Guimarães (2004). "Na Ante-sala da Discriminação: O Preço dos Atributos de Sexo e Cor no Brasil (1989–1999)." *Estudos Feministas* (Florianópolis) 12 (2): 177–200.

Boff, Leonardo (1985). *Church, Charism, and Power.* London: SCM Press.

Bourdieu, Pierre (1989). *Le sens pratique.* Paris: Editions de Minuit. (Trans., *The Logic of Practice*; Cambridge: Polity Press, 1990).

Bourdieu, Pierre, and Loïc Wacquant (1999). "On the Cunning of Imperialist Reason." *Theory, Culture, and Society* 16 (1): 41–58.

Bowen, William, and Derek Bok (1998). *The Shape of the River: Long-Term Consequences of Considering Race in College and University Admissions.* Princeton: Princeton University Press.

Boyer, Véronique (2011). "L'anthropologie des quilombos et la constitution de 'nouveaux sujets politiques': De l'ethnie à la race et de l'autodéfinition au phénotype." *Civilisations* 59 (2).

Boyer, Véronique (2014). "Misnaming Social Conflict: 'Identity,' Land, and Family Histories in a Quilombola Community in the Brazilian Amazon." *Journal of Latin American Studies* 46 (3): 527–55.

Boyer, Véronique (2015). "Énoncer une 'identité' pour sortir de l'invisibilité: La circulation des populations entre les catégories légales (Brésil)." *L'Homme* 214:7–36.

Boyer, Véronique (2016). "The Demand for Recognition and Access to Citizenship: Ethnic Labelling as a Driver of Territorial Restructuring in Brazil." In *The Crisis of Multiculturalism in Latin America*, edited by D. Lehmann. New York: Palgrave Macmillan.

Braga, Maria Lúcia de Santana, and Maria Helena Vargas da Silveira, eds. (2007). *O Programa Diversidade na Universidade e a construção de uma política educacional antiracista.* Brasilia: UNESCO, MEC, BID. http://unesdoc.unesco.org/images/0015/001545/154582por.pdf

Brandão, A.A., ed. (2007) *Cotas raciais no Brasil: A primeira avaliação.* Rio de Janeiro: DP&A.

Brandão, Carlos Rodrigues (2007). *Os deuses do povo: Um estudo sobre a religião popular.* New and unabridged ed. Uberlândia: Editora da Universidade Federal de Uberlândia.

Branford, Sue, and Jan Rocha (2002). *Cutting the Wire: The Story of the Landless Movement in Brazil.* London: Latin America Bureau.

Brinbaum, Yael, et al. (2012). *Les discriminations en France: Entre perception et expérience.* Paris: Institut National d'Etudes Démographiques (INED).

Brooke, Nigel, and Mary Wytoshinky (2002). *The Ford Foundation's First 40 years in Brazil: A Partnership for Social Change.* São Paulo/Rio de Janeiro: EDUSP/Ford Foundation.

Brubaker, Rogers (2002). "Ethnicity Without Groups." *Archives Européennes de Sociologie* 43:163–89.

Brubaker, Rogers (2015). "The Dolezal Affair: Race, Gender, and the Micro-politics of Identity." *Ethnic and Racial Studies* 39 (3): 414–48.

Brubaker, Rogers (2016). *Trans: Gender and Race in an Age of Unsettled Identities.* Princeton: Princeton University Press.

Brubaker, Rogers, and Frederick Cooper (2000). "Beyond 'Identity.'" *Theory and Society* 29 (1): 1–47.

Brysk, Alison (2000). *From Tribal Village to Global Village: Indian Rights and International Relations in Latin America.* Stanford, CA: Stanford University Press.

Burdick, John (1994). *Looking for God in Brazil.* Berkeley: University of California Press.

Burdick, John (2004). *Legacies of Liberation: The Progressive Catholic Church in Brazil.* Aldershot: Ashgate.

Burdick, John (2013). *The Color of Sound: Race, Religion, and Music in Brazil.* New York: New York University Press.

Capinan, Ubiraneila (2009). "O quilombo que remanesce: Estudo de caso acerca dos impactos da política pública de certificação e de titulação de territorio sobre a identidade étnica does quilombos remanescentes Barra e Bananal em Rio de Contas, Bahia." Masters thesis, Universidade Federal da Bahia, Salvador da Bahia.

Cardoso, F. H (1973). "Associated-Dependent Development: Theoretical and Practical Implications." In *Authoritarian Brazil,* edited by A. Stepan. New Haven: Yale University Press.

Cardoso, Fernando Henrique (1997). "Pronunciamento do presidente da república na abertura do seminário multiculturalismo e racismo." In *Multiculturalismo e racismo: Uma comparação Brasil-Estados Unidos,* edited by J. Souza. Brasilia: Paralelo.

Cardoso, Ruth (1983). "Movimentos sociais urbanos: Balanço critico." In *Sociedade e política no Brasil pós-64,* edited by B. Sorj and M. H. Tavares de Almeida. São Paulo: Brasiliense.

Cardoso, Ruth (1992). "Popular Movements in the Context of the Consolidation of Democracy in Brazil." In *The Making of Social Movements in Latin America: Identity, Strategy, and Democracy,* edited by A. Escobar and S. E. Alvarez. Boulder: Westview.

Carneiro, Suely (1999). "Black Women's Identity in Brazil." In *Race in Contemporary Brazil: From Indifference to Inequality,* edited by R. Reichmann. University Park: Pennsylvania State University Press.

Carroll, Thomas (1992). *Intermediary NGOs: The Supporting Link in Grassroots Development.* Boulder: Kumarian Press.

Carter, Miguel (2010). "The Landless Rural Workers Movement and Democracy in Brazil." *Latin American Research Review* 45:186–217.

Carvalho, José Jorge de (2005). *Inclusão étnica e racial no Brasil: A questão das cotas no ensino superior.* São Paulo: Attar.

Castells, Manuel (1983). *The City and the Grassroots: A Cross-Cultural Theory of Urban Social Movements.* London: Edward Arnold.

César, Raquel Coelho Lenz (2007). Politica de cotas na educação superiuor brasileiro: Um acerto de contas e de legitimidade. In A. A. Brandão, ed., 13–36 (2007).

Chartock, Sarah (2013). "'Corporatism with Adjectives'? Conceptualizing Civil Society

Incorporation and Indigenous Participation in Latin America." *Latin American Politics and Society* 55 (2): 52–76.

Chor Maio, Marcos, and Ricardo Ventura (2005). "Políticas de cotas raciais: Os 'olhos da sociedade' e os usos da antropologia: O caso da Universidade de Brasilia." *Horizontes Antropologicos* 11 (23): 181–214.

Cicaló, André (2008). "What Do We Know about Quotas? Data and Considerations about the Implementation of the Quota System at the State University of Rio de Janeiro (UERJ)." *VIBRANT* 5 (1): 65–82.

Cicaló, André (2012a). "Nerds and Barbarians: Race and Class Encounters through Affirmative Action in a Brazilian University." *Journal of Latin American Studies* 44: 235–60.

Cicaló, André (2012b). *Urban Encounters: Affirmative Action and Black Identities in Brazil.* New York, Palgrave Macmillan.

Contins, Marcia, and Luis Carlos Sant'Ana (1996). "O movimento negro e a questão da ação afirmativa." *Estudos Feministas* 4 (1): 209–20.

Costa, Haroldo, ed. (2009). *Fala crioulo: O que é ser negro no Brasil.* Rio de Janeiro: Record.

Cunha, Luiz Antonio (2003). "A Educação Superior no octênio FHC." *Educação e Sociedade* 24 (82): 37–61.

Cunha, Luiz Antonio (2006). "Zigue-zague no Ministério de Educação." *Revista Contemporânea de Educação* 1(1). https://revistas.ufrj.br/index.php/rce/article/view/1473

Cunha, Luiz Antonio (2007). "O desenvolvimento meandroso da educação brasileira entre o estado e o mercado." *Educação e Sociedade* 28 (100): 802–29.

D'Araujo, Maria Celina (2009). *A elite dirigente do governo Lula.* Rio de Janeiro: FGV/CPDOC. http://observatory-elites.org/wp-content/uploads/2011/11/D-Araujo-e-Lameirao-A-elite-dirigente-do-governo-Lula.pdf

Daflon, Verônica Toste, et al. (2017). "Sentindo na Pele: Percepções de Discriminação Cotidiana de Pretos e Pardos no Brasil." *DADOS—Revista de Ciências Sociais* 60 (2): 293–330.

da Matta, Roberto (1986). *O que faz o brasil, Brasil?* Rio de Janeiro: Rocco.

da Matta, Roberto (1991). *Carnivals, Rogues, and Heroes: An Interpretation of the Brazilian Dilemma.* Notre Dame, IN: University of Notre Dame Press.

da Matta, Roberto (1995). "For an Anthropology of the Brazilian Tradition: Or, 'A Virtude está no Meio'." In *The Brazilian Puzzle: Culture on the Borderlands of the Western World*, edited by David Hess and Roberto da Matta. Notre Dame, IN: University of Notre Dame Press.

da Silva, Paulo Vinicius Baptista, Evandro Duarte, and Dora Bertulio (2007). "Sobre políticas afirmativas na Universidade Federal do Paraná." In A. A. Brandão, ed., 163–220.

da Silva, Rodrigo Torquato (2008). "A formação de professores e os currículos praticados em um movimento de educação popular na Rocinha." *Educação em Revista* (Belo Horizonte) 48:61–80.

Davenport, Lauren D. (2016). "The Role of Gender, Class, and Religion in Biracial Americans' Racial Labelling Decisions." *American Sociological Review* 8 (1): 57–84.

Dávila, Jerry (2016). "Ações judiciais no contexto da 'Lei Anti-Discriminação' de 1951." *Varia Historia* 33 (61): 163–85.

de Almeida, Wilson Mesquita (2014). *ProUni e o ensino superior privado lucrativo em São Paulo: Uma análise sociológica.* São Paulo: Musa Editora.

de Fiori, Ana Letícia, et al. (2017). "O tempo e o vento: Notas sobre a arte de burocratizar políticas de cotas na USP." *Revista de Antropologia (São Paulo, Online)* 60 (1): 55–83.

de Theije, Marjo, and Cecília L. Mariz (2008). "Localizing and Globalizing Processes in Brazilian Catholicism: Comparing Inculturation in Liberationist and Charismatic Catholic Cultures." *Latin American Research Review* 43 (1): 33–54.

do Nascimento, Abdias (1989). *Brazil: Mixture or Massacre? Essays in the Genocide of a Black People.* Dover, MA: The Majority Press.

Degler, Carl N. (1971). *Neither Black nor White: Slavery and Race Relations in Brazil and the United States.* New York: Macmillan.

Doimo, Ana Maria (1995). *A vez e a voz do popular: Movimentos sociais e participação política no Brasil pós-70.* Rio de Janeiro: Relume Dumará.

dos Santos, David Raimundo (2007). "Como a Igreja Católica tratou negros e negras nestes 507 anos?" In *Brasil: país de todos?*, special issue, *Koinonia* 2 (5).

dos Santos, Ivair (2006). *O movimento negro e o estado: O Conselho de Participação e Desenvolvimento da Comunidade Negra no governo de São Paulo.* São Paulo: Coordenação de Asuntos da População Negra (CONE).

dos Santos, Renato Emerson (2006a). "Agendas e agências: A espacialidade dos movimentos sociais a partir do pré-vestibular para negros e carentes." Doctoral diss., Geography, Universidade Federal Fluminense.

dos Santos, Renato Emerson (2006b). "Políticas de cotas raciais nas universidades brasileiras: O caso da UERJ." In J. Feres Jr. and J. Zoninsein, eds. (2006).

dos Santos, Renato Emerson (2011). *Movimentos sociais e geografia: Sobre a(s) espacialidade(s) da ação social.* Rio de Janeiro: Consequência.

Earle, Lucy (2017). *Transgressive Citizenship and the Struggle for Social Justice: the Right to the City in São Paulo.* London: Palgrave Macmillan.

Eckstein, Susan, ed. (2001). *Power and Political Protest: Latin American Social Movements.* 2nd ed. Berkeley: University of California Press.

Eisenstadt, S. N. (2000). "Multiple Modernities." *Daedalus* 129 (1): 1–29.

Erickson, Kenneth (1977). *The Brazilian Corporative State and Working-Class Politics.* Berkeley: University of California Press.

Estatística, IBGE (2012). "Síntese de indicadores sociais: Uma análise das condições de vida da população brasileira 2012." Research Paper 29, Instituto Brasileira de Geografía e Estatística (IBGE).

Evans, Peter (1979). *Dependent Development: The Alliance of Multinational, State, and Local Capital in Brazil.* Princeton: Princeton University Press.

Falcão, Joaquim, and Rosa Maria Barbosa de Araujo, eds. (2001). *O imperador das idéias: Gilberto Freyre em questão.* São Paulo: Fundação Roberto Marinho/Topbooks.

Faoro, Raymundo (1975). *Os donos do poder: Formação do patronato político brasileiro.* 2 vols. Porto Alegre: Editora Globo.

Feres, J., Jr. (2008). "Ação afirmativa, política pública e opinião." *Sinais Sociais* 38:38–77.

Feres, J., Jr., et al. (2013). "O impacto da Lei no. 12.711 sobre as universidades federais." *GEMAA: Levantamento das políticas de ação afirmativa.* http://gemaa.iesp.uerj.br

Feres, J., Jr., et al. (2014). "Evolução temporal e impacto da Lei no. 12.711 sobre as universidades federais." *GEMAA: Levantamento das políticas de ação afirmativa.* http://gemaa.iesp.uerj.br

Feres, J., Jr., and J. Zoninsein, eds. (2006) *Ação afirmativa e universidade.* Brasilia: Editora da UnB.

Fernandes, Magda Fernanda Medeiros (2007). "Os Projetos Inovadores de Curso e seus atores da transformação." In Maria Lúcia de Santana Braga, and M. H. Vargas da Silveira, eds., 25–44.

Fleet, Nicolas, and César Guzmán-Concha (2017). "Mass Higher Education and the 2011 Student Movement in Chile: Material and Ideological Implications." *Bulletin of Latin American Research* 36 (2): 160–76.

Fox, Jonathan (1994). "The Difficult Transition from Clientelism to Citizenship: Lessons from Mexico." *World Politics* 46 (2).

Fox, Jonathan (1996). "How Does Civil Society Thicken? The Political Construction of Social Capital in Rural Mexico." *World Development* 24 (6): 1089–1103.

Fox, Jonathan, and L. David Brown, eds. (1998). *The Struggle for Accountability: The World Bank, NGOs, and Grassroot Movements*. Cambridge, MA: MIT Press.

Francis, Andrew, and Maria Tannuri-Pianto (2012). "Using Brazil's Racial Continuum to Examine the Short-Term Effects of Affirmative Action in Higher Education." *Journal of Human Resources* 47 (3): 754–84.

Francis-Tan, Andrew, and Maria Tannuri-Pianto (2015). "Inside the Black Box: Affirmative Action and the Social Construction of Race in Brazil." *Ethnic and Racial Studies* 38:2771–90.

French, Jan Hoffman (2009). *Legalizing Identities: Becoming Black or Indian in Brazil's Northeast*. Chapel Hill: University of North Carolina Press.

French, Jan Hoffman (2014). "Rethinking Police Violence in Brazil: Unmasking the Public Secret of Race." *Latin American Politics and Society* 55 (4): 161–81.

French, John D. (2000). "The Missteps of Anti-imperialist Reason: Bourdieu, Wacquant, and Hanchard's Orpheus and Power." *Theory, Culture, and Society* 17 (1): 107–28.

Friendly, Abigail (2016). "The Changing Landscape of Civil Society in Niterói, Brazil." *Latin American Research Review* 51 (1): 218–42.

Fry, Peter (1995). "O que a Cinderela Negra tem a dizer sobre a 'política racial' no Brasil." *"Revista USP* 28:122–35.

Fry, Peter (1999). Color and the Rule of Law. In *The (Un)Rule of Law and the Underprivileged in Latin America*, edited by Juan Mendez, Guillermo O'Donnell and Paulo Sergio Pinheiro, 186–210. Notre Dame, IN: University of Notre Dame Press.

Fry, Peter (2000). "Politics, Nationality, and the Meanings of 'Race' in Brazil." *Daedalus* 129 (2): 83–118.

Fry, Peter, ed. (2005). *A persistencia da raça: Ensaios antropologicos sobre o Brasil e a Africa Austral*. Rio de Janeiro: Civilização Brasileira.

Fry, Peter (2006). "Ciencia social e política 'racial' no Brasil." *Revista USP* 68:180–87.

Fry, Peter (2009). "The Politics of 'Racial' Classification in Brazil." *Journal de la Société des Américanistes* 95 (2): 261–82.

Fry, Peter, and Yvonne Maggie (2002). "O debate que não houve: A reserva de vagas para negros nas universidades brasileiras." *ENFOQUES—Revista Eletrônica*, Rio de Janeiro, 1 (1): 93–117. Reprinted in Fry, ed. (2005).

Fry, Peter, et al., eds. (2007). *Divisões perigosas: Políticas raciais no Brasil contemporâneo*. Rio de Janeiro: Civilização Brasileira.

Garretón, Manuel Antonio (1989). "Popular Mobilization and the Military Regime in Chile: The Complexities of the Invisible Transition." In *Power and Political Protest: Latin American Social Movements*, edited by S. Eckstein. Berkeley: University of California Press.

Gomes, Renato dos Santos (2015). "A formação histórica do pré-vestibular para negros e carentes: Nucléo vila operária." Masters thesis, PUC, Programa de pós-graduação em serviço social, Rio de Janeiro.

Gómez Bruera, Hernán (2015). "Securing Social Governability: Party-Movement Relationships in Lula's Brazil." *Journal of Latin American Studies* 47(3): 567–93.

Gonçalves e Silva, Petronilha, and Valter Silvério (2003). *Educação e ações afirmativas: Entre a injustiça simbólica e a injustiça econômica*, Brasilia: INEP—Instituto Nacional de Pesquisas Educacionais, MEC.

Goody, Jack (2006). *The Theft of History*. Cambridge: Cambridge University Press.

Granovetter, M. (1973). "The Strength of Weak Ties." *American Journal of Sociology* 78 (6): 1360–80.

Granovetter, M. (1983). "The Strength of Weak Ties: A Network Theory Revisited." *Sociological Theory* 1:201–33.

Grin, M. (2001). "Esse ainda obscuro objeto de desejo—políticas de ação afirmativa e ajustes normativos: o seminário de Brasília." *Novos Estudos CEBRAP* 59:172–92.

Guimarães, Antonio Sergio (1996). "Políticas públicas para a ascensão dos negros no Brasil: argumentando pela ação afirmativa." *Afro-Ásia* (Salvador) 18:235–64.

Guimarães, Antonio Sergio (1998). *Preconceito e discriminação: Queixas de ofensas e tratamento desigual dos negros no Brasil*. Salvador: Programa A Cor da Bahia, Universidade Federal da Bahia.

Guimarães, Antonio Sergio (2001). "Democracia racial: O ideal, o pacto, e o mito." *Novos Estudos CEBRAP* 61 (November): 147–62.

Guimarães, Antonio Sergio (2003). "Acesso de negros às universidades públicas." *Cadernos de Pesquisa* 118:247–68. (Also published in Gonçalves e Silva, P. B., and V. R. Silvério 2003.)

Guimarães, Antonio Sergio (2005). *Racismo e anti-racismo no Brasil*. 2nd ed. Sao Paulo: Paz e Terra.

Guimarães, Antonio Sergio (2012). "Para uma história da mobilização negra no Brasil." Review of Paulina Alberto (2011). *Afro-Asia* (Salvador) (46).

Guimarães, Antonio Sergio (2015). "Ação afirmativa, autoritarismo, e liberalismo no Brasil de 1968." *Novos Estudos CEBRAP* 101:5–25.

Guimarães, Antonio Sérgio (2017). "Racialisation and Racial Formation in Urban Spaces." *Social Identities*: 1–15. http://dx.doi.org/10.1080/13504630.2017.1418600

Hale, Charles (2005). "Neoliberal Multiculturalism: The Remaking of Cultural Rights and Racial Dominance in Central America." *PoLAR: Political and Legal Anthropology Review* 28 (1): 10–28.

Hanchard, Michael (1994). *Orpheus and Power: The "Movimento Negro" of Rio de Janeiro and Sao Paulo, 1945–1988*. Princeton: Princeton University Press.

Hanchard, Michael (2003). "Acts of Misrecognition: Transnational Black Politics, Anti-imperialism, and the Ethnocentrisms of Pierre Bourdieu and Loïc Wacquant." *Theory, Culture, and Society* 20 (4): 5–29.

Hasenbalg, Carlos (2005 [1978]). *Discriminação e desiguladades raciais no Brasil*. Rio de Janeiro: UFMG, IUPERJ. Portuguese translation of "Race Relations in Post-abolition Brazil: The Smooth Preservation of Racial Inequalities," PhD thesis, University of California, Berkeley, 1978.

Henriques, Ricardo (2001). *Desigualdades raciaias no Brasil: Evolução das condições de vida na década de 90*. Texto para Discussão, no. 807. Brasilia: IPEA.

Heringer, Rosana (2004). "Ação afirmativa e promoção da iguadade racial no Brasil: O desafio da prática." In *Ação afirmativa na universidade: Reflexão sobre experiências concretas Brasil-Estados Unidos*, edited by Angela Paiva. Rio de Janeiro: Desiderata, Editora-PUC.

Heringer, Rosana (2010). "Ação afirmativa à Brasileira: Institucionalidade, sucessos e limites da inclusão de estudantes negros no ensino superior no Brasil (2001–2008)." In Angela Randolfo Paiva, ed. 2010(a).

Hewitt, Ted (1991). *Base Christian Communities and Social Change in Brazil.* Lincoln: University of Nebraska Press.

Hochschild, Arlie Russell (2016a). "The Ecstatic Edge of Politics: Sociology and Donald Trump." *Contemporary Sociology* 45 (6): 683–89.

Hochschild, Arlie Russell (2016b). *Strangers in Their Own Land: Anger and Mourning on the American Right.* New York: New Press.

Hofbauer, Andreas (2006). *Uma historia de branqueamento ou o negro em questão.* São Paulo: Editora UNESP.

Holston, James (1995). "Spaces of Insurgent Citizenship." *Planning Theory* 13:35–51.

Htun, Mala. (2016). *Inclusion without Representation in Latin America: Gender Quotas and Ethnic Reservations.* Cambridge: Cambridge University Press.

Hulme, David, and Michael Edwards (1996). "Too Close for Comfort? The Impact of Official Aid on Non-governmental Organizations." *World Development* 24 (6): 961–73.

IPEA (2005). "Igualdade Racial." *Políticas sociais: Acompanhamento e análise* 11:135–47.

IPEA (2006). "Igualdade Racial." *Políticas sociais: Acompanhamento e análise* 12:158–66.

IPEA (2013). "Igualdade Racial." *Políticas sociais: Acompanhamento e análise* 21:422–80.

Iqtidar, Humeira (2012). "State Management of Religion in Pakistan and Dilemmas of Citizenship." *Citizenship Studies* 16 (8): 1013–28.

Jaffa, Amy (2017). Description of the PVNC Vila Operária. Personal communication.

Jaffrelot, Christophe (1996). *The Hindu Nationalist Movement and Indian Politics, 1925 to the 1990s: Strategies of Identity-Building, Implantation, and Mobilisation (with Special Reference to Central India).* London: Hurst.

Jaffrelot, Christophe (2010). *Religion, Caste, and Politics in India.* Delhi: Primus Books.

Junqueira, Rogerio Diniz (2007). "Prefácio." In Braga and Vargas da Silveira, eds. (2007).

Kapiszewski, Diana (2010). "How Courts Work: Institutions, Culture, and the Brazilian Supremo Tribunal Federal." In *Culture of Legality: Judicialization and Political Activism in Latin America*, edited by J. Couso, A. Huneeus, and R. Sieder. Cambridge: Cambridge University Press.

Keck, Margaret E. (1986). *From Movement to Politics: The Formation of the Workers' Party in Brazil.* New York: Columbia University Press.

Keck, Margaret E. (1992). *The Workers' Party and Democratization in Brazil.* New Haven: Yale University Press.

Keck, Margaret E., and Kathryn Sikkink (1998). *Activists beyond Borders: Advocacy Networks in International Politics.* Ithaca: Cornell University Press.

Kerstenetzky, Celia Lessa, et al. (2015). "The Elusive New Middle Class in Brazil." *Brazilian Political Science Review* 9 (3): 20–41.

LAESER (2010). *Relatório anual das desigualdades raciais no Brasil, 2009–2010.* Rio de Janeiro: Laboratorio de Analises Económicas, Históricas, Sociais, e Estatísticas das Relações Raciais.

LAESER (2012). "Assistência estudantil e ações afirmativas nas Instituições de Ensino Superior (IES)." *Tempo em Curso* (Laboratorio de Analises Económicas, Históricas, Sociais, e Estatísticas das Relações Raciais) 4 (8): 3–5.

Lamont, Michèle, et al. (2016). *Getting Respect: Dealing with Stigma and Discrimination in the United States, Brazil, and Israel.* Princeton: Princeton University Press.

Larkin Nascimento, Elisa (2007). *The Sorcery of Color: Identity, Race, and Gender in Brazil.* Philadelphia: Temple University Press.

Lehmann, David (1978). "The Political Economy of Armageddon." *Journal of Development Economics* 5:107–23.

Lehmann, David (1990). *Democracy and Development in Latin America: Economics, Politics, and Religion in the Post-war Period.* Oxford: Polity Press.

Lehmann, David (1996). *Struggle for the Spirit: Religious Transformation and Popular Culture in Brazil and Latin America.* Oxford: Polity Press.

Lehmann, David (2008). "Gilberto Freyre: The Reassessment Continues." *Latin American Research Review* 43 (1): 208–18.

Lehmann, David (2013a). "Intercultural Universities in Mexico: Identity and Inclusion." *Journal of Latin American Studies* 45 (4): 779–811.

Lehmann, David (2013b). "Religion as Heritage, Religion as Belief: Shifting Frontiers of Secularism in Europe, the USA, and Brazil." *International Sociology* 28 (6): 645–62.

Lehmann, David, ed. (2016a). *The Crisis of Multiculturalism in Latin America.* New York: Palgrave Macmillan.

Lehmann, David (2016b). "Introduction." In Lehmann, ed. (2016a).

Lehmann, David (2016c). "The Politics of Naming." In Lehmann, ed. (2016a).

Lehmann, David (2016d). "The Religious Field in Latin America: Autonomy and Fragmentation." In *The Cambridge History of Religions in Latin America,* edited by Virginia Garrard-Burnett, Paul Freston, and Stephen C. Dove. New York: Cambridge University Press.

Lehmann, David (2017). "A politica do reconhecimento—teoria e prática." In *Raça, racismo e genética em debates científicos e controversias sociais,* edited by Maria Gabriela Hita. Salvador: Editora da UFBA.

Levine, Daniel (1992). *Popular Voices in Latin American Catholicism.* Princeton: Princeton University Press.

Lima, Márcia (2011). "Access to Higher Education in Brazil: Inequalities, Educational System, and Affirmative Action Policies." Working Paper 111. Warwick University Institute for Employment Research, ESRC Pathfinder Programme on Collaborative Analysis of Microdata Resources: Brazil and India.

Lima, Márcia (2013). "Acesso à universidade e mercado de trabalho: O desafio das políticas de inclusão." In *Trabalho e sindicalismo no Brasil e Argentina,* edited by H. Martins and P. Collado. São Paulo, HUCITEC: 91–111.

Lino Gomes, Nilma, ed. (2006). *Tempos de lutas: As ações afirmativas no contexto brasileiro.* Brasilia: MEC, SECAD, UNESCO.

Lipson, Daniel (2008). "Where's the Justice? Affirmative Action's Severed Civil Rights Roots in the Age of Diversity." *Perspectives on Politics* 6:691–706.

Lopes, Maria Auxiliadora, and Maria Lúcia de Santana Braga, eds. (2007). *Acesso e permanência da população negra no ensino superior.* Brasilia: MEC, SECAD, UNESCO.

Lund, Joshua, and Malcolm McNee, eds. (2006). *Gilbert Freyre e os estudos latinoamericanos.* Pittsburgh: Instituto Internacional de Literatura Iberoamericana, Universidad de Pittsburgh.

Machado, Elielma Ayres (2004). "Desigualdades 'Raciais' e Ensino Superior: Um estudo sobre a introdução das 'Leis de reserva de vagas para egressos de escolas públicas e cotas para negros, pardos e carentes' na Universidade do Estado de Rio Janeiro (2000–2004)." Doctoral thesis, Universidade Federal do Rio de Janeiro.

Maggie, Yvonne (1994). "Cor, hierarquia, e sistema de classificação: A diferença fora do lugar." *Estudos Históricos* 7 (14): 149–60.

Maggie, Yvonne (2001). "Os novos bacharéis: A experiência do pré-vestibular para negros e carentes." *Novos Estudos CEBRAP* 59:198–202.

Maggie, Yvonne (2005). "Mário de Andrade ainda vive? O ideario modernista en questão." *Revsita Brasileira de Ciencias Sociais* 20 (58): 5–25.

Maggie, Yvonne (2008). "Does Mário Andrade Live On?" *VIBRANT* 5 (1): 34–64. Translation of Maggie (2005).

Maggie, Yvonne (2013). "La politique raciale dans le Brésil contemporain et l'accès au système publique d'enseignement supérieur: Un récit retrospectif à la première personne." *Brésil(s): Sciences Humaines et Sociales* 4:13–34.

Malloy, James, ed. (1977). *Authoritarianism and Corporatism in Latin America.* Pittsburgh: University of Pittsburgh Press.

Malloy, James (1979). *The Politics of Social Security in Brazil.* Pittsburgh: University of Pittsburgh Press.

Mariano, Ricardo (2011). "Laicidade à brasileira: Católicos, pentecostais e laicos em disputa na esfera pública." *Civitas* 11 (2): 238–58.

Mariz, Cecilia Loreto (1993). *Coping with Poverty: Pentecostals and Christian Base Communities in Brazil.* Philadelphia: Temple University Press.

Marteleto, Leticia J. (2012). "Educational Inequality by Race in Brazil, 1982–2007: Structural Changes and Shifts in Racial Classification." *Demography* 49 (1): 337–58.

Martin, David (1990). *Tongues of Fire: The Pentecostal Revolution in Latin America.* Oxford: Blackwell.

Martínez Casas, Regina, Emiko Saldivar, René Flores, and Christina Sue (2014). "The Different Faces of Mestizaje: Ethnicity and Race in Mexico." In Telles, ed. (2014).

Martins, José de Souza (1980). *Expropriação e violência: A questão política no campo.* São Paulo: Editora Hucitec.

Martins, José de Souza (1986). *A reforma agrária e os límites da democracia na "Nova República."* São Paulo: Editora Hucitec.

Matos, Mauricio dos Santos, et al. (2012). "O impacto do Programa de Inclusão Social da Universidade de São Paulo no acesso de estudantes de escola pública ao ensino superior público gratuito." *Revista Brasileira de Estudos Pedagógicos* 93 (235): 720–42. https://dx.doi.org/10.1590/S2176-6681201000400010

Massi, Luciana, and Salete Linhares Queiroz (2010). "Estudos sobre iniciação científica no Brasil: Uma revisão." *Cadernos de Pesquisa* 40 (139): 173–97.

McAdam, Doug, et al. (1996). *Comparative Perspectives on Social Movements: Political Opportunities, Mobilizing Structures, and Cultural Framings.* Cambridge: Cambridge University Press.

McCarthy, John D., and Mayer N. Zald (1977). "Resource Mobilization and Social Movements: A Partial Theory." *American Journal of Sociology* 82 (6): 1212–41.

Mendes, Alvaro, Jr., et al. (2016). "Affirmative Action and Access to Higher Education in Brazil: The Significance of Race and Other Social Factors." *Journal of Latin American Studies* 48 (2): 301–34.

Mendes Alvaro, Jr. (2014). "Uma análise da progressão dos alunos cotistas sob a primeira ação afirmativa brasileira no ensino superior: O caso da Universidade do Estado do Rio de Janeiro." *Ensaio: Avaliação e Políticas Públicas em Educação* 22:31–56.

Mericle, Kenneth (1977). "Corporatist Control of the Working Class: Authoritarian Brazil since 1964." In Malloy, ed. (1977).

Muniz, Jerônimo Oliveira (2010). "Sobre o uso da variável raça-cor em estudos quantitativos." *Revista de Sociologia e Política* (Curitiba) 18 (36): 277–91.

Neri, Marcelo (2010). "The New Middle Class in Brazil: the Bright Side of the Poor." Rio de Janeiro: Fundação Getulio Vargas. http://www.cps.fgv.br/cps/nmc/ (Also published as "Brazil's New Middle Classes: The Bright Side of the Poor," in *Latin America's Emerging Middle Classes*, edited by J. Dayton-Johnson. London: Palgrave Macmillan [2015].)

Neri, Marcelo (2011). "Desigualdade de renda durante a década." Rio de Janeiro: Fundação Getulio Vargas. http://www.cps.fgv.br/cps/bd/DD/DD_Neri_Fgv_TextoFim3_PRINC.pdf

O'Donnell, Guillermo (1977). "Corporatism and the Question of the State." In Malloy, ed (1977).

O'Donnell, Guillermo (1978). "State and Alliances in Argentina, 1956–1976." *Journal of Development Studies* 15 (1): 3–33.

O'Donnell, Guillermo (1984). *Y a mí, que me importa? Notas sobre sociabilidad y política en Argentina y Brasil.* Buenos Aires: CEDES.

O'Donnell, Guillermo (1988). *Bureaucratic Authoritarianism: Argentina, 1966–1973.* Berkeley: University of California Press.

O'Donnell, Guillermo (1996). "Delegative Democracy." In Guillermo O'Donnell, *Counterpoints: Selected Essays on Democratization and Authoritarianism.* Notre Dame: University of Notre Dame Press.

O'Dwyer, Eliane Cantarino, ed. (2002). *Quilombos: Identidade étnica e territorialidade.* Rio de Janeiro: ABA, Editora FGV.

Oliven, Arabela Campos (2008). "Universities and Affirmative Action: Comparing Brazil and the United States." *VIBRANT* 5 (1): 141–61.

Oxhorn, Philip (1994). "Where Did All the Protesters Go? Popular Mobilization and the Transition to Democracy in Chile." *Latin American Perspectives* 21 (3).

Oxhorn, Philip (1995). *Organizing Civil Society: The Popular Sectors and the Struggle for Democracy in Chile.* University Park: Pennsylvania State University Press.

Oxhorn, Philip (2011). *Sustaining Civil Society: Economic Change, Democracy, and the Social Construction of Citizenship in Latin America.* University Park: Pennsylvania State University Press.

Paiva, Angela Randolfo, ed. (2010a). *Entre dados e fatos: Ação afirmativa nas universidades públicas brasileiras.* Rio de Janeiro: PUC-Rio, Pallas.

Paiva, Angela Randolfo (2010b). "Ações afirmativas nas universidades públicas: O que dizem os editais e manuais." In Angela Randolfo Paiva, ed. (2010a).

Pallares-Burke, Maria Lúcia G. (2005). *Gilberto Freyre: Um vitoriano dos trópicos.* São Paulo: Editora UNESP.

Paschel, Tianna (2016). *Becoming Black Political Subjects: Movements and Ethno-Racial Rights in Colombia and Brazil.* Princeton: Princeton University Press.

Pereira, Anderson Lucas da Costa (2017). "Preto, gay e do Norte: Ações afirmativas na pele." *Revista de Antropologia (São Paulo, Online)* 60 (1): 35–46.

Pereira, Anthony (2016). "Is the Brazilian State 'Patrimonial'?" *Latin American Perspectives* 43 (2): 135–52.

Perla, Michelle (2004). "Ação afirmativa: Um estudo sobre a reserva de vagas para negros nas universidades públicas Brasileiras—o caso do Estado do Rio de Janeiro Museu Nacional, Programa de Pós Graduação em Antropologia Social." Masters thesis, Universidade Federal do Rio de Janeiro.

Pimenta, Simone Garrido, Maria Isabel de Almeida, Mauricio dos Santos Matos, Maria Amélia Campos Oliveira, and Quirino Augusto de Camargo Carmelo (2009). *Programa de Inclusão Social na Universidade de São Paulo—INCLUSP.* São Paulo: USP—Pró Reitoria de Graduação.

Pinto, Paulo Gabriel Hilu da Rocha (2006). "Ação afirmativa, fronteiras raciais e identidades acadêmicas." In Feres and Zoninsein, eds. (2006).

Power, Timothy (2010). "Optimism, Pessimism, and Coalitional Presidentialism: Debating the Institutional Design of Brazilian Democracy." *Bulletin of Latin American Research* 29 (1): 18–33.

Power, Timothy, and Marukh Doctor (2004). "Another Century of Corporatism? Continuity and Change in Brazil's Corporatist Structures." In *Authoritarianism and Corporatism in Latin America—Revisited,* edited by H. Wiarda. Gainesville: University Press of Florida.

Putnam, Robert (2000). *Bowling Alone: The Collapse and Revival of American Community.* New York: Simon and Schuster.

Queiroz, Ana Maria, and Dina Maria da Silva (2007). "O curso pré-vestibular Milton Santos e a Festa Afro-Junina do Grupo TEZ." In Braga and da Silveira, eds. (2007). http://unesdoc.unesco.org/images/0015/001545/154582por.pdf

Rawls, John (1972). *A Theory of Justice.* Oxford: Oxford University Press.

Reis, Dyane Brito (2007). "Acesso e permanência de negros(as) no ensino superior: O caso da UFBA." In Braga and da Silveira, eds. (2007).

Reis, João (1995–96). "Quilombos e revoltas escravas no Brasil." *Revista USP* (28): 14–38.

Ribas Guerrero, Natalia (2012). "Em Terra Vestida: Contradições de um processo de territorialização camponesa na Resex Quilombo do Frechal." Masters thesis, Universidade de São Paulo.

Ribeiro, Pedro Floriano (2014). "An Amphibian Party? Organisational Change and Adaptation in the Brazilian Workers' Party, 1980–2012." *Journal of Latin American Studies* 46 (1): 87–119.

Rich, Jessica A. J. (2013). "Grassroots Bureaucracy: Intergovernmental Relations and Popular Mobilization in Brazil's AIDS Policy Sector." *Latin American Politics and Society* 55 (1): 1–25.

Rosemberg, Fúlvia, and Nina Madsen (2011). "Educação formal, mulheres, e género no Brasil contemporâneo." In *O progresso das mulheres no Brasil, 2003–2010,* edited by L. L. Barsted and J. Pitanguy. Rio de Janeiro: CEPIA—Cidadania, Estudo, Pesquisa, informação e ação.

Sales, Augusto dos Santos, et al. (2011). *O processo de aprovação do Estatuto da Igualdade Racial, Lei no. 12.288, de 20 de julho de 2010.* Brasilia: INESC (Instituto de Estudos Socio-Económicos).

Salmi, Jamil, and Chloë Fèvre (n.d.). "Tertiary Education and Lifelong Learning in Brazil." Working paper, World Bank.

Sampaio, Helena, et al. (2000). *Equidade e heterogeneidade no ensino superior Brasileiro.* Brasilia: INEP.

Samuels, David, and Cesar Zucco (2015). "Crafting Mass Partisanship at the Grass Roots." *British Journal of Political Science* 45 (4): 755–75.

Sander, R. H., and S. Taylor (2012). *Mismatch: How Affirmative Action Hurts Students It's Intended to Help and Why Universities Won't Admit It.* New York: Basic Books.

Sansone, Livio (1998). "Racismo sem etnicidade: Políticas públicas e discriminação racial em perspectiva comparada." *Dados* 41 (4): 751–83.

Sansone, Livio (2002). *Blackness without Ethnicity: Constructing Race in Brazil.* New York: Palgrave.

Santos, José Raimundo J. (2007). "As estratégias de estar e permanecer da juventude negra na universidade: Representações e percepções dos(as) estudantes da UFAl." In Braga and da Silveira, eds., 89–109 (2007).

Saperstein, A. (2006). "Double-Checking the Race Box: Examining Inconsistency between Survey Measures of Observed and Self-Reported Race." *Social Forces* 85 (1): 57–74.

Sardenberg, Ronaldo Mota, and Hélio Santos (1997). "Ações afirmativas para a valorização da população negra." *Parcerias Estratégicas* 1 (4): 28–37. http://seer.cgee.org.br/index.php/parcerias_estrategicas/issue/view/4/showToc

Schmitter, Philippe (1974). "Still the Century of Corporatism?" *Review of Politics* 36 (1): 85–131.

Schwarcz, Lily (1999). "Questão racial e etnicidade." In *O que ler na ciência social brasileira (1970–1995)*, edited by Sergio Miceli. São Paulo: Sumaré / Anpocs / Capes.

Schwartzman, Luisa (2008). "Who Are the Blacks? The Question of Racial Classification in Brazilian Affirmative Action Policies in Higher Education." *Cahiers de la Recherche sur l'Éducation et les Savoirs* 7. http://individual.utoronto.ca/schwartzman/Schwartzman_who_are_the_blacks.pdf

Schwartzman, Luisa (2009a). "Does Money Whiten? Intergenerational Changes in Racial Classification in Brazil." *American Sociological Review* 72: 940–63.

Schwartzman, Luisa (2009b). "Seeing Like Citizens: Unofficial Understandings of Official Racial Categories in a Brazilian University." *Journal of Latin American Studies* 41 (2): 221–50.

Schwartzman, Luisa, and Graziella Moraes Silva (2012). "Unexpected Narratives from Multicultural Policies: Translations of Affirmative Action in Brazil." *Latin American and Caribbean Ethnic Studies* 7 (1): 31–48.

Schwartzman, Simon (2008). "A medida da lei de cotas para o ensino superior," 1 December 2008. https://archive.org/details/AMedidaDaLeiDeCotasParaOEnsinoSuperio

Scott, James C. (1998). *Seeing Like a State: How Certain Schemes to Improve the Human Condition Have Failed*. New Haven: Yale University Press.

Secretaria de Estado da Educação—São Paulo, Coordenadoria de Estudos e Normas Pedagógicas (n.d.). *São Paulo: Educando pela diferença para a igualdade: Ensino Médio; Ciclo 1* (Módulo 1 and 2); *Ensino Médio* (Módulo 1 and 2). 4 vols.

Sen, Amartya (2009). *The Idea of Justice*. Cambridge, MA: Harvard University Press.

Sheriff, Robin E. (2001). *Dreaming Equality: Color, Race, and Racism in Urban Brazil*. New Brunswick, NJ: Rutgers University Press.

Shorter, Aylward (1988). *Toward a Theology of Inculturation*. London: Chapman.

Silva, Graziella Moraes (2016). "After Racial Democracy: Contemporary Puzzles in Race Relations in Brazil, Latin America, and Beyond from a Boundaries Perspective." *Current Sociology* 64 (5): 794–812.

Silva, Graziella Moraes, and Marcelo Paixão (2014). "Mixed and Unequal: New Perspectives on Brazilian Ethnoracial Relations." In E. Telles, ed. (2014).

Silva, Nelson do Valle (1987). "Distância social e casamento inter-racial no Brasil." *Estudos Afro-Asiaticos* 14:54–84.

Silveira, Maria Helena Vargas da (2007). "Estratégias pedagógicas para a educação anti-racista nos projetos inovadores de curso." In Braga and da Silveira, eds., 25–44 (2007).

Silvério, Valter Roberto (2003). "O papel das ações afirmativas em contextos racializados: Algumas anotações sobre o debate brasileiro." In P. B. Gonçalves e Silva and V. R. Silvério, eds. (2003).

Skidmore, Thomas E. (1993). "Bi-racial USA vs. Multi-racial Brazil: Is the Contrast Still Valid?" *Journal of Latin American Studies* 25 (2).

Skidmore, Thomas E. (2002). "Raízes de Gilberto Freyre." *Journal of Latin American Studies* 34:1–20.

Skocpol, Theda (2003). *Diminished Democracy: From Membership to Management in American Civic Life.* Norman: University of Oklahoma Press.

Skrentny, John David (1996). *The Ironies of Affirmative Action: Politics, Culture, and Justice in America.* Chicago: University of Chicago Press.

Sorj, Bernardo (2008). "Deconstrucción o reinvención de la nación: La memoria colectiva y las políticas de victimización en América Latina." Paper prepared for the project Nueva Agenda de Cohesión Social para América Latina, iFHC (São Paulo) and CIEPLAN (Santiago). http://fundacaofhc.org.br/files/papers/450.pdf

Souza, Paulo Renato (2005). *A revolução gerenciada: Educação no Brasil, 1995–2002.* São Paulo: Pearson.

Sperber, Dan (1996). "The Epidemiology of Beliefs." In *Explaining Culture: A Naturalistic Approach.* Oxford: Blackwell.

Stepan, Alfred (1978). *The State and Society: Peru in Comparative Perspective.* Princeton: Princeton University Press.

Stepan, Alfred (1985). "State Power and the Strength of Civil Society in the Southern Cone of Latin America." In *Bringing the State Back In,* edited by P. B. Evans, D. Rueschemeyer, and T. Skocpol. Cambridge: Cambridge University Press.

Stepan, Alfred, ed. (1988). *Democratizing Brazil.* New York: Oxford University Press.

Tavares de Almeida, Maria Hermínia (1996). *Crise econômica e interesses organizados: O sindicalismo no Brasil dos anos 80.* São Paulo: EDUSP.

Tavares de Almeida, Maria Herminia (1997). "Unions in Times of Reform." In *Reforming the State: Business, Unions, and Regions in Brazil,* edited by M. d. A. G. Kinzo. London: Institute of Latin American Studies.

Taylor, Charles (1992). *The Politics of Recognition.* Princeton: Princeton University Press.

Taylor, Robert S. (2009). "Rawlsian Affirmative Action." *Ethics* 119:476–506.

Telles, Edward (1994). "Industrialization and Occupational Racial Inequality in Employment: The Brazilian Example." *American Sociological Review* 59:46–63.

Telles, Edward (2002). "Racial Ambiguity among the Brazilian Population." *Ethnic and Racial Studies* 25 (3): 415–41.

Telles, Edward E. (2003). "US Foundations and Racial Reasoning in Brazil." *Theory, Culture, and Society* 20 (4): 31–47.

Telles, Edward (2004). *Race in Another America: The Significance of Skin Color in Brazil.* Princeton: Princeton University Press. (Portuguese edition: *O significado da raça na sociedade brasileira* [trans. Ana Arruda Callado], http://www.soc.ucsb.edu/faculty/telles/uploads/8/7/5/2/87525260/livro_o_significado_da_raca_na_sociedade_brasileira.pdf)

Telles, Edward, ed. (2014). *Pigmentocracies: Ethnicity, Race, and Color in Latin America.* Chapel Hill: University of North Carolina Press.

Telles, Edward E., and Nelson Lim (1998). "Does It Matter Who Answers the Race Question? Racial Classification and Income Inequality in Brazil." *Demography* 35 (4): 465–74.

Thayer, Milly (2017). "The 'Gray Zone' Between Movements and Markets: Brazilian Feminists and the International Aid Chain." In S. Alvarez et al., eds.

Tilly, Charles (1998). "Social Movements and (All Sorts of) Other Political

Interactions—Local, National, and International—Including Identities." *Theory and Society* 27 (4): 453–80.

Touraine, Alain (1965). *Sociologie de l'action.* Paris: Editions du Seuil.

Touraine, Alain (1977). *The Self-Production of Society.* Chicago: University of Chicago Press.

Touraine, Alain (1985). "The Return of the Actor." *Social Research* 52 (4): 749–87.

Touraine, Alain (1988). *La parole et le sang: Politique et société en Amérique Latine.* Paris: Odile Jacob.

Valente, Rubia (2016). "The Impact of Race and Social Economic Status on University Admission at the University of São Paulo." *Latin American and Caribbean Ethnic Studies* 11 (2): 95–118. http://dx.doi.org/10.1080/17442222.2016.1170955

Valente, Rubia, and Brian Berry (2017). "Performance of Students Admitted through Affirmative Action in Brazil." *Latin American Research Review* 52 (1): 18–34. http://doi.org/10.25222/larr.50

Valenzuela, Arturo, ed. (1978). *The Breakdown of Democratic Regimes: Chile.* Baltimore: Johns Hopkins University Press.

van Dyck, Brandon, and Alfred Montero (2015). "Eroding the Clientelist Monopoly: The Subnational Left Turn and Conservative Rule in Northeastern Brazil." *Latin American Research Review* 50 (4): 116–38.

Venn, Couze (1999). "On the Cunning of Imperialist Reason: A Questioning Note or Preamble for a Debate." *Theory, Culture, and Society* 16 (1): 59–62.

Venturini, Anna Carolina, and João Feres Junior (2018). "Efeitos das alterações do PAAIS-Unicamp nos vestibulares de 2016 e 2017." *Textos para Discussão GEMAA* (16). Available from the GEMAA website, http://gemaa.iesp.uerj.br/

Véran, Jean-François (2003). *L'esclavage en héritage: Le droit à la terre des descendants de marrons.* Paris: Karthala.

Véran, Jean-François (2013). "Les avatars de l'engagement: l'Anthropologie brésilienne aux traverses du politique." *Brésil(s): Sciences Humaines et Sociales* 4:79–102.

Villardi, Raquel (2007). "Políticas de ação afirmativa no ensino superior: Notas sobre o caso da UERJ." In A.A. Brandão, ed., 37–48 (2007).

Villas Bôas, Glaucia (2003). "Currículo, iniciação científica e evasão de estudantes de ciências sociais." *Tempo Social* 15 (1).

Wade, Peter (2005). "Rethinking Mestizaje: Ideology and Lived Experience." *Journal of Latin American Studies* 37:239–57.

Waiselfisz, Julio (2012). *Mapa da violencia 2012: A cor dos homicidios no Brasil.* Rio de Janeiro: CEBELA, FLACSO, SEPPIR, PR.

Weinstein, Barbara (2015). *The Color of Modernity: São Paulo and the Making of Race and Nation in Brazil.* Durham, Duke University Press.

Weyland, Kurt (1995). "Social Movements and the State: The Politics of Health Reform in Brazil." *World Development* 23 (10): 1699–1712.

Wiarda, Howard J. (1981). *Corporatism and National Development in Latin America.* Boulder: Westview.

Wilson, William Julius (1987). *The Truly Disadvantaged: The Inner City, the Underclass, and Public Policy.* Chicago: University of Chicago Press.

Wolford, Wendy (2016). "State-Society Dynamics in Contemporary Brazilian Land Reform." *Latin American Perspectives* 43 (2): 77–95.

Žižek, Slavoj (1997). "Multiculturalism, or, the Cultural Logic of Multinational Capitalism." *New Left Review* no. I/225: 28–51.

Index